Kilkenn·

GW00870881

A Century of Change

100 Years of Vocational Education
in County Kilkenny

Edited by Tony Patterson

ISBN Number: 0-9557852-0-0

First Published 2007

County Kilkenny Vocational Education Committee

Seville Lodge, Callan Road, Kilkenny

Kilkenny Vocational Education Committee

ACKNOWLEDGEMENTS

Grateful thanks is extended to all those who helped to bring this book to publication.
I would like to acknowledge the following for their contributions:

- Mr. Tony Patterson for the hours which he spent going through the minutes of the many meetings of County Kilkenny Vocational Education Committee.
- Ms. Christine McGrath, Customer Services Officer for the many hours of work which she devoted to this project.
- Mr. Kieran O'Sullivan, Signiatec for his patience and professional advice.
- Ms. Eileen Curtis, Adult Education Officer for her work on the publication.
- The Arts Education Officer, Principals, Deputy Principals, Centre Co-Ordinators and staff of the Scheme for sourcing photographs and compiling the School/Centre sections.
- Ms. Moyra McCarthy and Mr. Chris Greene for their input into the school sections.
- Mr. Jim Cooke for access to some of his research on the history of the Irish Vocational Education Association.
- Mr. Denis Buckley, Ms. Teresa Buggy, Ms. Eleanor Parks, the Kilkenny Archaeological Society, the National Library (Lawrence Collection), students and parents past and present for supplying many invaluable photographs of historical interest and significance. In addition, we are indebted to photographers Mr. Tom Brett, Mr. Michael Brophy, Oliver and others who supplied photographs.
- Mr. Joe Flynn and Mr. Proinsias Ó Drisceoil for their assistance in relation to the translation of material.
- The Centennial Sub-Committee and the Vocational Education Committee for their support and advice.

Míle buíochas do gach éinne a chabhraigh leis an obair stairiúil seo.

Rodger Curran

Rodger Curran
Chief Executive Officer

Contents

An Reamhrá

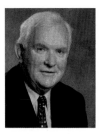

Is tréimhse fhada í céad bliain le bheith ag soláthar comhoideachais idir mheán is aosach ar fud Chontae Chill Chainnigh. Anois, is ceart agus is cóir dúinn mar Choiste an tseirbhís oideachais san a cheiliúradh.

Is mór an dul chun cinn í an réimse leathan ábhar atá á tairiscint do dhaltaí iarbhunscoile faoi chúram an Choiste Ghairmoideachais na laethanta seo thar mar a bhí ar fáil dóibh céad bliain ó shin.

Táimid go mór faoi chomaoin ag údar an leabhair staire seo as an taighde atá déanta aige ar conas a cuireadh an sórt san oideachais ar fáil do dhaoine nach raibh teacht acu ar a leithéid ag tús na haoise seo caite. Bíonn gach tosach lag, mar a deir an seanfhocal, ach ó shúilfhéachaint ar gach a thug Antóin fé ndeara trína chuid taighde is iontach an dul ar aghaidh ó thaobh oideachais den scoth atá curtha ar fáil anois , ní hamháin sa mheánoideachas ach san aosoideachas agus san oideachas ealaíon chomh maith.

Chuir an chéad Choiste Ghairmoideachais ábhair phraiticiúla ar fáil sa chontae ar Shráid na Parlaiminte i gcathair Chill Chainnigh. Cé go raibh easpa maoine orthu chun áiseanna cearta a sholáthar ag an am sin, ní raibh aon easpa muiníne ag na múinteoirí ná ag an gcoiste riaracháin chun an córas oideachais nua sin a thiomáint ar aghaidh.

Tá ár mbuíochas uile tuilte ag na ceannródaithe físeacha seo a chuir comhoideachas ar fáil in am an ghátair agus táim lánchinnte de go bhfuil ómós thar cuimse bronnta orthu sa saol ina bhfuil siad anois.

Bhí brú ar an Aire Oideachais i rialtas tosaigh na tíre seo bonn foirmeálta a chur leis an gcomhoideachas seo. Nuair a bhí an reachtaíocht á phlé sa Dáil bhí tuairimí ina taobh agus ina choinne ach de réir dealraimh bhí cuid mhaith den díospóireacht an-dearfach ar fad.

Pé scéal é, bhog an t-Aire ar aghaidh agus tháinig Acht um Ghairmoideachas na hÉireann i bhfeidhm i 1930.

Ó shin i leith, tá bonn níos láidre ag gairmoideachas na hÉireann faoi stiúir príomhoifigeach agus coistí bainistíochta, fochoistí de na comhairlí chontae.

Is féidir a thuiscint ó chuntais na miontuairiscí atá ar fáil cé chomh deacair is a bhí sé oideachas idir oideachas aosach is meánoideachas a chur ar fáil ar aon chéim leis an oideachas i scoileanna príobháideacha na laethanta sin.

Ba mhór an t-athrú a tháinig ar ghairmoideachas nuair a tháinig an saoroideachas isteach ag deireadh na seascaidí. Bhí an Ardteistiméireacht ar fáil anois i gcuid mhaith de na scoileanna agus réimse leathan ábhar á múineadh iontu.

Tháinig méadú mór ar líon na ndaltaí is na múinteoirí araon agus ar an bhfoireann riaracháin chomh maith. Chuir sin an-bhrú ar na háiseanna a bhí ann ag an am. Ba ghá don Choiste Gairmoideachais pleanáil cheart a dhéanamh chun na fadhbanna nua sin a réiteach.

Anois, tá scoileanna nua-aoiseacha ann agus teicneolaíocht ár linne ag gabháil leo uile. Is mór an dul chun cinn atá déanta in ionad na ndeacrachtaí a bhí ann i dtosach báire.

Táimse tar éis feidhmniú mar bhall den Choiste Gairmoideachais faoi cheathrar príomhoifigeach, le níos mó ná cúig bliana is tríocha agus caithfidh mé a rá fúthu gurbh oideachasóirí den scoth iad uile. D'oibríodar go dúthrachtach agus go físiúil le hídéil na mbunaitheoirí a chomhlíonadh chomh cumasach is ab fhéidir leo.

Níor cheart ná níor chóir an sliocht seo a chríochnú gan mo bhuíochas féin agus buíochas an Choiste a ghabháil leis na múinteoirí uile a thug a gcuid scoláireachta agus dúthrachta i seirbhís na ndaltaí a bhí faoina gcúram.

Mar a dúirt mé cheana, tá méadú mór tagtha ar líon na foirne riaracháin leis na blianta. Tá an tseirbhís uathusan in imeachtaí uile is i ngach gné den oideachas ar fheabhas ar fad.

Tréaslaím go mór le hAntóin as an éacht mór atá déanta aige chun an leabhar staire seo ar chéad bliain d'oideachas gairmscoile sa chontae a chur le chéile. Beidh sé úsáideach don taighdeoir, suimiúil don iarscoláire is don phobal araon agus éigeantach do lucht staire amach anseo.

Maith thú agus go maire tú i bhfad.

Cathaoirleach an Choiste Ghairmoideachais.

Risteárd ó Dubhlainn

An Comh. Richard Dowling
Cathaoirleach, Coiste Gairmoideachais Chontae Chill Chainnigh

Foreword

In this publication Mr. Tony Patterson has outlined the 'minuted' history of Technical and Vocational Education in County Kilkenny. As one would expect, the content of the 'Minute Books' varied over the years and depended greatly on the style of the secretary and the policy of the Committee at any given time. As he worked his way through the 'Minute Books', Tony found flamboyant descriptions of some events and little mention of others. This publication therefore documents the development of Technical and Vocational Education in County Kilkenny as represented in these minutes.

While there has been some discussion about the origins of technical education, historical evidence would suggest that it commenced in County Kilkenny in late 1906. One of the early significant developments in the county was the setting up of the Joint Technical Instruction Committee which in its third annual report, in 1909, cited the City Technical School as having three centres. This Committee was an amalgamation of the City Technical Instruction Committee and the Agricultural and Technical Committee for the county and was remarkable both in terms of the range of 'instruction' which it provided and the number of centres in which it operated. The 1909 report highlights activities such as Poultry-Keeping, Bee-Keeping, Laundry and Sewing, Manual Instruction, Cookery, Mathematics, English and Practical Mechanics that were being pursued in as many as twenty venues throughout the city and county. In 1910 three 'itinerant' teachers were employed to provide classes in the north, south and west of the county. In these early records Tony also found many references to the Committee's responsibility for the promotion of Gaeilge in the county and the efforts which were made to provide Irish classes in different areas as part of the Supplementary Scheme for the Teaching of Irish. Accordingly, County Kilkenny Vocational Education Committee can trace its inception to these origins and finds itself celebrating its centenary year in 2007.

Following the introduction of the Vocational Education Act in 1930 these responsibilities were handed over to the newly established Vocational Education Committee. The first meeting of County Kilkenny VEC was held on the 3rd of November, 1930. Chapter Two documents the early activities of the newly formed VEC and the appointment of its first Chief Executive Officer. With this

Act came the hope that more generous state funds would be made available for the setting up of new technical and vocational schools in the county. Many of the references in the early years of the newly formed VEC relate to the 'poor conditions' of the temporary school premises up and down the county. This was unfortunate and indeed reflects what many believe to be the poor regard in which this system of continuation education was held in the corridors of power for decades. This is clearly illustrated in the reply of the Minister for Education, Mr. John Marcus O'Sullivan to a question from Rev. D. Keane, Bishop of Limerick in October 1930 where he states that, "By their very nature and purpose the schools to be provided under this Act are distinctly not schools for general education ... When we can afford to make universal a system of general education for post-primary pupils it cannot be through the medium of these continuation schools".

In the remaining chapters the story of County Kilkenny VEC and the development of Vocational Education unfolds and in many ways this acts as a social commentary on the changing nature of Irish life over the decades. In particular, it illustrates how national policy on education impacted on local areas and documents the struggles of many communities to develop their local schools. The 1930s and 1940s were very difficult times for the VEC and while World War II is never mentioned in the minutes there are several references to rationing and its impact. The building programme of the VEC was interrupted during this period. In the early 1950s, mention is made of the first "demountable classroom" for the county, this was the precursor of the dreaded "prefab", discussion of which was to preoccupy the Committee for many years.

The 1960s heralded the dawn of a new era with the introduction of Free Education and free school transport. Together these transformed the educational landscape in County Kilkenny and led to the rationalisation of schools. In the succeeding years the deliberations of the VEC Committee were concerned with the stop-start school building programme, the introduction of the Junior and later the Senior Cycle, the commencement of Vocational Preparation and Training Courses as well as issues relating to staffing, finance and governance. While the Minutes act as a formal record of events this publication also profiles the personal journey of a number of individuals who worked with County Kilkenny VEC. These narratives reflect in a very real way the changing face of the VEC over the years and the effects of new developments on their day to day working lives.

The final section of the book brings the story up to date detailing the many changes that have impacted on this VEC in recent years, changes prompted by the introduction of the Vocational Education (Amendment) Act 2001 and the recommendations of the Rochford Report on staffing. Each school/centre and service is profiled thus adding to the rich and varied legacy of Vocational Education in the county. One of the weaknesses which Tony found in his research was that some aspects of the work were rarely documented and accordingly do not appear in the minutes of the meetings. The development of Adult Education receives scant mention and is more fully documented in this section. We are indebted to all those in our schools, centres and services for their contribution to this section.

The struggle to establish a system of Vocational Education in the county was long and often difficult and undoubtedly some were hurt along the way. I hope that anyone reading this book who was part of that story will be pleased with this account of their 'moment in history'. On the occasion of the celebration of our Centenary can I express the hope that your involvement with County Kilkenny VEC has been an occasion of growth and encouragement for you. A special word of thanks is extended to all those who supported Vocational Education in County Kilkenny over the decades. Thanks also to the many Committee Members, CEOs and staff members who have served County Kilkenny VEC so faithfully down through the years.

As we look forward to another 100 years of quality caring service the words of Gar in Brian Friel's *Philadelphia, Here I Come!* seem appropriate, "Its all over and its all about to begin".

Rodger Curran
Chief Executive Officer

CHAPTER 1

Technical Instruction before 1930

From the beginning technical education was bound up with the development of local government in Ireland. Although Boards of Guardians and other local authorities had been empowered since 1889 to strike a rate in support of technical instruction, very few attempts had been made to use this power. Things changed with the setting up of County Councils, Urban District Councils and Rural District Councils under the Local Government (Ireland) Act of 1898. In the following year, local elections were held in Kilkenny City and County. In that same year, 1899, the Agriculture and Technical Instruction Act became law, and within a few years, both local authorities had begun to provide for technical instruction.

The County Council set up an Agriculture and Technical Instruction Committee. In the first few years, a typical meeting would start with consideration of the licensing of stallions or some such matter pertaining to its agricultural remit, and then proceed to deal with night classes in various parts of the county, providing instruction in poultry keeping, bee keeping, laundry, dressmaking, needlework, domestic economy, horticulture, drawing, and woodwork. Their instructors travelled to the various centres.

The City Technical Instruction Committee didn't have any dealings with agriculture, but from the beginning had to consider the setting up of a permanent school. In May 1902, they met with inspectors from the Department of Agriculture and Technical Instruction. One of them, Mr. Fletcher advised the setting up of an evening school to start with. A month later, following an offer of an annual contribution of £500 from the Department, the decision was taken to lease premises and advertise for a principal teacher. The local contribution would be £75, the likely proceeds of a penny in the pound on the City rate. In addition there would be £875 available for equipping the premises. By September, the committee had leased a house in Parliament Street - the building then known as "The Library" and now the ACC bank - and the newly appointed principal, Mr. George Phillips was supervising the arrangements for opening the school. [1]

By 1906, the provision of technical education in Kilkenny was in the hands of a Joint Technical Instruction Committee which had responsibility for both City and County. The third annual report, printed in 1909 outlines the progress made. [2]

City Technical School

The city school now had three centres:
- The building in Parliament Street was in daytime use by boys of the Trades Preparatory School. In addition, evening classes were offered in preparatory Mathematics and English, Carpentry and Joinery, Building Construction, Practical Engineering, Practical Mechanics, Machine Construction and Drawing, Manual Instruction (wood), Practical and Theoretical Chemistry. The building was described as   quite inadequate, and there was great want of space. The metalwork room could only fit nine pupils, so the woodwork room had to be used as well. Some students had to be refused admission. English and maths had to be taught in the chemistry room. There were twenty-one boys in the Trades Preparatory School, spread over a three-year course, and they were taught by six teachers.
- In addition, the committee had got the use of three large, lofty, well-lit rooms in The Model School on the Ormonde Road, and there were eleven classes in domestic economy subjects, four in commercial subjects, and two in practical tailoring. The three rooms were used with the permission of the Commissioners of National Education. The rest of the building was a National School, attended by Protestant pupils.
- A room in the Court House, lent by the County Council, was used for two evening classes per week.

County Work

Three itinerant teachers were permanently engaged in instruction in the county at large:
- Manual instruction was given in six centres - Coon, Clogh, Castlecomer, Windgap, Owning and Kilmacow. In each centre there was one class for adults and one for boys in the upper standards of the National Schools, or who had just left school. A class was also held in Callan in the Christian Brothers' School.
- Laundry work and sewing was taught in seven centres - Gathabawn, Glashare, Johnstown, Galmoy, Urlingford, Clomantagh, and Ballyouskill. Laundry work included washing, bleaching, making-up of white clothes, flannels, coloured goods, silks and muslins, collars, cuffs, shirt fronts.
- There were centres for cookery, laundry work and home sewing at Listerlin, Inistioge, Ballygub and Dunnamaggin, with two classes in each centre, one for adults, and one for younger girls. Rooms were given rent free by Mrs. Tighe, Woodstock, Miss Brennan, Dunnamaggin, in the Glebe House at Listerlin, and by the Gaelic Society, Windgap. Miss Laracy, domestic economy instructress in the city conducted classes at Thornback and Ballyragget.

Accommodation was provided by Fr. J. Roe in Clogh, by Mr. Wandesforde in Castlecomer, and by Canon Barry in Ballyragget. In each case, a building was converted for the purpose.

Work in the city was held up by lack of accommodation. In the county the difficulty was trying to serve over thirty parishes with only three teachers available.

The Model School Building

The Model School system was set up in the mid-nineteenth century as a method of training teachers for the new National Schools. They were National Schools with a non-denominational intake and were intended also as models of good teaching practice for other schools in their area. They were directly controlled by the Commissioners for National Education, unlike most other national schools which were owned, in the case of Catholic schools by trustees for the local bishop. The Catholic bishops objected to the religiously mixed boarding character of this form of teacher training, where trainee teachers spent six months of supervised teaching, before seeking employment in ordinary schools. They ordered priests not to send teachers to be trained in these schools and to avoid employing anyone trained in them. In 1866, they ordered that Catholic pupils in the schools be withdrawn. As a result, the model school system, in its teacher training aspect, was replaced by teacher training colleges offering a two-year course, and mirroring the denominational make-up of the national school system.[3]

Some of the model schools survived as ordinary National Schools, although still under the patronage of the Commissioners for National Education. Kilkenny Model School on the Ormonde Road was one of these. It catered for the local Protestant children, and because it had been designed for a much larger intake, a large part of the building was unoccupied until the City Technical School got the use of three of the rooms.

As the years went by many of the members of the Joint Technical Instruction Committee cast covetous eyes on the whole building. [4]It was a beautiful stone building, centrally situated, with good space inside, and room for development outside. The obvious difficulty, stressed often by the Church of Ireland clergy on the Committee, would be in providing alternative and suitable accommodation for the pupils attending the model school. County Council and Urban Council representatives on the committee seem to have been very wary of putting a burden on the rates, and the possible electoral consequences for themselves.

In 1910, the Committee applied to the Commissioners for National Education to have the whole school building handed over for technical education. Eight commissioners voted to give the school, but nine voted against. In the same year, a deputation of the Committee was received by Augustine Birrell, Chief Secretary for Ireland, who admitted that their case was an obvious one, but they got no school.

In 1924, under the provisions of the Ministers and Secretaries Act,[5] responsibility for Technical Education was transferred from the Department of

Agriculture to the Department of Education. The passing of the Vocational Education Act in 1930 led to the setting up of County Kilkenny Vocational Committee in November of that year.

The Joint Technical Instruction Committee 1919-1927

One minute book of the Joint Technical Instruction Committee survives. It covers the years from 1919 to 1927. For the most part it covers routine matters - appointment of teachers, administration, finance, correspondence with the technical instruction department. However, read with the knowledge that these were the years of the war of independence, the civil war, and the setting up of the apparatus of native government, it takes on a different aspect.

In September 1919, a delegation from the Gaelic League urged the appointment of a second full-time teacher of Irish, and the Committee decided to do so, and wrote to the Department for approval. A week passed, and though the department's approval had not arrived, they decided to advertise for a teacher. Of twelve applicants considered, they decided to appoint Mr. Edmond Comerford, who was proposed for the job by Peter DeLoughrey, Mayor of Kilkenny, and seconded by E.T. Keane, Editor of the Kilkenny People. At the same meeting, Miss Nora Keenan was appointed a commerce teacher. At the next meeting the approval of the Department of Agriculture and Technical Instruction was received for Miss Keenan's appointment, but no mention was made of Mr. Comerford. The committee instructed the secretary, Mr. Phillips to tell Mr. Comerford to start work. Fr. Michael Gibbons, on behalf of the Gaelic League, guaranteed to indemnify the committee for any loss incurred if sanction wasn't forthcoming. This guarantee had a limit of £130, the amount of Mr. Comerford's first year's salary. It was December before his appointment was finally sanctioned by the Department. The delay becomes a little bit more comprehensible if one is aware that after the suppression of the 1916 rising, Ned Comerford was one of the Kilkenny men rounded up and interned.[6]

In February of 1920, several new members representing Kilkenny Corporation were welcomed on the committee, and a resolution thanking the replaced members for their long years of service was recorded. The context was the local election victory of Sinn Féin in January. From that same month, martial law had been extended to Kilkenny, Wexford, and Waterford.[7]

In May of 1920, the secretary, who was also Principal of the Technical School, referred to the receipt of a letter from the Department, concerning the training of boy mechanics in the Royal Air Force. He said he had brought the matter to the attention of the senior boys in the Trades Preparatory School. So far there had been no applications. Alderman DeLoughrey deplored the secretary's action. He was opposed, he said, to any influence being brought to bear on boys to join the English army. The letter was marked "read".[8]

In October of that year, a meeting was adjourned as a mark of respect to Terence McSwiney, Lord Mayor of Cork who had died on hunger strike. Schools were to close for the rest of the day. In March of the following year, a meeting was adjourned on account of the executions in Dublin that morning. This is a reference to the hanging in Mountjoy jail of Frank Flood, Thomas Whelan, Patrick Moran, Thomas Bryan, Patrick Doyle and Bernard Ryan.[9]

From the meeting of 13th December 1920, neither Peter DeLoughrey, Chairman, nor Sean Gibbons, Vice-Chairman (Mayor and County Council Chairman respectively) appeared at meetings. On Friday December 10, Ald. DeLoughrey had been arrested by the military and taken to Kilkenny Military Barracks. Next day he was brought by motor lorry to Woodstock House, Inistioge. There he was under the tender care of the Auxiliaries. On Tuesday, he was seen in Graignamanagh by Fr. Kearns who reported that he was in good spirits. He seems to have been taken in pursuit of a new policy of seizing prominent Sinn Féin people, and using them as hostages on lorries transporting military or Black-and-Tans. After a spell in Arbour Hill in Dublin, he was released but in April, Alderman Upton, editor of the Kilkenny Journal, was appointed temporary chairman in the "unavoidable absence" of DeLoughrey and Gibbons. As G.T. Phillips explained:

> They were in a rather awkward position at present and one that put him to
> some inconvenience at times, having no duly appointed chairman. Their
> worthy chairman, the Mayor, was not at home, and no one could presently say
> when he would be at home, owing to reasons of which they were aware; that
> was a regrettable thing and unfortunately the same was true of their vice-
> chairman.

It would seem that, following the introduction of martial law in Kilkenny, DeLoughrey and Gibbons felt that home wasn't a particularly safe or healthy place to be. It was October before they re-appeared at meetings, well after the truce.

In February of 1922, the Department notified the secretary that Mr. Comerford's salary for the period of his internment was to be paid. [10] This was a reference to a period of internment in 1921, not to his post 1916 incarceration.

The minute book refers to the Department of Technical Instruction all through the period, but up to the Treaty this was the Irish section of the British Department of Agriculture and Technical Instruction. Afterwards this was one of the ministries of Saorstát Éireann. In 1924, the Technical Instruction Section was transferred to the Department of Education of Saorstát Éireann. The re-organisation of public institutions and public bodies under the new regime led to clashes of meetings resulting in the abandonment of meetings in March and April due to absence of a quorum. [11]

Appointment of Temporary Chairman.

Owing to the unavoidable absence of the Chairman & Vice-Chairman it was decided to elect a Chairman until they returned to Kilkenny.

Proposed by Rev. Bro. Mc Goldrick
Seconded by Mr. J. W. O'Hanrahan
and unanimously passed :-
"That Ald. Upton be appointed Temporary Chairman of the Committee".

"That the meeting be adjourned until this day week on account of the executions which had taken place that morning in Dublin.

The Chairman supported the proposition and the meeting was adjourned.

Section from County Kilkenny
Joint Technical Instruction
Committee Minutes Book 1920s

The War of Independence gets very
little mention in the minute book.
The adjournment of a meeting on the
day that volunteer prisoners were
hanged in Dublin gives a hint of a
wider world in turmoil, as does the
election of an Acting Chairman to
replace Peter DeLoughrey and Seán
Gibbons who were "unavailable", or
in plainer terms "on the run".

Supplementary Scheme for the teaching of Irish in County Kilkenny

One of the consequences of the coming to power of a native government was a greatly increased effort to teach Irish, especially to adults. This work fell to the committees of technical instruction. County Councils were to strike a special rate of a penny in the pound to finance the new scheme. In May of 1923, the Kilkenny Joint Technical Instruction Committee received a letter from the local Gaelic League, pointing out that Kilkenny County Council had struck such a rate.[12] The committee, having been informed by the County Secretary that the rate would produce £1447 per annum, and that they could expect £163 from grants earned in the city and county, proceeded to draw up a scheme.

It was to be an experimental scheme for the first year. In addition to Éamonn Comartún (Ned Comerford) who was already a full-time teacher of Irish, earning £130 per annum, Conor Horgan was appointed at £120 and sixteen part-time teachers were chosen for centres scattered strategically around the whole county area. They were to get three shillings and sixpence per hour for their efforts. In addition there were cost of living bonuses for all the teachers under the Technical Instruction Committee.[13] Mr. Comartún's position caused some difficulty. He had been on the list of whole-time teachers on a permanent basis, and the department now listed him as being under the supplementary scheme. This was eventually settled to his and the committee's satisfaction.[14]

Over the years the scheme was varied, and improved as circumstances dictated. Some centres thrived, others attracted very few pupils. In July of 1924, the secretary reported that forty-five classes were held in the county and another eleven in the city. Some county centres obviously had two or three classes during each week.[15] By 1926, one of the whole-time teachers was also described as a temporary part-time organiser. In the General Election of 1932, the then organiser, Mr. Eamonn Kissane was elected a Fianna Fáil T.D. for County Kerry. He was succeeded by E. O'Kelly, and in 1934, in accordance with the provisions of the Vocational Education Act, 1930, his duties became part of the responsibility of the new CEO[16]

A report to the committee in November 1924 referring to the existence of classes in Ballydaniel, Revanagh, Castlewarren, Dungarvan, Gowran, Clodiagh, Inistioge, Listerlin, Tullogher and Harristown, and to the failure to get classes started in Tober Na Brone and Templeorum, gives an idea of the spread of the scheme. At the same meeting, a special sub-committee was set up to supervise the scheme. It had six members of the Technical Committee and four from the Gaelic League. The Editor of the *Kilkenny People* (at the time E.T. Keane) penned a blistering attack on the whole scheme, branding it a failure, maintaining that there had been more enthusiasm for the language before it started, proclaiming that the government's reliance on the schools was a better plan, and having a side-swipe at the Gaelic League for being dominated by one political party, which I take to be a reference to the fact that Fr. Michael Gibbons, one of the most prominent Gaelic League members was a brother of Sean Gibbons.[17]

A metalwork class in progress
in the City Technical School,
Parliament Street 1907.

Boys' Art Class

Tailors' evening cutting class

Kilkenny Model School before it was
acquired by County Kilkenny
Vocational Education Committee.

One curious provision which applied to teachers of Irish classes for adults required that they sign a "declaration of allegiance". In 1926, a motion calling on W.T. Cosgrave and the government to annul this requirement was debated and caused considerable disagreement. The matter was postponed and I cannot find a record of its having been voted on. [18] It was still a requirement in 1931, and the minutes note the reappointment of teachers of Irish "for the purposes of signing their declaration of allegiance". By October of the following year, Miss May Sparks was applying for arrears of an increase granted her by the Joint Technical Instruction Committee in July 1927. She stated that, as she could not conscientiously make the required declaration, she did not get her increase. The Vocational Education Committee granted her the arrears. I presume the change of Government in that year had something to do with the change.

In 1924, under the provisions of the Ministers and Secretaries Act, [19] responsibility for Technical Education was transferred from the Department of Agriculture to the Department of Education.

In September of 1926, the Commission on Technical Education invited the committee to appoint two members to give evidence on the working of technical education in Kilkenny. A draft of the evidence to be presented was approved by the committee beforehand. In the discussion, the members stressed the need for a new school in the city, the excellent work being done by the trades preparatory school, and the difficulties posed by being required to run the Irish language scheme as well as the normal technical education scheme. Nobody referred to the need for full-time schools outside the city, but a major expansion of the scope and extent of vocational and technical education was what the commission eventually recommended. The passing of the Vocational Education Act in 1930 led to the setting up of County Kilkenny Vocational Education Committee (hereafter referred to as the VEC) in November of that year.

The Model School Again

In 1931, a deputation from the newly set-up County Kilkenny VEC approached Mr. John Marcus O'Sullivan, the Minister for Education in the Free State Government. Their spokesman, Canon Staunton, President of St. Kieran's College, outlined their case:

> The school had been built for 515 pupils, and the present enrolment was 63; as a technical school it would be adequate for their present needs, and would have room for development; because of its distinguished appearance, it would give dignity and status to a neglected branch of education; they guaranteed to provide "to the pupils attending the Model School a school adequate for their number according to the regulations of the Department

of Education, without any contribution on their part towards the building...
..We are authorised by the Rt. Rev. Dr. Day, Protestant Bishop of Ossory, and Very Rev. Dean Phair, M.A., to state that they have no objection to the transference of the Model School to the Vocational Education Committee provided that adequate provision is made for the present occupants of the Model School.

In the subsequent discussion, the delegation pointed out that, if they were to build a new Vocational School in Kilkenny, the cost would be £15,000 to £20,000 of which the government would have to pay half, whereas a new national school to accommodate around sixty pupils could be built for about a tenth of that price, and a principal's residence would cost at most £2,000. They suggested that this cost of £3,500 could equitably be divided between the County and the Government. The minister replied that, if his department were to hand over a building belonging to the state, worth £15,000 to the people of Kilkenny, then the provision of accommodation for the existing pupils should be paid for in Kilkenny. Reporting back to the VEC the delegates felt that the Minister was aware that they had a building fund which would more than cover the cost, and that the Government would, as Canon Staunton put it "stand out for its pound of flesh". The Minister's final word was that he would give the school on condition that they provided a school for fifty to sixty pupils, built a teacher's residence and provided a sum for the upkeep of the school. He explained that, up to then, it was maintained by the Department, unlike a parish school, where the manager was responsible for the upkeep.

A year later, the committee were still awaiting the transfer of the property and called on the Minister of Education in the newly elected Fianna Fáil government to expedite matters. The Minister was Tomás Ó Deirg, who was actually a T.D. for the constituency. By early 1933, the conditions of the lease were forwarded by the Department, and accepted by the VEC.[20] It still remained to find a site for the replacement school, and to proceed with the building.

In June 1932, the members were incensed to learn that the Department were not providing for a teacher's residence in the plans for the National School to accommodate the Protestant children being moved out of the Ormonde Road. The Department claimed that the Principal's living quarters in the Model School were only held by Mr. Walker while he remained in the job, and that he had been told on appointment that he might be asked to vacate the premises at any time, on due notice. Further, they were not in the habit of providing teachers' residences with other new schools, and thought that Mr. Walker's case would be covered by an annual subvention to enable him to rent a house.

Canon Staunton, as a member of the original deputation to Professor O'Sullivan, objected strongly. They had promised Rt. Rev. Dr. Day and the Protestant community that a Principal's residence would form part of the complex and the VEC was in honour bound to see that this was done. The question was referred to a sub-committee consisting of representatives of the VEC, the Protestant Community, and the Ministries of Education and Finance.[21]

This building in Parliament Street housed the Kilkenny City Technical School for almost forty years. It is now the ACC bank.

Parliament Street as it is today, and as it was in the early twentieth century.

The matter seems to have been resolved. In the following April a departmental letter regarding the acquisition of the Model School was accepted, and a site of one to one-and-a-half acres was being sought for the replacement National School. A site on the Castlecomer Road which was acceptable to Dr. Day was on offer for £200, and it was decided to acquire it. [22] This caused a new difficulty as the acquisition of sites for National Schools was beyond the powers of VECs. The difficulty was surmounted by the committee giving £3,200 to the Minister of Education and letting him deal with site acquisition, building of the school and negotiations with Dr. Day.[23] It was 1937 before the site was finally transferred from the St. John estate to the committee and the Minister. In January 1938 the minutes note that the school was completed since December 20th 1937, but the staff and pupils had not yet vacated the Ormonde Road school, and the contractor was ready to move in there to get on with the renovations.[24]

Architects Downes and Kelly had been appointed for the Model School renovations since 1934. The plans caused some controversy, as they involved tearing down some stone buildings at the back and replacing them with concrete. Canon Staunton deplored the violence to "a model building designed by a capable architect" and objected to "the destruction of the artistic appearance of the building". It was finally agreed that the extensions would be faced in stone from the demolished buildings. [25]

While the conversion work was in hand, rooms were hired from the CYMS in William Street, so that the vocational school classes from the model school could continue in operation.

A delay in handing over the site on the date agreed resulted in the VEC getting £18-10-0 from the Board of Works in settlement of a claim for breach of contract. Defects in the coping of the front wall of the building led to the saturation of the wall, and this, together with the replacing of the rotten ground-floor windows was an extra cost that had to be dealt with. [26]

In July 1939, the VEC found itself embroiled in one last controversy regarding the renovation. It had sought tenders for the provision of bentwood chairs, and the successful tender involved the purchase of foreign-made chairs. Local and national papers castigated the committee for its neglect of Irish manufacture. The agreed reply said that the cost of the school to the County Kilkenny VEC was £18, 000, of which £17,000 was spent on Irish labour and materials. The chairs had cost £80-10-0.[27]

The thirty-eight year saga of the acquisition of the Model School for Vocational Education ended on the 9th of January, 1940, when Dr. Patrick Collier, Bishop of Ossory, and Chairman of the County Kilkenny VEC officially opened the school. the *Kilkenny People* described the newly refurbished school in glowing terms:

> The new technical school, formerly the Model school, provides
> accommodation for classes in joinery, engineering and metal work,
> technical drawing, housewifery, commercial and other subjects and has in
> addition a large assembly hall.
> The whole interior of the old building has been completely modernised

and three new wings have been erected. One of these contains the spacious metal workshop, another an entirely new staircase hall with cloakroom accommodation on two floors, and the third a large class room on the ground floor with a well equipped cookery room above.

Great care was taken by the architect to preserve the character of the original building, and a view of the school from Ormonde road gives very little indication of the extensive and thorough remodelling and rebuilding which has been accomplished.

A central heating system has been installed together with a most up-to-date system of electric lighting, especially designed to ensure that the correct intensity of illumination for various kinds of work is provided.

In his speech Dr. Collier referred to the early history of the model schools and to the Kilkenny school in particular:

These were schools to be proud of long ago, and I spoke to many who were educated here before Catholics left the Model School for purely Catholic schools, and there must be still a few alive in Kilkenny who received their early education here, and who share the pride of the old Catholic pupils of the early days of the model schools. Catholics and non-Catholics sat here side by side for many years.[28]

Eighteen years later, the VEC was offered the state's interest in the school for £20. They accepted and acquired the balance of a five-hundred year lease dating from August 1852.[29]

One teacher vocational school.
Listerlin, now used as a County Council store.

Miss Walsh with some of her Dunamaggin pupils in in
front of the county's first "demountable classroom".

CHAPTER 2

The Early Days of County Kilkenny Vocational Education Committee

The Vocational Education Act, 1930 introduced a more efficient administrative structure. Instead of the large, unwieldy technical instruction committees, each county was to have fourteen-member committees, with additional members for each urban area in the county. In the case of County Kilkenny, this meant fourteen members elected by the County Council, with at least five and not more than eight of these to be members of the County Council. In addition, Kilkenny Corporation elected two members.[30]

The term of office of the Vocational Education Committee was made concurrent with local government. After a local election, new nominations were made to the VECs. They were to provide continuation education for fourteen to sixteen year old pupils, and were also to provide technical education. The schools were to be secular, mixed, and locally controlled. Powers were conferred on the committees to establish and maintain schools, provide courses in the nature of technical education, and they could contribute to expenses incurred by people from their area in obtaining technical education within or without their own areas. [31]

The first meeting of County Kilkenny VEC was held on the Third of November, 1930. Most Rev. Dr. Patrick Collier, Catholic bishop of Ossory was elected Chairman, with Ald. John Magennis becoming Vice-Chairman. Rt. Rev. Dr. Day, Church of Ireland, Bishop of Ossory apologised for inability to attend. Apart from Ald. Magennis, other County Council members present were Sean Gibbons, James Brophy, P. Foley, J. Conway and E. Mahon. Dr. Staunton, President of St. Kieran's College, V. Rev. Canon Doody and Rev. Br. Franklin and Major J.E.B Loftus were County Council nominees. Pierce Tynan represented the Corporation. Councillors T. Hennessey and Geo. Dooley were not present.

In accordance with the act, Mr. G. T. Phillips, C. E.O. of the Joint Technical Instruction Committee became CEO of the VEC[32]

Over the coming months the committee set to work examining suitable locations for county centres, submitted a scheme for the coming year to the Department of Education, and got on with the routine work of administration. The department grant came to £4,050 for the year and this would have been supplemented by contributions from the County Council and Corporation.

Travelling expenses for teachers cannot have been a major part of the financial burden on the committee. Mr. E. O'Kelly (Eoghan Ó Ceallaigh, author of Cois Feoire, and An Dá Thaobh) got fourpence a mile for the use of a car in getting to Gowran and Goresbridge, but had to make do with the pedal cycle rate of a penny halfpenny a mile for nearer venues. Ned Comerford had the same car rate for some of his classes, with the maximum set at £40 per annum. He taught at Freshford, Danesfort, and Kilkenny Garda Station, and could only make up fifteen hours per week, whereas his minimum should have been twenty hours. A later minute notes that the attendance at certain Guards classes was quite low, and the Committee ordered that the Chief Superintendent should be notified.

Teachers' salaries, including bonuses, by 1934 ranged from £130 to £215, depending on length of service. A point of contention with the VEC was the demand of teachers for an incremental scale. Some members were in favour of following departmental guidelines, and of giving increments according to a national scale. Others favoured having each individual teacher apply for an increase which could be given or rejected by the committee.[33]

The greatest problem facing the committee was the appalling condition of the City Technical School premises in Parliament Street. I have outlined above how this problem was solved by the acquisition and renovation of the Model School premises on Ormonde Road. The first seven years of the committee's existence saw the solution of this difficulty, but concurrently the area outside the city had to be looked after. For over a quarter of a century there had been technical instruction classes in various centres around the county, but they were all of a temporary or part-time nature.

In early 1931 a sites and buildings committee report was presented to the Committee, but kept private as the scheme was a big one and the extra finance available was only £350. By the following year, it had been decided to proceed with centres at Castlecomer, Clogh and Listerlin, in the parish of Rosbercon. It was decided to apply to the County Board of Health to rent rooms in the old Castlecomer Workhouse. Tenders were to be sought for Listerlin. The Board of Health couldn't legally grant a lease for more than five years, and the VEC considered this too short. However by the end of 1932, the Department of Education suggested a year's trial of Vocational Education in Castlecomer. Specifications for refurbishment of the rooms were approved and the contract awarded to P. Kelly, to be completed in two months at a cost of £129. Five months later the contract was completed and a tender for electric wiring accepted.[34]

Dunnamaggin Vocational School opened in 1933 in the old National School building. The Parish Priest, Fr. O'Keeffe provided the building and the VEC set up a one-teacher school.[35]

A one acre site was acquired in Listerlin in July of 1933 at a cost of £60, and a new school built. It opened in February 1934.

Dr. Richard Walsh CEO

In January of 1933, the committee were advised by the Minister for Education that they should, "under the authority of Section 99 (5) of the Vocational Education Act 1930, proceed to abolish the position of Chief Executive Officer, award the present Chief Executive Officer, G.T. Phillips, the maximum pension which he will then be entitled to under Part IV of the Local Government Act 1925, and advising the committee to appoint Mr. Phillips as temporary Chief Executive Officer pending the appointment of his successor". This complicated-sounding device seems to have been intended to clear the way for the appointment of new CEOs to VECs all over the country. The VEC, with regret adopted this course and voted to give Mr. Phillips two thirds of his then salary, together with a cost-of-living bonus. Some time was taken up with a dispute between the Department, suggesting that Mr. Phillips' pension should be £152, and the VEC suggesting £203. The Local Government Officials Union encouraged the VEC, but eventually his pension was fixed at £157 per annum.

While this was going on, the committee was also trying to get around the requirement that the post should be filled through the Local Appointments Commission. The Department of Education turned down their request to be allowed appoint the new CEO by promotion from among the existing staff. Next, they wrote to Mr. B. Kavanagh, former teacher in charge of the Commercial School in Kilkenny, and recently appointed CEO in Laois, asking him to apply for the position in Kilkenny. He declined.

It was October before the Local Appointments Commission submitted the names of three candidates for the VEC to place in order of preference. Mr. Richard Walsh was placed first and was duly appointed to the position. Around the same time, the committee was notified that in future only one name would be submitted. A proposal to register a protest was narrowly defeated. [36]

Mr. Walsh attended his first meeting on the eighth of January 1934. During his term of office he added a master's degree and a doctorate to his qualifications, and was affectionately known to Kilkenny people as Doc Walsh. He was a Tipperary man, born in Ballybacon, near Ardfinnan, and had been Vice-Principal of Tullamore Vocational School in County Offaly. Outside working hours he was a historian, an Irish scholar, and an important figure in the artistic life of the community. He retired in 1962. [37]

Very shortly after his appointment, the new CEO found himself involved in a minor crisis in Castlecomer. On the Saturday before the new Vocational school was due to open, he was sent for by the Parish Priest, Canon MacNamara. The Canon announced that he could not allow the children to attend the school, because the teacher of English, Geography and Science, Mr. Boyd was "a non-Catholic", and that if the appointment were to be persisted in, the school would be a definite failure. At the monthly meeting on the following Monday, the CEO informed the committee that he had, on his own responsibility, installed Mr. Hickson in place of Mr. Boyd. The committee approved his action and urged that the CEO and an inspector from the department should find suitable employment for Mr. Boyd. As it happened, Mr. Boyd very quickly got a job in County Meath, and claimed payment from Kilkenny VEC for the six days he had been unemployed. The committee agreed to his request.

All this is recorded in the minutes, but, curiously enough, the *Kilkenny People* makes no mention of it in an otherwise very full report of the meeting. [38]

In June 1934, Kilkenny County Council was suspended, and its functions taken over by a commissioner, Mr. Meighan. The Councillors appointed to sit on the VEC could no longer do so, and for the next several years the only politicians on the committee were the Kilkenny Corporation representatives, John Magennis and J.P. Pattison.

The provision of schools in the county was proceeding apace. By March 1934 a site had been selected for a school at Mooncoin and the department had approved plans and specifications for Listerlin. The plans for Mooncoin were, however, considered too expensive.

With so much work under way or planned, it became necessary to borrow money. The CEO outlined a scheme for raising a loan: the committee could borrow £10,000 through the County Council; half the interest would be paid by the Department and the rest by the ratepayers. The commissioner, Mr. Meighan gave his consent, acting as Kilkenny County Council and the committee made a formal decision, under the provisions of Section 51 of the Vocational Education Act, to draw down a loan of £10,000 over the next five years. By autumn, work had started at Listerlin, and the £1,200 tender of P. Roche of New Ross to build the school at Mooncoin had been accepted. A setback to the development of the scheme was the closure of the day school in Clogh due to poor attendance, and a tendency locally to look for all materials to be provided free.[39]

In 1935 a deputation from Coon sought a school and in April, the purchase of a one-acre site for £50 was agreed. Listerlin opened in the same month and already there was discussion of renovating two extra rooms in Castlecomer. Amidst all this flurry of activity, the CEO had found time to acquire his M.A. and was congratulated on his achievement in November.[40]

Early in 1936, Edward Brennan's tender of £795-17 to build Coon school was accepted and Richard Walsh, having completed two years' probation, was made permanent. In March the committee expressed its sympathy with the relatives of G.T. Phillips who died in the second year of his retirement. He had given thirty years service as Principal of the City Technical School, as CEO of the Joint Technical Instruction Committee, and as the transitional CEO during the change-over to the new VEC. [41]

In May of 1938, Dr. Day, a member of the Committee while Bishop of Ossory, was congratulated on his elevation to the see of Armagh. Unfortunately, his tenure

Castlecomer Workhouse was opened in 1852. There were three ranges of buildings. The front range was partly demolished and the surviving part, seen here was opened as a Vocational School in 1933. It closed around 1940 and was re-opened in 1951. In 1963 students and teachers moved to a newly built school on the Kilkenny Road. The rooms vacated are now used by Kilkenny County Council as an Area Office.

Coon Vocational School is now a private residence.

The official opening of Kilkenny City Vocational School, January 1940
Dr. Richard Walsh CEO, County Kilkenny Vocational Education Committee, Professor J.V.Downes Architect, Most Rev. Dr. Patrick Collier, Bishop of Ossory and Chairman of County Kilkenny VEC.

Kilkenny City Vocational School Camogie Team 1939
Back L to R: Teacher Jim Byrne (R.I.P), Molly Dowling(R.I.P), Josie Dempsey, Betty Murphy, Mary Ryan, Clare Neary (R.I.P), Bridie Dowling.
Front L to R: M. Mc Grath, Unknown, Lily Curtin, Doreen Walton, Chrissie Millea.

Kilkenny City Vocational School Camogie Team 1940
Back L to R: Teacher Mai Sparks (R.I.P), Millie Holmes, Molly Dowing (R.I.P), Maureen Mc Grath (R.I.P), Bridie Lanigan, Bridie Dowling, Unknown.
Middle L to R: Molly Walsh, Mary Ryan, Hazel Burke, Mary Sinnott, Kitty Glennon (R.I.P)
Front L to R: Kitty McDonald (R.I.P), Molly Heffernan (R.I.P)

as Archbishop of Armagh was short. In October, the Committee offered their condolences to Mrs. Day on the death of her husband.[42] In the following January, congratulations were offered to Dr. James Staunton, another member, on his becoming Bishop of Ferns.[43] Dr. Day's successor, Rt. Rev. Dr. Tichborne joined the committee on becoming Bishop of Ossory, but died in April of 1940.[44]

By the end of the 1930s, the provision of schools in the county was going ahead quite well, with schools operating in Castlecomer, Mooncoin, Coon and Listerlin, and in the city, the Model School was renovated as the new City Technical School. There was still, however, a demand to be met. In 1937 and 1938, deputations were received from Conahy, Graignamanagh, Ballyhale and Johnstown. In each case, the committee agreed to acquire a site and have plans prepared.

In Conahy the site caused no problem but there was considerable delay over the plans. One sticking point was Departmental insistence on its policy of facing schools to the south, whereas the committee, and probably the local people, wanted the school to face the road.

In Graignamanagh, getting a site caused difficulty and delay. A first offer of a site of one and a third acres for £130 was considered too dear, with Johnstown costing £100 and Ballyhale £65. A very complicated offer was then brokered by the Graignamanagh Development Association. Mr. Hughes would sell an acre for £40, which was a very reasonable price even at that time, but in order to gain access to it, it would be necessary to purchase one sixth of an acre from a Mr. Cushen. As compensation for his plot of land, he wanted the committee to buy him an acre elsewhere for £60. The total cost of £100 was rejected by the VEC, who offered £55. The matter was eventually settled for £70. All that was now needed was finance, and Mr. Moynihan, the commissioner acting for Kilkenny Council gave consent to the taking out of a further loan of £5,000.[45]

100 Years of Vocational Education in County Kilkenny

The former Vocational
School in Callan which now
houses Callan Local Library.

**Mr. Christy Fewer(Teacher) and
Mr. P. Connolly with Mooncoin
Vocational School pupils 1942-43**
Back Row(from left:) Mr. C. Fewer,
P. Walsh, Mr. T. Tobin, Mr. P. Kelly,
H. Delahunty, J. Keever,
W. Walsh, T. Fitzgerald, Mr. P. Connolly.
Middle Row(from left:) M. McDonald,
J. Quinn, P. Lynch, M. Fitzgerald,
E. Brown, S. O'Keeffe.
Front Row(from left:) B. Keane, C.Rowe,
M. Holden, M. Moyhihan, J. Tobin,
J. Walsh, P. Wall.

Mooncoin Vocational School 1939-1940
Back Row(from left:) D. Mackey, J. Gorman, J. Delahunty, J. Deady, Mr. M.O'Hara, Mr. T. Foran.
Middle Row(from left:) K. Dunphy, T. Reddy, R. Wall, P. Keane, M O'Meara, J.J. Allen, W. Walsh, M. Crowley.
Front Row(from left:) J. Crowley, E. Falconer, K. Butler, M. Byrne, P. Burrows, J. Walsh, M. Quinn, E. Byrne,
A. Everett.

CHAPTER 3

World War II - Six Difficult Years

In September 1939, World War II began. The committee authorised the CEO to take whatever steps were necessary in the line of air raid precautions. At least one Kilkenny person must have expected more than bombs to drop from the sky, because, within three weeks of the start of the conflict, a letter was received requesting a class in the German language. The request was refused. The request was renewed in 1941, only to have consideration postponed indefinitely. At last, in 1943, the committee conceded the point after receiving a letter from twenty prospective students, and Miss Barron, the county librarian, was appointed as part-time teacher at 5/- per hour plus fourpence emergency bonus.[46]

This emergency bonus is first mentioned in April 1943. It was set at 5/- per week for unmarried teachers and 7/- for married. In the beginning caretakers and cleaners got a lesser rate, but by early 1945 the rate was 11/- for all employees, married, single, teacher, cleaner or caretaker. This bonus plus the cost of living bonus, and the employment of four extra teachers of Irish for two and a half years caused such a strain on the finances of the committee that in 1946 departmental approval was sought for an overdraft of £1,000 and in November the estimates sub-committee proposed that the local annual contribution be increased from 3 to 4 pence in the pound.[47]

Though it wasn't immediately apparent, the war was to have a dramatic effect on the expansion plans of the committee. In May 1940, a month after the committee had decided to build in Johnstown and Ballyhale, the architect, Mr. Downes gave his opinion that these two schools would between them cost more than the £5,000 available. In June, the reluctant decision was taken not to proceed with the building of schools in Conahy, Johnstown or Ballyhale.

The war itself is never mentioned in the minute books, but the consequences of the shortages of materials are clear.

Rationing of petrol could cause difficulties for teachers and VEC members. In early 1941, the committee agreed to provide evening classes at Castlecomer in mining, geology, mining science, physics, machine drawing, hand sketching and mathematics, all to be taught by Mr. Biltcliffe, a mining engineer. The introduction of petrol rationing prompted him to apply for a supplementary licence to purchase petrol in respect of his travel to and from his classes. The VEC passed on the request to the Department of Supplies, which refused his application.[48]

It became more expensive for VEC members to travel any distance to meetings, and they supported a call by their Westmeath colleagues for a shilling a mile travel expenses.

The problem was acute for Councillor E. Mahon. Ned lived at Clogh and couldn't get public transport from there to Kilkenny, so the committee agreed that he could hire a car, and they would honour his bills. Some months later, the CEO brought to their notice that they had paid £2-14 for one meeting to Cllr. Mahon, and this was more than he was allowed by the County Council for travel to their meeting. The VEC could not continue to pay this amount unless the member could establish with the County Manager his right to this rate from the County Council. When he did establish his right to the rate, the VEC submitted the whole question to the Department for a decision. After two refusals to sanction the amount, the CEO was instructed to write back, pointing out: that Ned Mahon was practically the only rural member left on the committee; that there was no public transport from Clogh to Castlecomer; that if he somehow got to Castlecomer, the 9.30 a.m. bus would have him in Kilkenny much too early for the meeting, and the 3.30 p.m. bus would arrive too late; that, even if he came on the early bus, he would still need a car to get to Castlecomer. After a year-and-a-half of letters to and fro, the committee was finally in a position, with departmental approval to pay for a car from Clogh to Castlecomer, and the bus to Kilkenny. The return trip would cost £1-5-6.[49]

Emergency conditions could affect schools in many ways. Fuel was in short supply and coal had to be ordered in bulk at high prices. In the summer of 1941, the CEO estimated that the city technical school would need twenty tons of coke or anthracite, Mooncoin six tons, and Listerlin five. For householders, turf was essential. Older people in Kilkenny can remember the long stacks of this fuel on the Fair Green, and even on the small number of bogs in County Kilkenny, turf production for local consumption was in full swing during the summer months. A fall in attendance at Coon school was blamed by the CEO on the wage available to boys in saving turf, at a time of labour shortages in rural areas. The impossibility of getting cycle tyres was also a factor in keeping students from school, even in the city school.[50]

With difficulty in importing food came the necessity for Ireland to feed itself from its own resources. Compulsory tillage was introduced and farmers, even in dairying areas, found themselves dealing with unfamiliar crops, particularly wheat. The VEC sponsored a series of lectures in their schools on farming and horticultural topics. The lecturers were supplied by the Royal Dublin Society. For instance, one proposed lecture at Mooncoin school was to cost £3 for the lecturer's fee and travelling expenses from Waterford to Mooncoin.[51]

Following a successful series of lectures in Kilkenny on farming subjects and on vegetable growing in allotment plots and small gardens, the Kilkenny farmers requested Agricultural Science classes for sons of farmers and farm labourers. The CEO outlined a scheme to appoint a teacher of Agricultural Science in the city school and to acquire a plot of land on the eleven month system. It took several months, but eventually a plot was rented which was close to the school and surrounded by a twelve foot wall. The rent was £40 per annum, a sum which would have bought a school site in a rural area some years before. Allotment plots were available near many towns. These would be taken by householders to raise potatoes and other vegetables. Mr. McDwyer wished to run a garden plot scheme for the students at Mooncoin and asked the committee to provide prizes for the most successful efforts. He was voted a sum of £9 for the year.[52]

Sites acquired for schools at Johnstown, Ballyhale and Conahy were offered to the former owners as grazing land on the eleven month system. The owners of the first two accepted the committee's offer, and at Conahy, the Parish Priest, Fr. Brady offered £2 per annum for the site, which would be used as a demonstration plot.[53]

Mr. Downes, the architect who had drawn up plans for Ballyhale and Johnstown wrote asking for payment for the work done. The committee thought he might be satisfied with an admission of their liability for the sums owed, and hoped to complete the schools "as soon as times were again normal". Mr. Downes was not impressed and was voted £99-9-5 for Johnstown and £75-15-11 for Ballyhale. [54]

During the war years, the schools undertook the testing of seed for farmers. The considerable work involved is clear from a submission by Mr. McDwyer, in Mooncoin, and Mr. Tooher, rural science teacher in the city. They had each tested 400 samples in the previous year, and at an hour for each sample, there was considerable interference with their normal work from February to April. They suggested getting a past pupil to do the work in his spare time under their supervision. The committee, with departmental approval, allowed £10 each at Mooncoin and Kilkenny and £5 at Coon.[55]

Difficulties in getting supplies were common. Sewing classes had problems by March of 1942, and there are references to purchases of second-hand electrical equipment and pottery equipment on a number of occasions.

Mooncoin took steps to deal with its electricity supply problem. A common sight near farmers' houses at the time was a windcharger. A large fan on top of a pylon operated a dynamo, which charged a battery or batteries, which served to provide light for the house. Mr. McDwyer, Mooncoin proposed to erect a windcharger for the school. He could have a pole, stays and cable provided locally for £30 if the committee provided the manufactured unit. Allowing £10 for a dynamo and rewinding, it was agreed to grant £40 for the complete job, subject to departmental sanction. Later on, a further sum of £12 was allowed to upgrade the batteries to give 290 amp. hrs. instead of the 75 originally proposed.[56]

In January 1946, with conditions beginning to return to normal, the stocktaker, Mr. Cotter reported a list of items worn out and missing in each school. The committee agreed, "that in the last six year period (when it was impossible to replace most items) practically no purchases of stock had been made and that worn-out items might now be replaced generally". By the end of the year, Mr. Cotter estimated that £85 to £95 would be needed to replace worn-out equipment throughout the county. The committee voted £50 in the current year, with the balance to be provided the following year.[57]

CHAPTER 4

The Post-War School Building Programme

The Second World War ended in 1945, but it wasn't until 1947 that the first mention of a renewed building programme was made at a VEC meeting in Kilkenny. In February of that year, it was noted that £5,000 was still available of the loan got through the County Council before the war. This would be insufficient for the building of much more than a single classroom school. The financial position at the time was not good. Already the committee was determined that Johnstown should have priority, and over the next year or two a consensus emerged as to what other locations should be considered. By November, it was decided to look for a site for a one-room school in Tullaroan. In February of 1948, the CEO reported that he and a Department Inspector, Morgan Sheehy had visited Tullaroan and agreed a price of £50 for a quarter acre site belonging to a Mr. Dillon. The VEC voted to accept the offer subject to department approval, and the following month Prof. J.V. Downes, B. Arch. reported that plans for Tullaroan were with the Board of Works.[58]

It was to be four more years before Tullaroan Vocational School opened. Downes first set of plans envisaged a school costing £3,600 and members wanted it redesigned to cost half as much. Four months later they accepted that this wasn't feasible and decided to put the school to tender in hopes that rural construction costs might be less than the architect thought. In February of 1949 he presented plans for the school and was instructed to prepare detailed drawings. Advertisements were to be published for contracts. By November, tenders had been opened and Mr. Dwyer was successful with a bid of £2,951. In the following January a letter from the Department complained that this price was excessive, and the CEO was to attend a conference with department officials, the architect and an inspector with the object of reducing the price to between £1,800 and £2,000. In February of 1950 the CEO reported the results: savings of £100 to £200 could be made. The committee members took the sensible view that spoiling the architect's conception of the building for that sort of minor saving would be silly. They wanted the tender price to stand and the school to be built. By August the Department too had seen sense and the school was sanctioned.[59]

The period of construction had its problems. In March of 1951 the minutes record that one workman had been killed and others injured in an accident on site. In the following month, it was learned that an action was being taken against the contractor, the architects and County Kilkenny VEC. However the Irish National Insurance Company advised the committee that, as they believed the contractor to have departed from the specifications, they would be defending the action on behalf of the VEC. By October the keys of the school had been handed over but, as the work contracted for was unfinished, the CEO was instructed to take action to have matters put to rights. In June of the following year the contractor was given until the 26th of the month to finish, otherwise the job would be given to another contractor to finish, using the retention money to pay for the work. [60]

In the late forties and early fifties, the VEC made several attempts to draw up a list of locations where schools would be built and to put them in order of priority. The order of priority changed several times, depending on the probable costs of the various proposals, and on the influence which local communities could bring to bear. That Tullaroan was the first new construction was probably due to its being a one-room school, and thus affordable out of the balance of the pre-war loan available to the committee. The re-opening of Castlecomer was another relatively cheap project.

Castlecomer had opened in 1934 but closed after some years. The premises in the old workhouse was still available and in 1950, there is a note of domestic economy classes being held on two nights a week, and of a payment of seven shillings and sixpence to a caretaker. In November of 1949, the committee decided to pay transport costs for pupils from Castlecomer who were attending Coon Vocational School. The pupils themselves were to pay a maximum of sixpence. The Department of Education took a month or more to consider the matter, and came up with the sensible idea of regarding the transport costs to Coon as scholarships. In July of 1950, a deputation from Castlecomer came before the VEC meeting and urged the re-opening of the school in their town. They were promised that the school would re-open by Christmas. An architects report in October made it clear that some refurbishment of the building would be needed first. In May 1951, P. Kelly's tender of £430-14-6 was accepted. In the following January, Mr. Peadar Madden was appointed Teacher-in-Charge. The re-opening of Castlecomer had an effect on attendance in Coon. As soon as the decision to re-open was taken, the scholarships formerly offered to Castlecomer boys were earmarked for pupils from Clogh and Moneenroe. In late 1953, word was received from the Department that there would be no further sanction for scholarships to Coon from the following year. Five pupils from Clogh who had been enrolled at Coon the previous year had transferred to Castlecomer. Members from the area pointed out that whereas the roads from Clogh or Moneenroe to Coon were bad, there was a good road to Castlecomer.[61]

Johnstown had been sanctioned just before the Second World War. A site had been purchased, and plans had been drawn up. Lack of money, particularly with building costs soaring due to the war, had forced the VEC to postpone plans to build in Johnstown, but as conditions eased in the late forties, there was still the awkward fact that Johnstown would be a bigger school and a much more expensive job than Tullaroan. In December 1950, Prof. Downes submitted plans for Johnstown school, and these were approved by the VEC in the following month. In June of 1951, the County Council was asked under Section 51 of the Vocational Education Act 1930 to grant a loan of £30,000 so that the VEC could proceed with its building programme, which included Graignamanagh, Thomastown and Ballyhale as well as Johnstown.[62]

Graignamanagh had got its position at number two on the VEC list due to some diligent work by the local Development Association. When they renewed their demand for a school in 1948, they were told that they should have a site of half to three quarters of an acre at a cost to the VEC not to exceed £50. They were back in October with a request that the CEO should inspect a site in Graignamanagh, with sewage and water connections available. As a result, they were given no definite promise, but were told that Tullaroan, Conahy and Johnstown had prior claims. In July of 1950, a deputation led by John O'Leary was able to promise a site of one acre in the town, which would be available free if the school were built. They were to be placed next on the list after Johnstown, and a three teacher school was envisaged, subject to the Department's approval. One slight hiccup delayed matters a bit. Messrs. Cunningham Bros. who were working on plans for Graignamanagh notified the committee that Mr. Clarke, the architect who was working on the plans, had left the firm. They proposed to hire an architect to replace him, but in the meantime had no architect in the firm as Mr. Cunningham was an engineer. The VEC asked the Department to approve continuing with Cunningham brothers, and by the following year, the firm was being referred to as Cunningham and Roche.[63]

While the projects for Johnstown and Graignamanagh were being progressed, construction was under way at Tullaroan, and advance moves on schools for Thomastown and Ballyhale were also occupying the minds of committee members, as well as the refurbishment of an old national school at Callan to provide a vocational school for that town, not to mention a bit of a crisis at Dunnamaggin. The work load of the CEO, Dr. Walsh must have been considerable, especially if one considers that his total office staff consisted of one secretary.

The Department didn't like the Graignamanagh site but the committee replied that it was too late now to change. The estimated cost would be around £9,000, slightly dearer than Johnstown which would be a bigger school. The extra expense at Graignamanagh was due to the nature of the site. Johnstown had been sanctioned by the Department in January of 1952, and on 24th November 1952 the Minister of Education performed the official opening ceremony. The teacher-in-charge was Mr. Paddy Taaffe, who transferred back to Kilkenny as woodwork teacher some years afterwards. Extra costs of £1,049 on the building of the school due to increased labour and materials expenses caused dissatisfaction and the committee resolved to have all future contracts include grounds, furniture etc. The cost of fitting out the school came to over £700, not including items like teachers' desks, sewing machines etc. Small wonder that by 1953, a further loan of £28,000 was being sought.[64]

In 1953, there was a gallant attempt to institute a national festival to bring tourists into Ireland. It failed eventually, but for three weeks or so in April of that year events were held all over the country. Graignamanagh extended its festival into May, and on the 11th of that month, Kilkenny VEC held its monthly meeting in the town to coincide with the turning of the first sod on the school site. The tender of W.K. Cleere had been accepted a month previously at £10,557-5-6, considerably more than the architect's estimate. The Graignamanagh Development Association would have liked a plaque on the school grounds acknowledging the fact that the site had been donated free by Miss Keating. The VEC, while sympathetic, replied that it couldn't use its funds for such a purpose. The school was officially opened on 9th December 1954. There were four teachers and the teacher-in-charge was Mr. Daly.[65]

In March 1951 Dr. Hughes, the curate at Slieverue in Ferrybank Parish near Waterford offered the newly extended hall at Slieverue to the VEC at a nominal rent, provided they set up a vocational school there with both day and evening classes. The chance to start up in the area without massive capital expenditure was too good to miss and the committee agreed to have a department inspector visit the hall and report on its suitability. The concept of a nominal rent led to some months of tough negotiation, with the committee's opening offer of £40 per annum being somewhat removed from Dr. Hughes's idea of £100 as being more appropriate. The matter seems to have been settled for £65 per annum. By January of 1952, H.C. Fewer is noted as the Teacher-in-Charge. By the end of that year, Dr. Hughes was asking for £120 - with some justification. He had been billed for an extra £25 in rates on the newly extended hall, and he asked that the VEC should bear the increased cost. He was informed that school buildings should be exempt from rates, and that he should make a claim for exemption to the County Council. By the end of the year, he was able to inform the VEC that the County Council refused to remit the rates on the building as it was merely rented to a local authority. The VEC voted to increase the rent paid from £65 to £80, which didn't quite cover the extra cost to Slieverue parish of the £25 increase in rates.[66] The VEC established a school at very little capital outlay, except for equipment, but Slieverue climbed way up the waiting list.

Dr. Doyle, the Parish Priest of Callan approached the VEC looking for a vocational school for the town and offering the old national school as a site. The committee received a report from its architects late in 1950, and agreed with Dr. Doyle to buy the building for £450. When the Department approved the purchase, sketch plans were prepared. In late 1951 a slight snag appeared. The Primary Branch of the department wanted £120 for its interest in the old primary school and refused to remit this sum despite representations. County Kilkenny VEC decided to increase the amount paid to Dr. Doyle by £120 and let him settle with the Primary Branch. The architects, Cunningham Bros. estimated that putting the old building in good condition would cost approximately £3,500. To fund this from its own resources would be a problem for the VEC, and there was mention of approaching the Local Loans Society. After a chat with the County Secretary, the CEO was confident that it would be cheaper to go through the County Council and was authorised to seek a loan of £5,000 which was thought to be necessary for refurbishment and fitting out. In May of 1953, Dowling Bros. tender of £4,783-6-0 was accepted. The school opened 14th February 1955. The VEC meeting for that month was held in Callan after the opening and the minutes record that Cllr. John Holohan deplored remarks made by Dr. Doyle at the official opening, suggesting

Slieverue Vocational School Official Opening
Front L to R: Canon Ryan, Dr Walsh, CEO County
Kilkenny VEC, Dr. Hughes PP, Mrs. Walsh, Fr. Stapleton.
Back L to R: John Carey, Principal, Slieverue NS,
Pat Connolly, Mooncoin,
Mona Hearne Department of Education Inspector,
Christy Fewer, Desmond Kelly, Ferrybank, Michael Griffin,
Seamus Doran, Mooncoin.

Slieverue Vocational School - Turning of the Sod 1963
L to R: Canon Ryan, Dr. Walsh, CEO County Kilkenny
VEC, Unknown, Dr. Hughes PP, Mr. Bob Alyward MCC,
Mr Paddy Edwards, Department of Education Inspector, Mr.
Tom Walsh, MCC, Mr. Christy Fewer.

Site of Slieverue Vocational School.

that poor attendance at the day school was due to negligence by the committee. Mr. Peadar O'Dwyer was Teacher-in-Charge.[67]

In October 1949, in response to a letter from the Department of Education, the VEC ordered a report on the condition of Dunnamaggin school. At the following meeting they had a report from Mr. John Gillman B.E. The roof of the building was in very bad condition but there was no immediate danger of collapse, unless in a violent gale or after a heavy fall of snow. It was sufficiently strong to protect the pupils in case of a minor collapse. It would cost £700 to make the roof safe, and this was not advisable as it was on a dangerous junction and the County Council was considering its removal. His recommendation was to discontinue using the building as a school within the next few years.

"A demountable classroom" - a hint of things to come

These were the years when the committee was preoccupied with the Johnstown, Graignamanagh, Thomastown and Ballyhale projects, but in March 1953, Dunnamaggin again claimed their urgent attention. A deputation from the area said the old school was too dangerous, with the roof partially stripped, and ceilings ready to collapse. They asked for a new one-room school, and after a discussion the CEO was asked to investigate the possibility of putting up a wooden structure. In July the committee agreed to the purchase of a wooden structure "as approved by the Department of Education". This was to be got from Lee Joinery and would cost £800. A plot of three eighths of an acre was to be had at Baurscoob for £35 plus legal costs. In October the members were told that the department had approved this "demountable classroom" and the purchase of the plot of land. The building had been designed by Mr. Thomas Bridgeman, and his fee of £42-8-0 was to be shared between Kilkenny and Wicklow VECs. The cost of transporting the school to the site was £36-10-0, paid to CIE. It was erected on site in July '54 by two woodwork teachers who got £9 travelling expenses. One of them got more than the other because he drove home to Kilkenny each day to have his lunch. The structure was evidently just bare timber inside, because the minutes record expenditure of £67 on lino and £45 to line the walls and ceiling with Lignatex.[68]

Conahy, which had once enjoyed a high priority for the building of a one-room school as soon as Tullaroan was completed, was gradually pushed down the list, until in February 1954, the decision was taken to abandon the project and sell the site which the committee had owned since before the war.[69]

The committee owned a plot in Ballyhale, and in 1948 they got a demand for fourteen shillings in rates. Although school buildings were exempt, they were liable for the rates on the vacant site until such time as the school was built. A deputation was told that the school would be built although Graignamanagh and Johnstown would have priority. Around the same time Thomastown began to make its claim to a school. In March 1952, the committee decided to have plans drawn up for a

Official Opening of Johnstown Vocational School 1952

Billy Holmes, caretaker, Johnstown Vocational School (1952-1976)

Tullaroan Vocational School.

Graignamanagh Vocational School-Turning the Sod 1953

Teresa Buggy with Boys Cookery Class, Graignamanagh Vocational School 1961-62
Also pictured in the photo is Brian Hunt, Woodwork Teacher.

two-room school in Ballyhale and a three-room one in Thomastown. The Department almost immediately sent the first of a number of letters expressing reservations about building two vocational schools five miles or so apart. In the meantime, an inspector viewed a one-and-a-half acre site at Thomastown which was on offer for £150. The Department approved the site but suggested that two acres would be better, and the VEC agreed to pay £225 for the two acres. It was late in 1955 before Ballyhale and Thomastown reached the top of the VEC's list, and by then pressure was coming from Slieverue and Castlecomer for new schools to replace what were by then seen as inadequate buildings.

In June 1956, tenders for the two schools were discussed at a special meeting of the committee. Also present were Mr. Edwards, an Inspector with the Department, and Mr. Colm Ó Cochláin, an architect with Cunningham Brothers. The tenders were much higher than the members had expected, and Ballyhale was as expensive for three rooms as Thomastown was for four. Mr. Edwards explained the reasons for this, but it was decided that both schools should be re-advertised. This resulted in threats of legal action from the builders who had tendered, but the legal adviser told the committee that they were not bound to accept the lowest or any tender. Another special meeting resulted in the tender of Dowling Brothers for Thomastown being accepted at £13,852-5-5, while it was decided to re-advertise for tenders for Ballyhale. In December, Departmental approval for the Thomastown scheme came through, but Ballyhale was postponed indefinitely. When the CEO said that funds were insufficient to build and then equip Thomastown, the members decided to go ahead with the building and worry about the equipment later. By January 1958, approval had also been given for Ballyhale and a contractor given the go-ahead. [70]

All through these years the VEC had constant need for overdrafts. Each time the consent of the Department was needed to run an overdraft, but in large measure, the problem was a result of slow payments from the Department. In March of 1957, the bank was anxious to have the overdraft wiped out. The problem had been caused because money from the revenue account had been spent on the completion of schools, an expense which should normally have come from the capital budget. There was a debt of £3,320 on schools completed to that date. It was not permissible to ask the County Council for a loan to cover that amount. In addition, no refunds had been received from the Department on Expenditure connected with Ballyhale and Thomastown. It didn't help that the department of education notified the committee that cuts of 6% imposed the previous year were to continue in 1957/58. Grants were cut by £286 and the local contribution went down by £365. [71]

The tender for electric lighting at Thomastown came to £622. R.J. Ryan's tender was the lowest but only £420 had been allowed in the main contract. The difference was mainly due to a duty of 40% on all electrical goods imposed in the meantime. Doherty Brothers' tender of £661 for central heating was accepted. The partial destruction of the partly built school by fire in early 1952 was a blow, but apart from the delay caused, the fire, which was malicious, had no financial implications for the committee. Mr. Ó Cochláin assured them that the insurance company would cover the cost of putting things right. He reckoned that £3,000 worth of damage had been done, but in the event the tender for reconstruction came to £1178-18, a figure the members regarded with surprise, but equanimity, considering the matter of academic interest since somebody else was paying. Over £2,000 worth of equipment was put into the school, and the official opening was held on the 13th of October 1958. By that time work had started on Ballyhale. In May of 1959, the committee were told of problems with the septic tank there. In August, a further report said that due to its being in yellow clay, with consequent poor drainage, and also due to the presence of springs in the field, the tank very soon overflowed. To "remedy" the situation, a proposal was accepted which would be considered environmentally unfriendly nowadays: an overflow pipe was to convey the surplus to a nearby stream at a cost of £30 for cutting the trench and providing a pipe. Two local farmers through whose lands the stream flowed were to receive compensation of £15 each. Planning acts were some years in the future. In the event it took eight months to get department sanction to fix the problem, with bitter complaints from the committee about the health hazard involved.[72]

In early 1955, the meeting held in Callan to coincide with the opening of the school there, received a deputation from Slieverue. They pointed out that the school based in the Parish Hall had been three years in operation, was highly successful, and was not able to cater properly for the numbers attending; the population was growing; there was a keen demand for classes in metalwork and engineering; a purpose-built four room school was needed. They also pointed out that Waterford City Vocational School would soon refuse to take pupils from outside the city area, throwing an extra burden on Slieverue. At its next monthly meeting the committee decided that the schools then at an advanced stage of planning at Thomastown and Ballyhale would be completed, and that the next step in their building programme would be the replacement of unsuitable premises at Castlecomer and Slieverue with permanent schools. A deputation from Glenmore wanted any replacement school built halfway between Slieverue and Glenmore, but the committee members were unsympathetic.[73]

The pressure of work on the CEO and his one clerk must have been considerable with all this construction and planning of schools, together with the increase in the number of schools and the resultant routine administrative duties. On several occasions the committee asked the Department to sanction extra office staff. In 1955, the department replied, requiring the committee to justify hiring a second clerical assistant. They pointed out that in 1934 they were responsible for one eight teacher school in Kilkenny and one temporary rural school. Now they had forty whole-time teachers, ten to twelve part-time teachers, eleven permanent schools, twelve caretakers and an annual expenditure of £33,000. Six months later they got a refusal of an extra assistant, but an offer of £100 per annum to hire temporary secretarial assistance. They didn't consider this practical, due to the difficulty of getting somebody competent to work on this basis, and to the necessity of having somebody whole-time who knew the system. They opted to continue as at present and if work piled up, it was out of their control. Eighteen months later they renewed their plea, on the grounds that the clerk, Mary Rabbit was overworked. At a time when VECs all over the country were considering a Department circular urging economies, their plea fell on deaf ears. By 1959, Miss Rabbit had resigned and her successor Carmel Darcy was similarly overworked. The Department finally relented and Patti Burke was appointed temporary whole-time shorthand typist and a month or so later made permanent in the newly-created post.[74]

Slieverue and Castlecomer

Three years after the committee had decided to provide permanent schools at Slieverue and Castlecomer, the Department wrote requesting a statement as to why these schools were needed. Since the committee already had inspectors' reports recommending new buildings at both locations, they felt that the officials were engaged in delaying tactics. In the meantime the committee acquired sites at both locations. In Castlecomer the Castlecomer Estate was paid £200 for 3.4 acres alongside the Kilkenny Road, part of which was sold on to the local convent, leaving two acres for the vocational school. In Slieverue Dr. Hughes sold three quarters of an acre of parish land adjoining the curate's house for £170. By March 1959, plans for Slieverue had been approved by the Department and sketch plans for Castlecomer amended by them and approved by the committee. The Department questioned the sale of part of the site to the local convent. The committee replied that it was mostly a narrow neck of land along the road, useless for school purposes and used as an unofficial dump. The Department sanctioned the sale.[75]

Getting plans approved by both the committee and the Department took a long time. When the architect presented plans to the committee in early 1960, he estimated that Slieverue would cost £25,000 and Castlecomer £30,000. He was instructed to bring in revised plans to keep the building costs for each to £19,000, including fees, site costs and legal costs. In each case £5,000 was to be kept for fitting out. This process was gone through and resulted in severe cutting back on the plans, bringing the estimated costs down to £18,000 for Slieverue and £17,500 for Castlecomer. It was the Department which considered that the plans needed improvement at that stage. And it was late in 1961 before the committee submitted final plans for sanction. Tenders for Castlecomer were considered in January of '62, and for Slieverue in July of that year.[76]

There was some controversy about the Castlecomer tenders. The lowest was by Dowling Brothers, but the committee decided on a four to three vote to give the contract to P. Kelly of Castlecomer the second lowest bidder, on the basis that he was locally based, and might have fewer extras during the course of the contract in transport costs. The Department took a dim view of this decision and the committee was eventually obliged to award the contract to Dowlings at a figure of just over £22,000. The two lowest tenders for Slieverue were so close that both builders agreed to have their bills of quantities opened and checked by the quantity surveyor. He made some small adjustments to the tots but Sisk and Son of Cork were still the lowest bidders at £23,351-9-6, and got the contract. In January 1963, the CEO informed the members that the £48,000 borrowed to build and equip Slieverue and Castlecomer would be sufficient to build but not to equip the schools. He was asked to estimate the amount needed for furniture and equipment, and to approach the County Council for a loan.[77]

Dr. Walsh's long tenure in the position of Chief Executive Officer was drawing to a close. In March of 1962 the Department told the committee to advise the local appointments commission to recommend a person to the position of CEO when the position became vacant. His retirement date was August 31st 1960, but he continued in office until his successor was appointed.[78]

Since his appointment in November 1933, he had presided over two periods of expansion and guided the County Kilkenny VEC through the difficulties of the Second World War. At his retirement the committee was responsible for schools at Kilkenny, Mooncoin, Listerlin, Ballyhale, Dunnamaggin, Thomastown, Graignamanagh, Callan, Castlecomer, Johnstown and Coon. Tullaroan was closed but there was still a possibility of its re-opening. Coon and Listerlin were not attracting enough pupils, Callan was threatened, and Dunnamaggin would eventually lose out to Ballyhale. The others were thriving. Kilkenny City VS was a large school with a day school, a domestic economy school, and commercial school. Five schools were purpose-built; Mooncoin (1935), Johnstown (1952), Graignamanagh (1954), Thomastown (1958) and Ballyhale (1959). Temporary premises at Castlecomer and Slieverue were being replaced. In addition to the permanent schools, night classes were held in various centres in the county, the main subjects being woodwork, domestic economy and Irish. Adult education in the wider sense was also coming to prominence. Mr. Connolly of Mooncoin outlined his duties in this regard in 1959. In the course of his work with Adult Education groups in County Kilkenny, he had travelled over 2000 miles to arrange talks and lectures, and spent 200 hours in preparation work.

Slieverue and Castlecomer schools occupied a great deal of the committee's time in 1963 and 1964 both before and after they opened. The sewage scheme for the town of Castlecomer was delayed, leaving the school with no connection to sewage. The committee, aware that schools at Dunnamaggin, Listerlin and Coon were using Elsan chemical toilets, decided to install these at Castlecomer. There was an immediate protest from the Health Authority, and the architect was asked to put in a temporary overflow to the nearby river Deen. The architect notified them that the landowner involved objected, so £130 was voted to fix the problem. The architect came back with an estimate to put in a septic tank for £275. The committee decided to put in the Elsans after all.[79]

In Slieverue a water supply was the problem. Several local sources were tried but eventually it was decided to hire a water diviner to locate a site for boring a well on the school land. Tenders from three diviners were considered. I couldn't find a reference to a report but in 1965 a payment of £245 was made to the contractor who had drilled the well.[80]

Buying equipment for the two schools required a new loan of £5,000 each, and provision for the building of a school sanctioned for Gowran, and the erection of a Principal's office and other rooms in Kilkenny City Vocational School increased the amount borrowed through the County Council to £41,800.[81]

There were defects in both schools and the architect said that these would be put right before the openings. In the case of Castlecomer however, there were some extras not in the contract and these would have to be paid for. Dealing with a steep bank at the back and additional painting were mentioned. These extras arose from the committee's determination to cut costs at the design stage.[82]

The greatest problem with both didn't become apparent until the schools were actually in operation - the heating in both was inadequate. The burners were not working properly and the architect proposed to fit inducer fans to improve the draught. These would be fitted at no extra cost to the committee. Two months later, this had been done and the heat was adequate but the cost of coal was outrageous at 20/- a day. In March of 1964 the Committee were informed that, when the caretakers learned to manage the burners properly, matters would improve. Hearing that the caretakers were obliged to give constant attention to the burners, the committee decided to hire a heating expert to report. The man chosen was Mr. L.C.C. Leonard and his report became available to the committee in October of 1964.

The cross-section of the flue at Castlecomer was less than that demanded by the specifications. To deal with the burner fitted, the chimney would need to be taken down and rebuilt to specification. Slieverue had an adequate cross-section, but both it and Castlecomer would need to have an extra ten feet added to their chimneys to produce a decent draught. At Castlecomer the contractor would be liable for replacing the chimney, and could then tender for raising it to thirty feet. At Slieverue the extension could go to tender immediately. The committee however decided to ask the architects about the effect on the appearance of each school.

Some time before this, Mr. Colm Ó Cochláin informed the committee that he had purchased the Kilkenny end of the practice from Cunningham Brothers, that he would be taking responsibility for Castlecomer and that they should contact Cunninghams in Waterford regarding Slieverue. Both firms gave it as their opinion that thirty foot chimneys would spoil the appearance of the schools. The committee asked Mr. Leonard to recommend a new boiler and make other recommendations. He advised new boilers in both schools as well as extra radiators. The committee consulted their legal adviser, who contacted the architects.

The eventual solution agreed was that both schools would get new hopper-fed coal-burning boilers costing £433 each, of which the architects would pay £217, the amount of the original tender. Cllr. John Holohan remarked that he hoped in future there would be no cheese-paring. If they had employed a clerk-of-works to supervise construction and a heating expert to design the systems, a lot of trouble and expense would have been spared. It must have been cold in the schools during the three winters involved. One piece of good news was the connection of Castlecomer to the town sewage scheme. [83]

The construction of Tullaroan VS had begun in early 1951, and by 1963 had been joined by new schools at Johnstown, Graignamanagh, Thomastown, Ballyhale, Castlecomer and Slieverue. A "demountable school" had been erected at Dunnamaggin, and it is interesting to note that the dreaded word "prefab" so familiar to a generation of teachers hadn't yet gained currency. A school had opened in Callan in a refurbished building. The amount of borrowing through the County Council was very large by the standards of the time, and meeting half the cost of repayments must have been a considerable burden. As well as that the minutes record regular annual increases in the local demand, the VEC being regularly obliged to raise the rate by the maximum allowable amount of threepence in the pound annually.

The committee decided on new schools at Freshford, Gowran and Ballyragget, and even got sanction for the first two - a great comfort to Cllr. Tom Waldron of Freshford, and the Parish Priest of Gowran, Canon Murphy, who were both members of the committee. These schools were never built however, and the planned extension at Kilkenny was put on the long finger. The 1960s saw a great rethink on Irish educational provision, and very great changes at post-primary level, which were being planned while the VEC in Kilkenny were watching their own territory.

Mr. Sean O'Regan took office as CEO in April of 1964. At about the same time a salary increase had been granted to teachers and to CEOs. Teachers had also got a status increase, but this did not apply to CEOs of VECs. The result was that Mr. O'Regan was earning less as a Grade III CEO, than he would have if he had remained as Headmaster in Swinford. The members were sympathetic and called on the Department to grant him five extra increments. There is no reply to this recorded. By December, he announced to the Committee that he had been appointed as CEO in Mayo and was resigning with effect from 1st April 1965. During the period before the appointment of a new CEO, an acting CEO would be needed. No principal or senior teacher in the county was interested so the committee appointed Dr. Richard Walsh, retired CEO to the temporary post. He served for a year until April 1966.

Boat Building Course at the City Technical School, Ormonde Road 1965 includes Matt Kennedy and Denis Buckley.

Picture of a group of staff from the City Technical School, Ormonde Road
Back L to R: Jim Timmons, Matt Kennedy.
Front L to R: Kate Hennessy, Moyra McCarthy, Sean Dignan, Patti Burke, Carmel Darcy.

Pictured at the presentation to Mr. James Phelan of Coolnaleen, Glenmore, a former pupil of Slieverue Vocational School who won the 14th International Apprentices' World Competition for Carpentry and Joinery, which was held in Glasgow
Left to right: Mr. S. Power, Department of Education, Rev. R. Phelan, C.C,
Dr. F. O'Callaghan, Department of Education, Mr. C.Fewer, Mr. James Phelan, Very Rev. M. McGrath, PP,
Dr. R. A. Walsh, CEO, County Kilkenny VEC.

Group taken at the annual dinner of the County Kilkenny Vocational Teachers' Association in the Metropole Hotel 1957
Front row (left to right)
Mr. John Walsh, Chairman,
Miss M. Feeney, Ald. S. Monahan, Chairman, Vocational Education Committee,
The Mayoress, Mrs. Holohan,
The Mayor, Mr. J. Holohan,
Dr. R. A. Walsh, C.E.O, Mr.
J. A. O'Donnell, Secretary.
Middle row- Mr. P. Connolly,
Mr. P. Taaffe, Mr. J. Daly, Mr. M. O'Neill,
Mr. S. Dignan, Miss G. Kelly,
Mr. M. Purcell,Mr. J. O'Byrne, Headmaster,
City Vocational School, Mr. M. Leahy,
Miss B. Lynch, Mr. W. Cleary,
Miss M. Morris, Miss M.Chambers.
Back row-Mr. J Colter, Mr. M. Loughman,
Mr. D. Canning, Miss M. Aughney,
Mr. D. Buckley, Mr. P. Madden.

Mooncoin Vocational School: 1945-1946
Back Row: James Kelly, Jer Delehunty,
Jimmy Foley, Sem Hayes, Michael Croke,
Pat Coffey, A. Henderson,
Joe Walsh, Pat Walsh (R.I.P.), Joe Anthony,
Lar Digens.
Middle row: Mary Fitzgerald,
Maura Malone, Maura Carroll,
Eileen Walsh, Greta Hennebry, Eda Carroll,
Myra Dunne, Mary Greene,
Josephine White, Cathleen O'Hara
Third row: Tes Hayes, Mary Grant,
Mr. Connelly, Miss Goulding,
Mr. McDwyer, Mr. Fewer,
Catherine Delahunty, May Carroll.
Sitting: Jim Anthony, Jimmy English,
Mary O'Keeffe, Statia Phelan,
Cosmas Maguire.

CHAPTER 5

The Dawn of a New Era

In 1963, the committee had voted an honorarium of £5 each to the two typists in the CEO's office for the after-hours work involved in compiling records for the study Investment in Education. This report was published in 1965 and provided the information on which reforms were based in the following years. It found that participation rates in second-level education were unacceptably low, and that making better use of existing facilities would be one way of improving matters.

In January of 1966, the Minister of Education wrote to the authorities of secondary and vocational schools. His letter called for equality of educational opportunity, reminded schools that the school-leaving age would be raised to 16 by 1970, looked forward to the provision of post-primary education for all children, and looked forward to the provision of an education suited to the different aptitudes and abilities of the children. From 1969, the Intermediate Certificate examination would be open to Vocational schools as well as Secondary Schools with new subjects added and revised syllabuses. The Department wanted to find out how many children in an area needed post-primary education, what facilities were needed for them, what the existing facilities were, and what additional facilities were needed. [84]

On the 24th of January 1966, County Kilkenny VEC held a special meeting to consider the Minister's letter. The acting CEO, Dr. Walsh reported on a meeting a week before at which the principals of St. Kieran's College, the CBS Secondary School, St. John's College and the CEO discussed the letter. Dr. Walsh seems to have visited girls' schools in the city and Secondary and Vocational schools in the county, because he was able to give the VEC a quite detailed report on the requirements and facilities in each centre. In the city it seemed that there might be as many as six groups of boys seeking woodwork classes from the Vocational school, and these could only be provided after four in the afternoons or after half past seven at night. The Presentation might require typing and shorthand classes which could be fitted into the Day School's hours. In Callan, Thomastown and Mooncoin local Secondary Schools would require the same sort of facilities. At Ferrybank no facilities were needed from Slieverue. In Castlecomer the convent wanted classes in Science and Commerce.

The committee decided to invite Secondary authorities to meet with three members of the VEC, the Acting CEO, an Inspector from the Department of Education and three Vocational School Principals to discuss co-operation in the matter of classes. A preliminary meeting was held on 26th February and afterwards the CEO prepared a list of the facilities and extra teachers needed in each Vocational school and their probable cost: Callan £2,135; Thomastown £2,175;

Castlecomer £400; Mooncoin £400; Kilkenny City £38,330.

The meeting of the city principals, VEC representatives and CEO with Mr. Ó Nualláin, a Department Inspector, took place on March 24th and the requirements of some secondary schools had fallen dramatically in the meantime. In the city only St. Kieran's College and St. John's College would still require woodwork. The other three schools would provide their own facilities. When the Vocational School Principal, Mr. Byrne enquired about the possibility of his students using the CBS language laboratory, he was told there was unlikely to be a vacancy.

The CEO and the Inspector visited schools in the county area. There was less change of position in these centres. Callan Convent would require classes in typewriting, and these could be provided. Mooncoin Convent School and the Vocational school would be able to make similar arrangements for commerce. In Castlecomer there could be reciprocal arrangements. The Convent School would require classes in Commerce and Science and were offering French classes if required.

It was explained that teachers would be credited with hours of work done in either school in which they worked, that they would be subject to their own employer, that the school of employment would be responsible for insurance travelling between schools, that discipline would be the responsibility of the receiving school.

A month later Dr. Walsh retired for the second time and Mr. Eamonn Gibson of Renmore, Co. Galway became Chief Executive Officer.[85]

During Dr. Walsh's tenure as CEO, huge social changes had taken place. Only now and then are these reflected in the minutes of the VEC. Mooncoin school had its first connection to the Electricity Supply Board grid in 1948. In the following year, the provision of an electric cooker in the school was requested, on the grounds that several people in the area had bought electric cookers and there was a demand for demonstrations in their use, which the domestic economy teacher could meet if there were a cooker in the school. Mooncoin, in a populous area and on a main road, would have been an early beneficiary of the rural electrification scheme, which took a lot longer to reach more remote areas. The same meeting in 1958 which considered tenders for electric connections in the almost finished Ballyhale school, was informed that rural electrification had reached Coon and that it would cost £37 to provide fifteen lights, six ironing points, heat and cooker points. Listerlin was connected in 1960.[86]

Sanitation in rural areas changed over the period. In 1960 Johnstown VS depended on Elsan chemical toilets. A new main sewer was planned for the area and would run by the school, but it was nine years from the opening of the school before the connection to the main sewer went to tender. Ballyhale was built with a septic tank system and Castlecomer was planned for a similar sewage disposal scheme, but the construction of a new main running by the school made a mains connection possible.[87]

Farm work changed dramatically. In 1948, a course in farriery was held in Kilkenny City. It included smithwork and welding, but the main focus was on the shoeing of horses. In 1953 when the Department proposed a similar course, the members felt that there was little demand as the craft had practically died out. In the intervening five years, many farmers had turned to the tractor for ploughing and other farm tasks, and increased prosperity had seen the first signs of the dominance of the motor-car in transport, both on and off the farm.[88]

One of Dr. Walsh's interests was the Kilkenny Arts Society and his involvement led to the City Vocational School becoming the focus of national interest in 1954, when the Arts Society held a debate in the school on the subject "That Ulster's best interests lie with the United Kingdom". In an era when the anti-partition movement was dominant, this was treading on dangerous ground, and when the speakers to the motion became known, considerable controversy ensued. Colonel W.W.B. Topping MP, the Unionist chief whip, and Mr. W. Douglas, Secretary of the Ulster Unionist Council, were the targets of criticism in their own community for debating partition "with men holding extreme views for the destruction of the British Empire". The *Kilkenny People* was equally critical from the other end of the political spectrum, their ire being directed at the Arts Society and its sub-committee, the Kilkenny Debating Society for holding the debate in the first place. The newspaper had been to the fore some years before in condemning Hubert Butler, for an alleged insult to the Papal Nuncio when he referred to forced conversions in war-time Yugoslavia. Opinion was divided in Kilkenny and although Butler himself was not prominent in the Kilkenny Arts Society, it was dominated by his sympathisers, and he worked in the background. When the night of the debate arrived, armed special branch officers and a sniper on the roof to protect the speakers against any attack proved unnecessary and the debate passed off without incident. It was widely reported north and south of the border and even made the pages of the *Manchester Guardian*. There were further debates on various worthy topics in subsequent years, but none that aroused the same interest nationally. The minutes of County Kilkenny VEC are silent on the matter, although a year or two later a resolution on the hiring out of the hall carried the proviso that the Arts Society should inform the committee of the title of any lecture or debate contemplated. Half a century later, after so much destruction and so many deaths in the North of Ireland, the mind-set of all the participants seems as remote as that rural landscape with its absence of electricity and piped water.[89]

Great as the changes were during Dr. Walsh's tenure of the office of CEO, the changes of the next thirty years were to be much greater. Vocational Education was transformed to the point where the very words "technical" and "vocational" could no longer describe the huge range of responsibilities which the VECs undertook.

The scheme for the teaching of Irish begun in the 1920s continued. Finding teachers for the night classes was often a problem, as there was an expectation that the teacher would recruit the students, teach them, encourage a good attendance and, in some areas, run a local Feis. Teachers of Irish tended to be part-time and often moved on after a few months in the county. In January 1947, when the committee found it impossible to get Irish teachers, several National Teachers were recruited, and later in the year, twenty-four of them were appointed in various parts of the county to teach night classes in Irish. Over the next few years the numbers declined.[90]

The case of one long-serving Irish teacher occupied the committee a great deal over the years. Eibhlín Ní Chróinín had spent most of her life in Kilkenny teaching Irish, first with the Gaelic League branch in Kilkenny City, and later for nineteen years as a temporary part-time teacher, with the Joint Technical Instruction Committee and with the VEC. In 1933, she was made temporary whole-time, and the committee wanted to make her permanent. The Department refused on the grounds that she was over the age limit of fifty-four. They sanctioned her temporary whole-time status, and two years later, after a good deal of pushing, sanctioned her as permanent. In 1947, the committee was notified by the Department of the age limit for officers of VECs. The two teachers affected were John S. Gibb, a woodwork teacher in the city, and Eibhlín Ní Chróinín, who had only thirteen years pensionable service. The committee wanted ten years added on as recognition of her long service temporary part-time, and they pleaded to have her service in a local secondary school recognised. They failed and she was awarded a pension of £155 per annum, although in the following year as part of a general increase in pensions this was raised to £226. For fifteen years after her official retirement the VEC employed her as a temporary part-time teacher of Irish, allowing her to supplement her meagre pension by teaching some hours in the Gaelic League rooms in Rothe House. In 1962, the minutes note that she had not returned to work after a recent illness. She must have been in her mid-eighties at that stage.[91]

Mr. Eamonn Gibson CEO

Mr. Gibson attended his first committee meeting as CEO in May 1966. His five-year tenure of the office of chief executive saw the beginning of the new era in Irish second-level education and a dramatic expansion in the numbers catered for in vocational schools in County Kilkenny. This was accompanied by the closure of some of the small schools, and by a continuous struggle to match classrooms to pupil numbers. The minutes of the three meetings held before the summer break that year give an early indication of some of the main problems that were to occupy the committee for the next several years.

- Some of the older schools badly needed upgrading, as exemplified in the case of Mooncoin, where the water supply was from roof tanks, leading to supply problems in dry weather.
- Posts of responsibility were few at the time. A vacancy for headmaster in Kilkenny was to be filled, the committee decided, by competition open to all teachers in the permanent employ of County Kilkenny VEC. Within a few years, the filling of posts of any kind was to be strictly regulated and the number of posts of responsibility to be greatly increased.
- Mrs. O'Hea, who had had to retire on marriage, was working as a part-time teacher in Kilkenny City Vocational School. The Department notified

Prize Winners at the Fish Cookery Competition
Breda Brownrigg, Dunnamaggin, first from left, having received first place in the County in the Fish Cookery
Competition. Miss Walsh is third from left. Shown also are some of the competitors.

Pictured in 1959, Moyra
McCarthy, Domestic Science
Teacher coaches the first Boys
Cookery class at second level
in Ireland. This was initiated
by Dr. Walsh CEO.

Kilkenny Junior Chamber of Commerce Secondary School Question Time 1968-69 in Ballyhale Vocational School

Ballyhale Macra beat Tullaroan in County Final 1965
L to R: Paddy Dermody,
David Rice,
Kevin Connolly,
James O'Keeffe,
Ned Fitzpatrick,
Jim Devereux, School Principal.

Graignamanagh Vocational School Staff 1960
L to R:
Teresa Buggy, Student Teacher,
Sean Buckley,
Rural Science Teacher,
Gerry Daly, School Principal,
Brian Hunt,
Woodwork Teacher,
Maeve Feeney,
Home Economics Teacher.

45

the committee that she was working more than 700 hours per year which was not allowed for temporary teachers. When the committee pointed out that there was no alternative, the department relented and allowed the hours. Within a few years, the bar on married women teachers was abolished.

- Listerlin, with an enrolment of eight was under threat. Pupils from the area were going by car to New Ross in County Wexford or to Thomastown. A deputation to the Department was told that Gowran would not get the school that had been sought for many years.

- Accommodation needs were assessed by the Department and considered by the committee in July. Extra accommodation was to be rented in Kilkenny City, Graignamanagh, Castlecomer, Slieverue and Johnstown. Woodwork stores at Thomastown and Mooncoin were to be adapted as classrooms. The prefabricated classroom as God's gift to Irish education was only months in the future. Of all the problems besetting the VEC, accommodation was to be the most frustrating and the most expensive.

- In July the committee's schools employed thirty-one permanent whole-time teachers, and eleven part-time, of whom all but one were women. There were of course thirty-one clergymen who taught religion part-time. Over the next few years the problem of filling the increased number of teaching posts was to be an annual headache.[92]

The other major change lying ahead was the provision of free transport to schools of all kinds. Early in 1967, the Department requested that the CEO of County Kilkenny VEC act as Transport Liaison Officer for the state-financed transport scheme to post-primary schools in the area. [93]The setting up of catchment areas gets no mention in the minutes of the VEC, but their creation implied a decision as to which schools should survive and which should close. The provision of free transport to schools was at least as important as the introduction of free second-level education in transforming Irish life over the coming decades.

Listerlin, Coon, Dunnamaggin and Callan Vocational Schools were closed. Tullaroan had closed some years before. The decision on Listerlin was taken in October 1966. Dunnamaggin was kept open until the summer of 1967, when the teacher-in-charge, Miss Walsh, who had taught there since its opening retired. She had thirty-seven years reckonable for pension purposes, leaving her short of the full amount. Four years which she had spent teaching in schools of rural domestic economy were not taken into account. The buildings at Listerlin and Dunnamaggin were sold to local voluntary organisations while Coon was sold as a dwelling to Mr. Phillip Keane. It seemed at first that Mr. Jack Lanigan, Teacher-in-Charge would lose his allowance for that post, but after representations, the department conceded the continuation of the allowance. Tullaroan was used for night classes for some time, and later served as a temporary Primary School during the building of a new school in the village. It later served as a temporary church while the parish church was having its roof replaced. Callan wasn't so easy to dispose of. Interest in purchasing it was minimal, and it became a target for vandals. Eventually the

County Librarian asked for its use as a branch library and got a twenty-five year lease for ten pence a year.[94] The only one which made a reasonable price was Coon. The building originally cost £50 for the site, construction cost £800 and extras £50. Mr. Keane bought it for £1,051.

Rationalisation of second level schools saw some gains for the vocational sector. It was decided that convent schools at Thomastown and Mooncoin would leave the provision of second level schooling in their areas to the local vocational schools. They were guaranteed that two places in each of the amalgamated schools would be reserved for nuns. These would be nominated by the Reverend Mother of the local convent and appointed to the posts by the VEC under what was described as a gentleman's agreement similar to that which obtained in hospitals. In Castlecomer the local convent secondary school and the vocational school were to operate a joint arrangement which would see managements unchanged, but pupils from each of the schools being offered subjects in the other. For many years, the sight of groups of boys and girls heading up and down the footpath joining the two schools was common.

The Prefabricated Classroom

All these changes called for extra classroom space in the surviving schools. In September of 1966 Carroll System Buildings got the contract to provide a prefabricated classroom each for Ballyhale and Johnstown schools at a cost of £846 each. Kilkenny City Vocational School also needed prefabs, but the problem was where to put them. The VEC entered into negotiations with the agent for the Ormonde estate to buy a plot of ground immediately behind the school. This had been leased by the estate to the County Club which fronted onto Patrick Street. The garden behind the club had been sub-let on the eleven-month system to Lady Bellew who lived across the street. After an appeal to the Marquis of Ormonde who visited Kilkenny in November, the purchase of the site was agreed for £1,700 plus fees. The estate and the County Club would give immediate possession and Lady Bellew was willing to give up immediately that part of the garden which the school was ready to build on, and to rent back the remainder on a yearly basis until it was needed.

The renting of St. Patrick's Hall near Kilkenny City Vocational School (KCVS) had not provided the most comfortable of learning environments, with a local professional band of the showband era rehearsing in another part of the building. Two prefab classrooms were needed on the Ormonde Road site, and a prefab had been erected by teachers and students to accommodate the Principal's office. The Department had also approved a garage workshop and fitter's workshop to accommodate apprentices on block release and a proposed Bord Na Móna apprentices training course. Kilkenny City had been designated a centre for Senior Stage Courses for Motor Trade Apprentices and the apprentice block could now be

Members of staff attending TUI Dinner Dance 1967
L to R: Maura Ryan, Bernie Ryan (Woodwork Teacher 1952 to 1984), Mary Mc Grath,
Maurice McGrath (Vice Principal 1967-1981), Lily Walshe(Home Economics Teacher in the 1960s).

Mooncoin Secretarial Certificate Class 1963-1964
Back Row(from left:) B. Faulkner, M. Howley, A. Kennington, R. Phelan,
A. Power(R.I.P), A. Gilmartin, J. Kinsella, M. Healy, M. Hayes.
Middle Row(from left:) M. Maguire, E. Farrell, K. Coady, K. Dunphy,
M. O'Brien, B. Walsh, K. Walsh.
Front Row(from left:) E. Cody, J. Dale (R.I.P), P. Allen, J. O'Gorman,
M. Foskin, K. Mackey, J. Meaney.

Pictured with the Minister Jack Lynch, are Nicholas Hayes, Willie Walsh, Vincent Long (front), Dick O'Gorman(back), Patrick Dalton, George Butler, Edward Hughes, David Doyle, John Raggett and their instructor Mr. James Devereux, Headmaster, Ballyhale Vocational School.

Ballyhale students win All-Ireland Titles in the Tractor and Implement Maintenance Competition
This prestigious award was much in demand in the Vocational Sector. The competition was sponsored by 'David Brown' and involved repairing faults on a faulty tractor and then writing up a project on their findings.
Presentation of tropies by Mr. C.J. Haughey, Minister for Justice to Mr. David Rice and Mr. Patrick Walsh, All-Ireland Winners of the Tractor and Implement Maintenance Competition 1964.

put on the new site behind the school. With all this proposed development it was probably just as well that Kilkenny Corporation, in its draft development plan, had listed the Talbot Castle for preservation. This surviving bastion of the medieval city wall was in the school grounds, was in poor condition, and is only now, forty years later destined for some sort of restoration. [95]

Elsewhere in the county, the VEC had assessed its needs for September 1967. In April the CEO reported to the committee. Some ordinary prefab classrooms were needed at Mooncoin, Thomastown, Ballyhale, Castlecomer, Graignamanagh and Slieverue, but in the case of Science units, the preferred solution at Graignamanagh and Thomastown was to install semi-permanent Bantile units manufactured by Banagher Tiles Ltd. In all twelve classrooms were needed, two toilet blocks and two Bantile Science units. The County Council was to be asked to make a loan of £20,000 available. It was also estimated that Mooncoin needed a new block for woodwork, metalwork and science, to be ready for September 1968. The committee's architect was to be asked to design this as soon as the Department approved the project in principle. In the event, this approval was problematic.

The twelve classrooms needed were provided in time through a new initiative from the Department. A bulk purchase of pre-fabricated classrooms had been made by the Department through City of Dublin VEC, and erection in various parts of Ireland was to be supervised by their architect. All twelve for County Kilkenny were erected by August. It was four years before the County Kilkenny VEC got a Department claim for re-imbursement of the money spent, which had been borrowed under Section 50 of the Vocational Education Act. County Kilkenny VEC was advised to use the same procedure rather than using the local loans fund. [96]

These measures may have eased the immediate accommodation crisis, but a new school year revealed long-term problems. Halls were still being rented at Johnstown, Slieverue, Thomastown and Kilkenny, the provision of heat, light and other services caused problems at a number of centres, and the pressure of increased enrolments in all schools, together with the imminence of Leaving certificate provision meant that there was going to be an increased demand for classrooms.

In Kilkenny City Vocational School, the tender of Banagher Tiles (Bantile) for the provision of an apprenticeship block was accepted. The cost was £12,859, with prime cost sums provided for fittings, £896, and heating and light, £3,680. For some time it was thought that the more economical course of installing one heating system to heat the new block and the old school would be adopted, but Departmental delay in sanctioning this meant that the new block was completed and in need of heat, while the Department was still reviewing the situation. In the event, an electric air system was installed and gave considerable trouble, with frequent replacement of expensive heating elements. At the same school, a tender of £3,825 from Carroll System Buildings for the provision of a prefab extension was accepted, with electrics to cost £350 and equipment estimated at £315. [97]

In November the CEO presented a draft development plan. Already fifteen prefabs supplemented forty permanent rooms. Over a quarter of the accommodation was in prefabs, and if we remember that students move from one room to another, especially where practical subjects are concerned, it would seem that a very high proportion of students spent at least part of every day in these units. In the immediate term, the CEO estimated a need for an art room in Kilkenny, with the apprentice block ready to go, a two-room science block at Thomastown, the acquisition of a plot of ground at Graignamanagh and the provision of tarmac at several schools to cater for increased numbers of students at breaks. In the medium term, there was a need for gyms in three schools, and science units in two. Long term needs were also considered. The most pressing of these was the acquisition of more land to extend Kilkenny City VS. There the old art room was available as a gymnasium at a cost of £850 for equipment and £53 to sand and seal the floor.

Of a loan of £20,000 already approved by the County Council, £12,586 would be taken up by existing projects, and a new loan of £31,400 would be needed to fund the new needs.[98]

From about this time, planning permission was necessary for all of these building projects. The decision by the VEC to build or extend was subject to departmental sanction and to planning regulations, and delays were common.

The school at Mooncoin had been built thirty years previously and major renovation was needed. Following a survey, the architect recommended demolishing the existing building and erecting a prefab. A decision on this was deferred because of the probable cost of £30,000 and the dilemma of whether to build on the original site or to seek a new site. By late 1968, the VEC had decided to accept the Department's suggestion that the existing school should be incorporated into any planned development. The committee's architect stressed that it would be impossible to remodel the existing practical rooms in a way that would meet Department standards. It would be better to build new practical rooms and remodel the old ones as ordinary classrooms. At that stage Mooncoin had been awaiting sanction for its building needs for over a year. It had already seen the conversion of a woodwork storeroom into a classroom, and been given two mobile classrooms. These were to be moved to Ballyhale when Mooncoin got its permanent extension. By October 1968 the situation in Mooncoin was described as explosive. In the following January purchase of a site had been completed and in February the Department had seen sketch plans for the building. In October the department promised a mobile classroom to be supplied by Messrs Hull of Belfast. In June 1969 a Department architect visited Mooncoin. There was no possibility of sanction for the £48,000 needed for the planned refurbishment, but toilets, heating, science room, a staff room and redecoration would be priorities. A month later they announced a limit of £3,500 on minor reconstruction. What this meant became plain when a reconstruction tender of £1950 was accepted but heating had to be referred back to the person making the lowest tender as, at £2,152, it would bring the total for the two projects outside the department limit. In the event the Department did sanction the amount. In mid 1971, Department approval was refused for extensions at Ballyhale, Thomastown, Johnstown and Mooncoin. By late 1972, VEC members were describing the mobile classrooms at Mooncoin as very poor value. The idea of mobile classrooms had been that they could be used at one location to fill a temporary need and they moved elsewhere. The ones at Mooncoin showed signs of deterioration caused by their move there. By then opinion of prefabs and mobile classrooms all over Ireland was fairly low. They couldn't really be moved without risk of damage, they needed a fair bit of maintenance, and even with care would show signs of deterioration within ten years. They were cold in winter and stifling in warm summer weather, and were hated with equal vigour by students, teachers and parents. The VEC, as the nearest official body, got most of the criticism, although the CEO and committee were powerless in the face of departmental financial stringency.[99]

The increase in enrolments was dramatic over the years following the introduction of free second-level education. Starting from a base of 767 students in all the committee's schools in 1966, there was an increase of 237 the following year, a growth of thirty percent. By 1971 the total had passed 1,200 and by September of 1972 had reached 1,512, almost doubling the enrolment over a six-year period.

Staffing in the new era

This increase, as well as putting pressure on space and creating a demand for extra classrooms, toilets, play space and sports facilities, called for extra teachers. Again taking 1966 as a base line, we can see the results. Thirty-one whole-time and eleven part-time teachers catered for the needs of County Kilkenny Vocational schools in that year. Eight new posts were created the following year, and in 1968, twelve new posts. By September 1970 the VEC had an allocation of ninety-eight whole-time teaching posts and felt that they needed two to six extra. There was a severe shortage of metalwork teachers for some time.

The availability of so many new posts, not only in the vocational sector, but in all second-level schools brought about a teacher supply crisis. Posts were advertised; vacancies were filled; quite a few of the successful candidates subsequently got jobs which they preferred to the first one they had accepted; they moved on and the post had to be filled all over again. In 1969, to fill their allocation of new posts, as well as vacancies caused by resignations, County Kilkenny VEC made one hundred appointments. Two of the resignations were notified to harassed Principals on the morning that the schools opened after the summer holidays.[100]

Conditions for teachers changed over the period as well. The disappearance of the marriage bar was only one of a range of reforms. In January 1967 committees were notified of a new procedure for the appointment of teachers. For some years previous to this County Kilkenny VEC had voluntarily set up an appointments sub-committee. Normal procedure was to accept their recommendations - a considerable improvement on the previous method of an open vote of the committee, following a round of vigorous canvassing of members by candidates. The voluntary system could be set aside - as in the case of the appointment of a Headmaster in Kilkenny City by a nine-to-six majority of the committee. Now a uniform mandatory system was imposed by the Department of Education on all VECs. An appointments committee was to decide between candidates and the VEC members' role was simply to give formal approval. There was resentment in Kilkenny that the new system was to be mandatory, but apart from expressing that resentment, no further action was possible, and in July 1967 the names of the selection board members were entered in the minute book; Dr. D.F. O'Callaghan representing the Department, and four VEC members - Monsignor Thomas Murphy, Canon John Holohan, Councillor John Holohan and Deputy Seamus Pattison. Their first nominations were accepted at the August meeting. [101]

The Tribunal on Teachers Salaries, chaired by Prof. Louden Ryan, reported in April 1968. It recommended a common basic salary scale for all teachers, a scheme of allowances for qualifications and eight graded posts of special responsibility. A scheme of conciliation and arbitration was to be introduced, to ensure industrial peace. All three teachers' unions went on strike in 1969 and it was some years before all three were satisfied with the outcome of negotiations. In 1973 the secondary teachers accepted the common basic scale and the scheme of conciliation and arbitration. The minutes of County Kilkenny VEC make little mention of the strikes in the vocational sector, except to note that labour was to be withdrawn on certain days, and to note department circulars arranging for the deduction of pay for strike days, and notifying the committee that pension rights would not be affected. [102]

The filling of posts of responsibility created a system of promotion for teachers in VEC schools. Up to 1967, the only form of promotion was to become a Principal or a Teacher-in-Charge. In that year assistants to the headmaster were appointed in Kilkenny City, Castlecomer, Thomastown, Mooncoin and Johnstown. By early 1970 the filling of the new graded posts of responsibility were being discussed. These would be worth between £100 and £625 per annum. By September it was clear that Vice-Principals would be appointed in all schools, that B posts were to be created in Mooncoin, Castlecomer and Graignamanagh and temporary Grade B posts in the remaining schools. The total cost in the first year was estimated to be £6,023. The filling of the post of Vice-Principal in Kilkenny caused some controversy. The appointments board recommended Miss Moyra McCarthy for the post, but Mr. Paddy Taaffe felt that, as he was appointed Assistant to the Headmaster some years before, he should have been made Vice-Principal. The committee sought legal advice and were told that the appointment was made in a proper manner and was valid. The Department took the same view. The controversy took a new turn in July 1971, when the Department notified the VEC that the allowance paid to Mr. Taaffe as assistant to the Principal was to be continued, but that the payment of this allowance would block a Grade B post. The Irish Vocational Education Association was asked to take the matter up with the Department. It was fourteen months before the department conceded that the payment of the allowance need not block a B post. [103]

Thomastown Vocational School Leinster Vocational Schools Under 15 Football Champions 1972

First Kilkenny team to win a Leinster football title for 54 years.
Back Row: Luke Murtagh, Johnny Phelan, Paudie Lannon, Sean Reid, Pat Minogue, Noel Duggan, Seamus Caulfield, Johnny O'Brien, Dan Breen, T. O'Callaghan.
Front Row: Eugene Gibbons, Ger Lyster, Christy Beck, Dick O'Hara, Bryan O'Keeffe, Walter Lanigan, Eugene Kavanagh.

Leinster Senior Colleges Camogie Champions 1978

Back Row: Brid O'Neill, Joan Lanigan, Mairead Lee, Catherine Hennessy, Áine Kerwin, Kathleen Drea, Joan Holden, Rita Wemyss.
Front Row: Maura Lee, Bridget Walsh, Brid Farrell, Margaret Farrell, Kay Dowling, Hazel Diamond, Ann Aylward, Ann Roche.

Thomastown Vocational School created camogie history on the double. It was the first time that a school had won Leinster Senior and Junior titles in the one year. It was also the first school to win 3 senior Leinster Colleges titles in a row.

Leinster Junior Colleges Camogie Champions 1978

Back Row: Marie Ryan, Olive Galway, Kathleen Farrell, Peggy Cody, Maura Lee, Anna Grace, Annette Lannon, Jacqueline Kelly, Ann Naddy, Carmel O'Reilly.
Front Row: Kathleen Rowe, Marie Behan, Kay Dowling, Brid Farrell, Eileen Lanigan, Joan Lanigan, Frances Behan, Helen Galway.

Pictured in 1975 at Johnstown Vocational School Sports Day.
L to R: Bernie Ryan, Pat Connolly, Seamus Doran, Betty Buckley, Jim Walsh, Brian Ryan (Child)

CHAPTER 6

Kilkenny City Vocational School and St. Kieran's College

Meeting accommodation needs at Kilkenny City Vocational School took up a lot of the committee's time. It was by far the largest of their schools, and even after the site behind the school was bought, there was need for a great deal of extra land, which was not easy to get in the centre of Kilkenny City, and comparatively expensive when available. The Ormonde Estate had already sold one piece of ground to the committee and in early 1969, negotiations commenced for the purchase of part of Kilkenny Castle Park. This provoked a response from Mr. Jim Gibbons, Parliamentary Secretary to the Minister for Finance who had contacted the Marquis of Ormonde to oppose the sale of the land. Mr. Gibbons was a local T.D. and was in charge of the Office of Public Works, so his opposition was a serious matter. He was invited to a special meeting of the VEC at the end of March and outlined the reasons for his opposition: the Marquis of Ormonde had given the Castle and part of the Castle Park to the people of Kilkenny; it was now in state ownership and in the care of the Office of Public Works; the entire walled area had been classified for preservation, including the part still owned by Lord Ormonde; Mr. Gibbons hoped to see the entire area become the centrepiece of a national park for which Kilkenny had been chosen as a pilot scheme. [104]

The committee, which had honestly thought that the southern end of the park was available for purchase now looked for another site. By mid 1969 the matter had become urgent, as the school had twenty-eight classrooms as against thirteen in 1966, and more were needed. For a time the acquisition and conversion of Butler House on Patrick Street was considered. This was a fine Georgian building and considering the note in the minutes that it wouldn't be necessary to retain the decorative ceilings, it may be just as well that this project wasn't carried through. [105]

Protracted negotiations for a site in New Street owned by Mahon and McPhillips eventually fell through. At first part of the site was on offer and its purchase was actually sanctioned by the Department, but when the vendors decided that only the whole site would be offered and asked for £25,000, the Department refused sanction. Many years later this site was to be developed as Ormonde Street, a new thoroughfare connecting Patrick Street with New Street. The price asked in 1971 may have been steep, but one wonders. [106]

The VEC had succeeded in the meantime in buying Statham's yard immediately to the west of the school, at a cost of £3,000, with the demolition of four stables and two houses costing a further £300. Carroll System Buildings had the contract for erecting prefabs and wanted to breach the wall adjoining the Talbot Tower to get access to the site. Since there was doubt as to whether this was part of the medieval city wall, the Office of Public Works were to be consulted as to whether an archway could be made in the wall.[107]

In 1970 the question of co-operation between Kilkenny City Vocational School (hereafter referred to as KCVS) and St. Kieran's College was raised in the context of providing a Senior Cycle between the two schools. The CEO and Canon Holohan, President of St. Kieran's College met Department officials and reported the proposals which emerged to the staffs of the schools and to the VEC.

- The senior cycle facilities were to be built on a site provided by St. Kieran's College and shared with KCVS.
- A sports hall and four handball alleys were to be provided on a site also given by St. Kieran's College and these would be used by both schools.
- Junior cycles were to be separate.
- There was to be separate enrolment for the Senior Cycle but a joint board of management. A co-ordinated time-table would be necessary.
- Costs would be shared equally, making allowance for the sites given by St. Kieran's College.

Both staffs rejected the proposals, as did the VEC.

The situation became critical by 1971. KCVS had an enrolment of 432 and was providing facilities for 224 pupils from St. Kieran's College. In April 1972 the two schools took the initiative. A case was prepared by the Principal of St. Kieran's College, Fr. Delaney and the Acting CEO, Mr. Sean Dignan. Mr. Gibson had resigned after five years as CEO to take up a position as CEO in Donegal, and Mr. Sean Dignan, Principal of Kilkenny City Vocational School became Acting CEO. On 6th July the VEC considered the report of a meeting between the authorities responsible for the two schools.

Report of meeting of Trustees and Principal, St. Kieran's College with representatives of County Kilkenny VEC on 6th. July 1972

Present: Monsignor Murphy, Canon Holohan and Fr. Delaney from St. Kieran's College; Dean Harvey, Councillor Holohan and Mr. S. Dignan representing the VEC; Mr. S. Lynch, Curriculum Planner, City Vocational School attended at the request of the Committee's representatives.

The meeting was held at the request of the County Kilkenny VEC on the initiative of Canon Holohan, as member of the Committee and President of St. Kieran's College, to discuss areas of co-operation between St. Kieran's College and the City Vocational School and in order to expedite the Department's decision on the provision of accommodation at both schools.

With a view to (a) making available to pupils of both schools a wider curriculum than at present possible in either school, (b) making the most economic use of specialised facilities, a detailed proposal, worked out by Fr. Delaney and the Acting CEO was outlined to the meeting concerning the provision of subjects at Senior Cycle level and discussed at length. The recommendations of the meeting which Fr. Delaney and the Acting CEO were asked to formulate are:

1. That St. Kieran's College only would be responsible for the provision of Latin, Greek, History, Geography, Modern Languages, Physics, Chemistry, Physics and Chemistry Joint, Applied Mathematics and Music for the students of both schools and that any special facilities required would be provided at St. Kieran's College.

2. The provision of Building Materials and Processes, Engineering Workshop Theory and Practice, Technical Drawing, Mechanics, Biology, Agricultural Science, Agricultural Economics and Home Economics would be the responsibility of the KVCS only (under County Kilkenny Vocational Education Committee) and any special facilities required would be provided at the City Vocational School.

3. The special facilities required for Business Studies subjects and Art to be provided at the City Vocational School only while both schools remain free to teach those subjects.

4. In the case of Irish, English and Mathematics and any other subject not already restricted to one school that the principals of both schools consult - on a year to year basis - how best to provide them at Higher and Ordinary levels in the most economic way possible.

5. That every student would be given a choice of subjects from the combined curricula of both schools.

6. The provision of any subject at either level shall be dependent upon demand and the availability of staff.

7. All special facilities provided in either school in accordance with the above terms shall be available to the County Kilkenny Vocational Education Committee for the purpose of adult education outside normal school hours.

8. That this agreement shall be reviewed and assessed three years after its inception.

At the VEC meeting, the report was endorsed and, if it was acceptable to the Bishop and the Trustees of St. Kieran's College, the Department of Education was to be asked to receive a deputation.[108]

The Senior Cycle Question

Throughout this period, KVCS was providing a Leaving Certificate course. In September 1970, nineteen pupils from Ballyhale were being bussed to Kilkenny to do a Technical Leaving Certificate course. In June 1971, the VEC considered a request from Thomastown Parents' Association for a leaving certificate course in their own town. There were currently no students travelling from there to Kilkenny, so the VEC members felt that it would be best if the Department of Education were to examine the whole question of Senior Cycle education in South Kilkenny. The Department, which had had the same request from the Thomastown parents, replied in February. They suggested one Senior Cycle between Thomastown, Ballyhale and Graignamanagh. In April 1972, Mr. Coyle, an official of the department was present at a VEC meeting to explain new proposals. The survey of the areas had been carried out and the Department were prepared to concede one Senior Cycle for the three towns and favoured Thomastown to provide this. Members were worried about the effect on Ballyhale and Graignamanagh. Mr. Coyle said the Department had no plans to close these two schools, but, when pressed, said that he couldn't give an indefinite guarantee.

The committee held public meetings in each of the three schools, with four VEC members asked to be present at each. The Graignamanagh and Ballyhale meetings rejected the proposals. The committee decided to notify the Department of the results, but to point out that the issue should not be regarded as closed. Negative reactions were due to fears that the two schools might be closed, and that, with a Leaving Certificate course available in Thomastown, the right of Ballyhale students to be transported to Kilkenny would be lost. In reply the Department said that it would be best to preserve the status quo for another year to give parents at Ballyhale and Graignamanagh time to consider. Canon Holohan proposed "that the Department would guarantee that existing schools would remain provided numbers did not drop substantially and that the Senior Cycle programme as promised by the Department would be available provided the numbers attending Thomastown would be 400 and that the Department would authorise the committee to put this to the communities not at present in agreement". Councillor Devoy seconded and the committee agreed. In March 1973, the committee accepted in principle the latest letter from the Department on the subject. They asked that an official should attend the next meeting of the VEC, to which the Principals of the three schools would be invited.[109] In the event it was June before an official was able to attend and by then the new CEO, Mr. Brendan Conway had taken up office.[110]

Mr. Brendan Conway CEO

Mr. Conway was welcomed to his first meeting of the County Kilkenny VEC on May 7th. 1973. For the first few meetings of his term of office, Mr. Sean Dignan was also present and members expressed their gratitude to him for his service as Acting CEO and to Miss Moyra McCarthy who had acted as Principal at Kilkenny City Vocational School while Mr. Dignan was looking after the affairs of the VEC.

One of the new CEO's first initiatives was to work out a possible compromise on the question of the Senior Cycle in the Thomastown/Ballyhale area. He proposed that each student would do the core subjects in his or her home school, with the other subjects divided between the schools at Thomastown and Ballyhale.

This would involve one bus journey four days a week and would cost £500 per annum. Mr. O'Carroll, a Department official who was present, rejected the proposals. Some subjects would not be covered and the Department wanted one centre to avoid fragmentation. They would want an enrolment of sixty students in the first year for viability. He outlined what would be considered an adequate range of subjects and promised prefabs at Thomastown to supplement the existing accommodation. In answer to protests that the proposals could lead to the closure of the other two schools he said that the only guarantee the Department could offer on the continuance of schools was the setting up of a sub-committee under Section 21 of the Act. The interests of all communities would be represented and this should ensure the continuance of Ballyhale for at least another decade.

An appeal to the Department was unsuccessful and the CEO was left with the job of trying to launch the Senior Cycle course for Thomastown by September. Ballyhale parents would have to be consulted and VEC members wanted them represented on a sub-committee formed to promote the course. Canon Holohan pointed out that by accepting the Thomastown centre, Ballyhale parents would be abandoning their right to free transport into Kilkenny. Hitherto, some Ballyhale students had attended Leaving certificate courses in Kilkenny City, some at KVCS, others at other second-level schools. From September Thomastown would be their nearest centre and free transport would be available only to there.

A letter from Graignamanagh parents seeking transport to Thomastown indicates the possible effects on public opinion and on the reputations of the two outlying schools of the refusal of the Senior Cycle. The VEC replied that it had no function in the matter of providing transport. It was true that the CEO acted as Transport Liaison Officer for the area, but this was an administrative task undertaken for the Department of Education, unconnected with his work for County Kilkenny VEC. The parents were informed that there were places available to the pupils in question at Graignamanagh. From this it would seem that some parents were seeking transport for prospective first-year entrants, rather than prospective Senior Cycle candidates.

Early in 1974, the Headmasters at Ballyhale and Thomastown wrote to the CEO on the distribution of points accruing from the joint Senior Cycle. This would affect the number of posts of responsibility available at each school. They wanted all pupils transferring from Ballyhale to Thomastown for senior cycle to be reckonable at Ballyhale and vice versa for a secretarial course proposed for Ballyhale, at which Thomastown pupils would attend. Three years later, the Department approved a Senior Cycle for Ballyhale, a measure of the desire of parents to have their children educated to Leaving certificate level, and of the public perception that five years of second-level schooling was a minimum educational standard in the late 1970s.

The decision to locate the Senior Cycle at Thomastown was welcomed by parents in that town, but led to a protracted struggle to get extra accommodation, in the first place as prefabs, and later as a new school. Even levelling the field for the prefabs ran into trouble when the Department insisted on no more than £900 being spent on the job. The architect felt that the levelling could be done for that price and two prefabs were sanctioned for the site by the Department. The VEC accepted the tender of Carroll System buildings at £11,775. The Principal and parents at Thomastown provided evidence that enrolment there would reach 425 by 1981, doubling the present numbers. Three additional prefabs would be needed in September and advance planning was needed immediately to be ready for the situation that would arise by 1981. This dilemma of providing immediate accommodation at the school, planning for a new school, and dealing with departmental parsimony was to occupy much committee time over the next few years.[111]

The Joint Extension Project in Kilkenny City

It was to prove considerably less troublesome than the Kilkenny City problem. The overcrowding at KCVS had become acute. The CEO was seeking to rent office accommodation for himself and his staff, to relieve overcrowding in the school where he was based at that time. A deputation to the Minister for Education in June 1973 presented a portfolio of photographs taken by the Principal, showing the extent of the overcrowding. The Minister promised to give a decision on the matter of a joint complex for KCVS and St. Kieran's College (hereinafter referred to as St. Kieran's). The CEO met with the newly appointed President of St. Kieran's, Fr. Thomas Maher and was empowered by the VEC to draw up with him a joint document for submission to the Department. In August, both men met with department officials who welcomed the progress made and supplied work-sheets and booklets on the programme of building. When the work-sheets were completed, a proposal for sanction would be made to the Minister. No serious setbacks were envisaged on the way. The same VEC meeting which welcomed this report was told of a successful outcome to the Leaving Certificate examinations for thirty-five students at KCVS. By November Fr. Maher was a member of the VEC, having been co-opted to replace his predecessor, Canon Holohan. He and the CEO had presented the filled-in worksheets to the Department together with a map of the site. The Department official expressed his pleasure, but insisted on a joint worksheet. When they reported back to a VEC meeting, members deplored the delay. The year ended on a more hopeful note with the appointment of Mr. Colm Ó Cochláin as architect, and the offer of the position of consultant heating engineer to Mr. Cecil Buggy. The architect was to appoint a consultant structural engineer. Fr. Maher assured the meeting that St. Kieran's would accept the same design team as appointed by the VEC.

Early in 1974 the committee was informed that the file had gone from the building section of the Department to planning and statistics. The VEC appointed Cllrs. Holohan, Dowling and Waldron with Deputy Pattison to meet with St. Kieran's authorities. The report of this meeting said that a Memorandum of Agreement drawn up by the legal adviser was to be finalised by the CEO and Fr. Maher and forwarded to the Department.

The Memorandum provided for the transfer of over an acre of land from St. Kieran's to the VEC, reserving their own right of way to the remaining parts of their property. The VEC were to erect a two storey building on this land, and St. Kieran's trustees were to erect a two storey building on adjoining land. In both cases classroom and other facilities were to be provided by agreement between the trustees and the VEC. Each was to be responsible for the heating, lighting and maintenance of its own property, and the staff and students of either school were to have the use of all rooms jointly for instruction and study during normal school hours. The management of the KCVS part of the complex was to be under a Sub-Committee of the VEC comprising the Chairman of the VEC, the CEO, the President of St. Kieran's and a nominee of the trustees. Supervision and control were to be the duty of the host school of either part of the complex. It was the intention of the agreement that students of either school should have available to them the widest possible course of studies. The agreement was to come into effect upon the Minister for Education approving of it.[112]

The Department expressed some reservations: they wanted clarification of the operation of the joint Senior Cycle arrangements, a majority of members on the management sub-committee of the KCVS building to be VEC representatives, all specialist rooms in the complex to be erected by the VEC, the price of the plot of ground being transferred by St. Kieran's to the VEC to be stated, and the road widening costs to be borne by the local authority.

In response the VEC pointed out that the schools were at present sharing facilities, with mixed classes, that they would seek sanction for the provision of all specialist Senior Cycle rooms in their new building, and that the price of the plot of ground was ultimately a matter for agreement between the trustees of St. Kieran's and the Department. They decided on a three-man management committee for their new building to consist of the Chairman of the VEC, the CEO and the President of St. Kieran's. Fr. Maher and the CEO had a meeting with the Town Clerk of Kilkenny and it was expected that Kilkenny Corporation would shortly be in a position to announce the beginning of work on the road widening to coincide with the start of work on the building. The CEO and Fr. Maher were authorised to negotiate with the Department.

In May of 1974 the VEC considered a letter from the Department stating that they were prepared to approve the joint development.
1. St. Kieran's would erect a block of general classrooms and ancillary facilities for which the department would sanction the normal school grants.
2. The County Kilkenny Vocational Education Committee would erect a building with all the special subject rooms required for the two schools, general classrooms, and ancillary facilities on a site to be acquired from St. Kieran's at an agreed price.
3. The new buildings would be in the closest possible proximity.
4. Between them the two schools would conduct a joint Senior Cycle with each school taking responsibility for the teaching of certain subjects and with

61

every pupil getting a choice of subjects from the joint curriculum of the two schools.

5. The VEC would set up a sub-committee comprising two of their own representatives and one from St. Kieran's to manage their new building and ensure that the joint development as agreed would be implemented.

6. The two school authorities would enter into a written agreement formalising these arrangements.

Fr. Maher said that St. Kieran's had been assured of financial support for the sports complex and that the facilities would be made available to the KCVS students. The VEC members accepted the Department proposals. Local and national papers were to be told of what was an unprecedented arrangement.

In July at its first meeting following on from the local elections, the new VEC appointed a sub-committee to advance the joint project. The VEC representatives were to be the Chairman, Cllr. John Holohan, the Vice-Chairman Monsignor Thomas Murphy, Deputy Pattison, Cllrs. Waldron and Dowling and the CEO, while Fr. Maher, Fr. Delaney and Mr. John Collins were to represent St. Kieran's. The Principal of KCVS was later co-opted on to this sub-committee.[113]

A note in the minutes for December 1974 that final plans for the complex were almost ready and that construction might commence by July proved to be somewhat optimistic. It was July 1977 before the contract for construction was awarded to M. & J. Wallace, Wellington Bridge, Co. Wexford and it took the Department another four months to sanction the awarding of the contract. The cost was to be £572,833.65 and the building unit outlined the method of financing through the local loans fund to a figure of £585,000 to be repaid over twenty years. Three years of delays had caused great frustration among VEC members, not to mention the staffs of the two schools. The refusal of the Department of Local Government to provide funds for the widening of New Street wasn't resolved until September of 1977. There was difficulty in January 1977 over a request by Fr. Maher that the plans should be altered to make the complex easier to manage. He was supported in this by the Principal of KCVS but the Department refused to sanction the changes. After an initial threat to withdraw from the project, Fr. Maher accepted the Department decision. A more serious dispute involved the price of the land set in 1974 at £10,000. St. Kieran's claimed that this was now worth £15,000, but the Valuation Office advised the Department that this price was not acceptable. No money had been paid by the Department from the monies promised to St. Kieran's for the building of the sports complex, although this had at that stage been available to KCVS students for two years. The dispute was resolved in May with a decision by the Department that costs could be split on a twenty/eighty basis provided a case could be made for this. They also would pay a sum on account to St. Kieran's for the Sports complex. The preparation of plans and tender documents would account for some of the time which elapsed but it is hard to escape the conclusion that most of the delays occurred in the Department of Education.

At the October meeting in 1977 members expressed pleasure that after decades of effort a start could be made.[114]

The construction phase seems to have gone relatively smoothly, although early

**Official Opening of the joint complex in New Street, Kilkenny 1984
by the Minister for Education, Mrs Gemma Hussey, T.D.**
On the left is Mr. Brendan Conway, C.E.O. and on the right is
Fr. Martin Campion, President of St. Kieran's College.

in 1978 the architect, Colm Ó Cochláin attended a meeting to address some misgivings of the KCVS teachers. They complained that the ceiling in the speech and drama room was too low at nine foot one inch. Department sanction would be sought to increase this. He defended changes which he had made to the second entrance to accommodate a teachers' toilet and said that the installation of showers had been ruled out by the Department. In response to a request for a barrier between the two sections he said that he had no brief to provide this but could provide demarcation. Provision for wheelchair access could be made. The same meeting heard that Kilkenny Corporation had refused planning permission for an overpass of New Street to connect the new complex with the Ormonde Road buildings. A month later the VEC meeting was told that a meeting between teacher representatives and the Department had agreed alterations to the plans, but the CEO had no official notification and accounts from the teachers' side and the Department differed. A meeting in the Department on March 22nd with teachers, officials and VEC representation brought agreement on additions and alterations to the plans at an extra cost of £26,833. The parents' representative complained to the next VEC meeting about the refusal to provide showers or to raise the ceiling height in the speech and drama room. An allegation that the building sub-committee had been disbanded on the appointment to it of the Headmaster was denied by other members of that sub-committee.[115]

In June 1978 a letter from the Teachers' Union of Ireland (TUI) was considered. It referred to the union's policy of seeking a common enrolment for the Senior Cycle in the New Street complex. It was pointed out at the meeting that there was no mention of common enrolment in the agreement between St. Kieran's trustees and the VEC. It was decided to invite TUI delegates to the next VEC meeting. At that meeting the Assistant General Secretary of the TUI, with J. Walsh and T. Hunt represented the union. They pointed out that teachers feared for the security of their jobs, were worried about the future development of Vocational Education in County Kilkenny, and wished to avoid friction with any other persons engaged in the project. Their union had had bad experiences with other such projects around the country where Vocational Schools had virtually disappeared. They wanted to see common enrolment set down in a written agreement and didn't consider the undertaking by St. Kieran's to limit their first year intake to 108 students to be an adequate guarantee. A swing in enrolments could take place in the future. Their head office would be holding discussions with the Association of Secondary Teachers in Ireland (ASTI) on the subject.

When the VEC considered these points, it was decided to request a meeting with the trustees of St. Kieran's to discuss common enrolment and to negotiate with the TUI at national level. In contrast to the union, the VEC members considered the offer by St. Kieran's to limit enrolments to be adequate. They didn't see any fall-off in enrolments in KCVS since the start of the project and felt that population trends would favour an enhanced enrolment in the school.

In November the VEC heard of a meeting between their own delegates and the trustees of St. Kieran's who would agree to add the undertaking on enrolment to the agreement between the schools. They would accept the idea of a common enrolment but this would have to have the consent of the ASTI. Over the course of the following year, 1979, there were several meetings of the various parties, VEC, Trustees and the two unions. All four were represented at a Conference on the problem held in the Rose Hill Hotel on Thursday May 24th 1979. There was disagreement between the two unions on common enrolment. With executives of each union due to meet shortly, it was felt that it might help if a mediator were engaged locally

With the complex due to open in September, a sub-committee met with the officer board of the TUI. The union said that from September their members would not teach any students of St. Kieran's who had not been taught by them already. In effect this was a refusal to teach first years. The VEC responded that guidelines for the coming school year had been set on the basis that the full programme would be available to first years, and they appealed to the union to operate the complex from September without prejudice to their long-term policy. The TUI agreed to negotiate on a local level and said that their executive would not necessarily provide obstacles to the branch recommendations. They would take account of the fact that enrolments at St. Kieran's had already taken place. In the beginning of September the VEC was notified that TUI members in KCVS would be directed not to teach first-years from St. Kieran's. In October, with the complex in use by both schools the Vocational School Principal notified the VEC that "first year students from St. Kieran's College are not being taught Woodwork, Metalwork or Mechanical Drawing, as teachers are abiding by a Union Directive to with-hold such services." Fr. Maher said no timetable was in operation in the school because rooms were not available. In response to complaints from TUI that rooms in the complex had not been furnished, the CEO said that orders had been placed weeks beforehand. The heating in the new building wasn't working and the heating in the old building wasn't finished. A joint working party was proposed to help resolve the dispute. In the beginning the ASTI would not attend this working party as they saw it as a sub-committee of the VEC but by year's end this problem had been resolved and Mr. Paddy McAlinney, Principal of Mother Of Fair Love School, Kilkenny was appointed to chair the working party with the consent of the TUI, ASTI, St. Kieran's trustees and the VEC. A month earlier the TUI had lifted their ban on the teaching of first years.

The appeal of the VEC to An Bord Pleanála on the refusal of planning for the overpass of New Street was turned down, with the Parents' Council at KCVS claiming that the VEC had mishandled the appeals process. By the end of the year there was still no equipment for the metalwork room.[116]

In May of 1980 there was hopeful talk of a September official opening if the future operation of the school could be agreed beforehand, but by June an emergency meeting was informed that the TUI was to re-impose its ban from September. Mr. Hunt complained that the working party had dragged its heels all year. Fr. Maher disagreed that there had been undue delays, but saw no hope of an agreed statement. Mr. Hunt proposed discussion of a St. Kieran's Community

School, but got no support from the other members. When the schools opened after the summer holidays, the ban on teaching first years from St. Kieran's was again in force. In January of 1981 some work was still uncompleted in the complex. The joint working party didn't succeed in resolving the dispute to the satisfaction of all parties, but in March of 1981 the TUI requested a joint consultation meeting to discuss an agreed position between TUI and the trustees of St. Kieran's contained in a highly confidential document. A month later the VEC considered the document which had been agreed at the Joint Consultation meeting on 24th March. It dealt with matters concerning the smooth running of the joint complex: a joint timetable facilitating the taking of subjects in either area of the complex by students of either school; a joint prospectus outlining the total curriculum of the two schools; a date for enrolments to be advertised jointly by both schools; the holding of regular joint staff meetings with the chairmanship rotating; the use of specialist rooms, gymnasium, and handball alleys; the appointment of a liaison officer from each school to further co-operation between the schools, and the smooth running of the complex. In retrospect, Paragraph 1 seems the most significant: "In consideration of the implementation of all the clauses in this agreement, County Kilkenny Branch of TUI will at this time withdraw their demand for Common Enrolment as a minimum requirement for their co-operation in the New Complex". [117]

A certain amount of criticism by the Board of Management of the city school was considered by the VEC. Complaints about the equipping of the new building and the lack of progress in reconstruction at the old premises on Ormonde Road were noted with the comment that these could be taken in hand when the final account had been agreed and the final instalment of monies had been received from the Department. A demand for computer equipment would be considered as part of a package for the whole county already proposed to the Department. A request for additional secretarial services was dismissed as not justified by increased enrolment.

A slight note of reproof can be detected: "It was noted that the meetings of the Board of Management of the City School had become occasions for complaint on lack of support for the school by the VEC administration more than any other school and that the City Board of Management meeting had been given the impression that the VEC had under-spent its due allocation of money over a five year period and that the students of the city school were being treated less favourably than students of other schools". In November of 1981 suggestions from the TUI were considered as to how a decline in numbers at KCVS might be reversed - whole time adult day courses, repeat Leaving certificate classes, the setting up of an out-centre for Regional Technical College courses, for example in Computer Studies. In May of the following year a report of the meeting of the KVCS Board of Management was finally considered, having been postponed on at least three occasions. VEC members who were on that Board of Management expressed displeasure at the mood of the meeting. A demand for drinking water to be supplied for the school from a rising main was agreed but the demand for extra secretarial services was again referred back. In January the headmaster was told to get a price on the provision of drinking water "which seemed to be a minor undertaking". In such matters he had discretion to spend up to £200 without consultation. In July 1984, in response to a plea from the Board of Management that any diminution of staff in the school would be unacceptable, the CEO informed the VEC members that KCVS had 27% of the teachers in the scheme, and 18% of the pupils. Cutbacks imposed by the Department might have an effect on the agreement between the VEC and the trustees of St. Kieran's, as one of the bases of the joint project was that vocational teachers should be available to teach practical subjects to St. Kieran's pupils. A letter from the Department gave permission to appoint two teachers for the current year to facilitate cooperation between the two schools.[118]

In late 1983, the TUI claimed at a joint consultation meeting that declining numbers of apprentices at the city school apprenticeship block had reached crisis level. A further meeting was attended by Mr. Swan of the Motor Industry who said that new regulations imposed by AnCo (An Chomhairle Oiliúna) would affect Kilkenny, though rejected by the motor industry. He foresaw seven to ten apprentices coming on stream over the next five years. The TUI, VEC and the motor industry were to plan a joint programme designed to preserve the Kilkenny operation. As VEC members commented when they considered the report of this meeting, they had to "sit back and watch the erosion of a very successful amenity in the school even though the trade interest had a preference for the services of the Vocational School".[119]

In summer of 1984, the word that the Minister for Education, Gemma Hussey T.D. was available to perform the official opening of the complex was received. The opening ceremony took place on October 19th 1984. This was fourteen years after the first proposal by the Department that there should be joint Senior Cycle facilities in Kilkenny, eleven years after the VEC and St. Kieran's trustees had made their joint proposal to the Department, ten years after they were told that approval would be forthcoming, seven years after the contract was awarded and five years after classes commenced in the buildings.

Under the headline "Minister opens £1m school complex" the *Kilkenny People* of October 26th 1984 reported:

> A new one million pound joint schools complex in Kilkenny was officially opened by the Minister for Education on Friday. The school complex, which caters for almost one thousand pupils, is a joint venture between St. Kieran's College and the City Vocational School. Situated at New Street, the massive building was completed in 1979 and has been in operation for the past five years. The building contains woodwork rooms, metalwork/engineering rooms, art room, science laboratories, assembly hall, library, music/drama room and six general classrooms.

The co-operation between the two schools which led to the new complex began in 1966. The Vocational school provides teaching facilities at junior and senior level for pupils from St. Kieran's in Metalwork, Woodwork, Mechanical Drawing and Business Organisation. St. Kieran's provides teaching facilities for Vocational school pupils at Senior level in Physics, Chemistry, Applied Maths, Honours Maths, Irish, French, Accounting and Computer Studies".

Mayor Tom Crotty, welcoming the Minister paid tribute to the hard work of the CEO Brendan Conway, VEC Chairman John Holohan and Monsignor Tommy Maher for the dedication they had shown and which he had witnessed as a VEC member. Speaking after a joint Ecumenical Service conducted by himself and Bishop Noel Willoughby, Bishop Laurence Forristal said that in addition to the building now completed for St. Kieran's and the City Vocational School, Kilkenny City had, in recent years, seen extensive building programmes at Kilkenny College, the Christian Brothers' Secondary School and the Loreto, while the Presentation Order was just beginning construction of a new school. The Minister, Gemma Hussey praised the shared facility as an example to the country especially in view of the government's stated determination "to achieve the greatest possible rationalisation of school facilities and resources". The President of St. Kieran's, Fr. Martin Campion challenged the Minister to allow on a permanent basis the current arrangement of allowing extra teachers to the VEC in Kilkenny to facilitate the integration of the two schools. Conceived in better times, the straitened economic circumstances of the 1980s had made the realisation of the integration a bit of a struggle.[120]

CHAPTER 7

The 1970s

Thomastown Extension

During the years that the Kilkenny City complex occupied so much of the committee's time, the schools in the rest of the county also needed attention. In Thomastown, with a Senior Cycle in operation and an enhanced enrolment, the existing facilities soon proved inadequate. In October 1974, a meeting in the town, called by the Parents' Association of the school called for an extension. Mr. Luke Murtagh, the Principal of the school, presented estimates of enrolment for the next seven years, based on the current enrolments of feeder Primary schools in the Thomastown catchment area. Three TDs were in attendance to lend their support. Shortly afterwards the department sanctioned the erection of toilets at the school and there was an implication that the extension would be considered favourably, and in October of 1975 the CEO and the School Principal were invited to attend at the department for the first stage of a planning programme for a new building at Thomastown.

It was May of 1976 before a schedule of accommodation was agreed with the Department and VEC members were told that a visit to the site would be the next step.

The refusal of a prefab was a disappointment, but the CEO had arranged that Johnstown, which had been assigned three prefabs, could manage for the present with two, and Thomastown was to get the third.

In November, the VEC heard of discussions between the Principal in Thomastown and Bord na gCapall about developing a course at Thomastown for young people anxious to make a career in the non-thoroughbred horse industry. Bord na gCapall were prepared to second their instructor Mr. John Hall, and Major McCalmont was prepared to give facilities for field work for the course. Mr. Jim Finnegan assured them that horses would be made available by owners. Sixteen places were to be available at a fee of £75 per annum. The VEC agreed to offer four free places.

In September 1977, the CEO was nominated to the Equitation Sub-Committee of Bord na gCapall and land was acquired for the equitation school. Mr. Doody offered land to the VEC at £12,500, described in the minutes as a special price for the purpose intended. A deposit of £1,200 was to be paid immediately from fees for the course and the balance was to be repaid over five years from leasing fees to be paid by Bord na gCapall to the VEC.

At the same meeting, members heard of an offer from the Department planning section to allow for a new school at Thomastown with a capacity of 375 pupils. Members felt that 450 would be better but were forced to accept what was on offer as the Department was adamant. The CEO made a submission to the Department showing that the 450 places would be needed, and in reply the Department invited him to postpone matters for a year to ensure further proof of this. The CEO advised the members not to accept this offer as the same attitude would probably prevail a year from then. Members were reasonably satisfied with the accommodation except for the failure to provide a metalwork room. Mr. Herbert Devoy pointed out that it would be particularly necessary as there were 85 to 100 jobs in engineering in Thomastown.

In the event, the Department listened. The building unit allowed for Junior and Senior Metalwork in the revised schedule of accommodation. In December a design team was appointed: Colm Ó Cochláin as architect, with Vincent Drum as quantity surveyor, and J.B. Barry and partners as structural engineers and Cecil Buggy as heating engineer. In the meantime Mr. Luke Murtagh resigned as Principal at Thomastown on getting a position as CEO with Mr. Patrick Cronin becoming Principal and Mr. Tim O'Mahony becoming Vice-Principal.

The new building was to be erected on the playing pitch of the school, and the Parents' Association set about acquiring land for a new pitch. They raised a sum of £1,500 by local fund-raising, and a loan was needed for the rest. The VEC agreed, subject to the agreement of the Minister for Education to pay the interest on the loan. Two fields were acquired for £15,000 and vested in the school. VEC member, Jim Kelsey donated fertiliser to the value of £50 and the parents took 500 bales of hay off the land that summer. The hay was used in the equestrian centre. At the June 1979 meeting, members were told that the design team were working on the Development Sketch Plan stage.

By the following February, the Thomastown Board of Management were complaining at the delay in getting the project started and the CEO said that he had got no reply on the subject from the Department since the previous December. The anxiety in Thomastown cannot have been lessened by the knowledge that the Kilkenny City Complex was by then in operation. In March 1980, the announcement of a capital loan of £430,000 from the Office of Public Works for the Thomastown building must have gladdened a few hearts. The design team were instructed to prepare tender documents. Seven months later Cllr. Michael O'Brien was expressing total dissatisfaction with the lack of progress on Thomastown School, and members of the VEC decided that the minister should be written to on the subject and that local deputies should be lobbied to use their influence. [121]

In June the arena for the Equestrian Centre was officially opened and two teachers were congratulated at the subsequent VEC meeting for the splendid meal served to two hundred guests.

A report in the *Kilkenny People* seven years later outlined the progress of the school in the intervening years. The original three-month course was a pilot project leading to the Irish Certificate in Equitation Science. Nine of the eleven participants were successful in gaining certification, and the course was made permanent in September 1977, and its duration was extended to six months. From 1981, it became possible for students to do Equestrian Studies for the Leaving certificate examination. Candidates attended the centre for some hours weekly and took the examination after two years.

"The Vocational School has stabling facilities for 17 horses. The horses are borrowed from owners around Ireland, and they are kept free in return for their use. Young horses are also taken and broken for a nominal fee. The employment prospects are good with 80% staying in the horse industry".

Senior Cycle Demands

In 1972 the school at Johnstown was the second largest in the scheme, with 210 students on rolls. As at other schools, prefabs were showing signs of age and the toilets were so bad that the acting Chief Medical Officer of the South Eastern Health Board threatened to close the school if the situation continued. By early 1974 a new toilet block had been completed at a cost of £9,639. Parents in Johnstown wanted a Senior Cycle in the school and early in 1975 the CEO met with parents and teaching staff there. He pointed out that the establishment of a Senior Cycle in Johnstown would mean that transport to other centres would be curtailed, and that the range of subjects would be limited until numbers justified additional teachers. A special meeting of the VEC, called to consider the provision of a Senior Cycle at Johnstown, heard that twenty-one girls and eighteen boys were prepared to commit to the course, and that the parents understood that the VEC would not be able to provide finance for any school extension or for new teachers in 1975. The staff had been consulted and it appeared that subjects could be provided as follows: Irish, higher and lower; English, higher and lower; Mathematics, lower; Technical Drawing; Home Economics; Biology; French; Building Construction; with optional subjects from History, Geography and Business Organisation. VEC members were unanimous in their support and the CEO, following a telephone conversation with a Department official, was hopeful that the course could be set up. [122]

Boards of Management at Slieverue and Mooncoin demanded Leaving Certificate provision in their schools in 1976 and in July of the next year the VEC were told that the department would sanction Senior Cycles in both schools from the following September. The committee pressed the department to sanction a Senior Cycle in Ballyhale and were successful in April 1977.[123]

Castlecomer was a less straight-forward case. Since the late 1960s the Vocational School there had operated a reciprocal arrangement with the local Presentation Convent Secondary School. In 1976 the VEC heard of discussions with the Convent on broadening the Senior Cycle curriculum to include technical subjects. When a cheque for £700 was sent by the convent for the services of Vocational teachers, members felt that this was a way of saying that the convent authorities did not wish to promote further co-operation between the schools. The

CEO was instructed to return the cheque with all due courtesy and that a meeting with the convent authorities be sought to allay any fears of a take-over by the VEC.

The numbers at the Vocational School would not justify a Senior Cycle there, but the Principal proposed that they should extend their programme of leaving certificate subjects to offer Technical Drawing, Workshop Engineering Theory and Practice, and Chemistry. If they did so, fifteen boys now completing Junior Cycle would enrol in Presentation Convent on the understanding that they would have the facilities sought at the Vocational School.

In 1978 the CEO met with the Principals and Vice-Principals of the two schools. In that year Presentation students took the following Leaving Certificate subjects at the Vocational School: Workshop Engineering Theory and Practice, Technical Drawing, Art and Biology. Junior cycle students took allied subjects with the effect that four teaching posts at the Vocational School were solely required for pupils enrolled at the convent school. Now the convent proposed to appoint two science teachers in their own school, which would duplicate facilities in the Vocational School in these teaching areas. When the results of the meeting were reported to the VEC, members requested the committee members who were on the board of management of Castlecomer Vocational School to meet as a working party and make recommendations to the VEC.

A meeting in the following month with teachers at the Vocational School concluded that the present situation could not continue, as there was a possibility of the disappearance of the school. Following the meeting the Mother Superior of the Convent telephoned the CEO to the effect that they were not insistent on the appointment of a science teacher, that an agreement for the future development of both schools was necessary, and that the appointment of a new head-mistress was imminent. The CEO, with the Principal and Vice-Principal of the Vocational School met with the Mother Provincial of the Presentation Order, the Mother Superior of the convent, the Headmistress of the convent school, and Messrs. Hester and Johnson. A proposal to limit the convent school intake to 75 first-years was not acceptable to the convent side. The VEC began to consider the phasing out of co-operation over a three year period. The failure of a second meeting to reach agreement between the sides meant that this course was adopted. The CEO issued a statement to the *Kilkenny People* outlining the future relationship between the schools. The VEC agreed in principle to a motion from the Board of Management of their school calling for the offering of a Leaving certificate course in the school, which would encourage first-year enrolment, and for the establishment of a second-chance Saturday course for young adults who were at work. A modest increase in enrolment in the following September gave some cause for hope, as did the proposal to establish a whole-time CERT course for twenty-four students. The following September however saw a big fall in new enrolments, and in early 1981, the CEO was still having no success in getting the department to sanction Senior Cycle courses at Castlecomer and Graignamanagh.[124]

Boards of Management

Mention has been made of Boards of Management at Vocational Schools. These were set up as a result of the issuing of Circular letter 73/74 by the Department in July 1974. Such boards were already in operation in comprehensive and community schools and were in the process of being established in primary schools following agreement with the Irish National Teachers Organisation. Now the Minister for Education suggested that VECs should use their powers under Section 21 of the Vocational Education Act to set up a sub-committee in respect of each school in their scheme which would act as a Board of Management of that school. An attached memorandum set out the proposed composition of the boards, their functions, and their financial relationship with the VEC and the principal of the school. [125]

County Kilkenny VEC first considered these proposals when their delegates to the Congress of the Irish Vocational Education Association (IVEA) reported on the Minister's speech to that body. A letter from the IVEA, the umbrella body for VECs advised the committee to take no action on boards of management pending discussions with the Department. A meeting between the CEO and School principals discussed the proposals and the CEO reported back to his committee. Principals considered that the present structure was satisfactory, and that the establishment of the boards would lead to duplication of the work of VEC members who would be members of two boards each. They felt that parental involvement should be through Parents' Associations, and that the provision of secretarial assistance for Principals would be an essential pre-requisite for the establishment of boards of management in their schools. They expressed surprise that teacher representation was not included in the current proposals and requested the VEC to postpone the establishment of the boards, provide clerical assistance and arrange for teacher representation. The VEC expressed general agreement with the proposals but Cllr. Dick Dowling said that it was incumbent on the committee to establish these boards irrespective of their personal opinions. To opt for an alternative would provoke a possible dissolution of the committee.

A special meeting of the committee decided to recommend that the boards should have six VEC members, two parents and one elected teacher besides the Principal. Senior Cycle schools were to have the Vice-Principal in addition. Otherwise they expressed general agreement with the terms of circular 73/74. Boards had been set up in some counties and steps were being taken in most counties to do so. By the end of 1975 draft lists were being prepared matching members to the various boards in County Kilkenny. By February of the next year, most boards of management had been set up but members were informed that the TUI were unwilling to attend until secretarial services were provided. A clarification of their position by the Union that, if secretarial services were provided, their members would participate as an interim measure led to agreement by the VEC to pay for these services. [126]

By May of 1976, Boards of Management had met and the VEC considered

Aontas Executive members pictured with the local organising committee and Mayor McGuinness at the opening of the successful Aontas Adult Education Conference in the Newpark Hotel
Seated: (from left) Ms. Mary Enright, Mr. Kevin McBrien, President of Aontas, Mayor McGuinness, Ms. Naomi Sargant (guest speaker), Mr. Chris Greene.
Behind: Mr.Robin Webster, Director, Mr. Brendan Conway, C.E.O,
Mr. Michael O'Hanrahan, Mr. Prionsias Ó Drisceoil, Arts Education Organiser,
Mr. Martin O'Grady, Adult Education Organiser.

demands from Slieverue and Mooncoin for Senior Cycle courses, and from Thomastown and Ballyhale for Post Leaving Certificate courses. Castlecomer reported discussions with the local convent on a Senior Cycle curriculum to include technical subjects, as outlined above. A Department offer of eleven pounds per month for secretarial services was considered totally inadequate by the TUI and with their members not attending, the VEC decided in November not to hold meetings of boards for the present. [127]

In April 1978 the Department allocated extra clerical posts to County Kilkenny VEC: one senior clerk, two clerical officers and four clerk typists. The Chairman was hopeful that this would help to resolve the dispute with the teachers' union about Boards of Management and the lack of clerical services. Arrangements for advertising of posts, setting up of an interview board and appointment of the extra secretarial staff were set in train by the summer and in October a letter from the TUI requested a meeting to discuss the re-activation of the Boards of Management in the schools. The letter set out some points which the union wanted clarified. The CEO said that all except the question of representation of teachers formed part of the existing charter of the boards. The current representation was Principal, Vice-Principal and one elected teacher in Senior Cycle schools, while Junior Cycle schools had the Principal and one elected teacher. The VEC agreed to offer boards composed of six VEC members, the Principal and Vice-Principal ex officio, two parents and two teachers elected by the school staff. With the current VEC members nearing the end of their term of office, it was agreed that the parent representation might be increased by the next VEC. This would necessitate cutting the VEC members to four on each board. In December the TUI agreed to participation on the boards.[128]

Posts of Responsibility

Concurrently with the dispute on Boards of Management, the VEC found itself at odds with the teachers' union on the question of posts of responsibility. In November 1977, the committee was informed of the procedure for filling two vacant posts of responsibility. The job descriptions had been agreed with the Principals of the schools concerned but TUI policy was that such descriptions should not be attached to the posts before appointments were made. It was decided to hold a joint consultation meeting with the union before any further action would be taken. A special meeting of the VEC was held to consider the results of the joint consultation. Some points were acceptable to both sides - notably the idea that holders of posts of responsibility would form a management team for their school. Members questioned whether the TUI had a national policy on posts. Mr. J. Walsh the TUI representative outlined a ten point programme of action which was to be discussed at the next meeting. A further joint consultation meeting failed to agree an interim policy on filling posts of responsibility pending agreement of the Irish Vocational Education Association and the teachers' union at national level.

A letter from the General Secretary of the TUI outlining their policy on Posts of Responsibility was received in January 1978, and members felt there was some common ground with the views of the committee. However a further letter from the Kilkenny branch secretary notified the VEC that all teachers had been instructed to withdraw applications for Posts of Responsibility before January 20th and all except one had complied. The VEC decided not to hold any appointment boards in the current circumstances and Mr. Walsh was asked to notify the TUI that the VEC were available to meet with them on this issue. At the following meting, Mr. Walsh conveyed the decision of his branch not to meet with the committee. [129]

The April meeting was delayed for twenty-five minutes to allow discussions between the Assistant General Secretary of the TUI, local branch officers and the CEO to finish. Later the CEO reported to his committee that a programme of action for filling vacant posts of responsibility was to be put to the union branch by the TUI, and that he was putting the same proposals to the VEC. The proposals were adopted at a special meeting a week later.

Basis for Agreement on the Appointment Procedure to Posts of Responsibility in County Kilkenny Vocational Educational Committee

1.   A schedule of acceptable duties to be assigned to Posts of Responsibility within scheme will be compiled by Headmasters in consultation with their staffs, agreed by VEC and TUI Branch Officers.
2.   This schedule of duties will be subject to annual review by the parties mentioned at 1. The date of appointment of new posts is suggested as an appropriate date for this review.
3.   This schedule of duties is equally available to all teachers and to members of the Selection Board.
4.   Posts will be advertised as Grade A or Grade B Posts and candidates will be informed that duties will be assigned to the successful candidate by apportionment from the agreed schedule.
5.   The successful candidate will be informed of his appointment from a stated date, subject to his/her agreeing to assume the duties agreed for the post.
6.   Apportionment of duties to newly appointed post-holders will be made by a meeting of Principal, Vice-Principal and existing post-holders at the school.
7.   This apportionment of duties will be placed before the VEC for approval,
8.   The teacher on first appointment to a Post of Responsibility will be ratified in the position by letter from the CEO which will confirm to him/her the duties agreed for the post.

The VEC decided to proceed with the filling of posts following compilation of a list of duties by headmasters, and the minutes for July contain a list of Posts of

Responsibility in all schools together with the names of successful applicants. In the following school year a scheme for filling posts was proposed at the October VEC meeting with the proviso that, "there remained the establishment of posts from the distribution of part-time points monies and the clarification of some posts now becoming a personal entitlement thus providing for the establishment of further new posts. It was on this section that a position required agreement with TUI". By December a revised schedule had been agreed between the parties.

Adult Education

In November 1979 County Kilkenny VEC appointed its first Adult Education Officer, Mr. Michael O'Neill. A new approach to lifelong learning for adults led to a number of initiatives in adult education over the coming years. The Vocational Education system already had a very long experience in this field to draw upon. The Joint Technical Instruction Committee, even before it acquired its one permanent school, had employed what were called itinerant teachers to conduct night classes in various parts of the county. When the Vocational Education Committee took over the running of the City Vocational School, night classes became a valued part of community life. As Vocational Schools opened in other centres around the county, other smaller communities benefited in the same way. The subjects were mostly but not exclusively the practical ones - Domestic Economy, Cookery, Dress-making, Woodwork, Typewriting, Shorthand, Book-Keeping, Irish and European languages. Classes were were very well attended and gave excellent results. They were held in the committee's schools for the most part, but centres which didn't have a Vocational School were not neglected. The classes in these places were held in national schools, parish halls and so on. Some were in better condition than others and few were ideal.

From 1980 onwards Michael O'Neill was faced with implementing a new approach: adult literacy classes, continuation education, second-chance education and whole-time day classes for adults joined the familiar old-style night classes as part of the Adult Education Organiser's remit. An advertisement for night classes in the autumn of 1980 listed over sixty subjects offered in various schools and centres.[130]

By May of 1981, Mr. O'Neill submitted a report to the VEC outlining a major expansion in adult education enrolment, particularly in out centres. A month later the committee members were told that he had not reached the necessary standard in Irish. The requirement was that he should have the same qualification as any vocational teacher, the Ceard Teastas Gaeilge. The committee recommended to the Department that his temporary appointment be extended for one year, but this appeal seems to have been unsuccessful. In an interview with a local newspaper he outlined the efforts he had made to learn Irish. Born in England, he had been working in Northern Ireland and studying Irish when he was appointed to the job of Adult Education Organiser with County Kilkenny VEC. The committee recommended to the Department of Education that his temporary contract be extended for one year but his appeal seems to have been unsuccesful. In September, Mr. O'Neill resigned his position, expressing his sense of grievance at having to do so through lack of a qualification in Irish.

On November 1st his successor, Mr. Martin F. O'Grady took up office. A sub-committee of the VEC had been set up to look after adult education and they were recommending the setting up of whole-time day classes for adults in the city school. By September KVCS was offering a pilot programme for adults. English and Commerce subjects would be taught for two hours on each of three mornings each week. The Adult Education Organiser was also inviting applications from people who had reading difficulties and from tutors willing to help. Mr. O'Grady spent four years in the post of Adult Education Organiser and died tragically in a road accident in December 1986.

Finance

Finance in the 1970s and 1980s proved a headache for the committee, with inflation affecting costs and poor economic conditions putting a severe strain on resources. Cutbacks in education not only affected the provision of services, but Government delay in repaying capital expenditure left the VEC with large overdrafts most of the time. New banking rules in 1972 resulted in the Hibernian Bank requesting the committee to convert its overdraft to a term loan. The size of the overdraft was commented on, and the CEO explained to members that capital costs of £47,969 had to be met from revenue. The most expensive items over the previous four years had been the apprentice block at Kilkenny, new buildings at Slieverue and Castlecomer, mobile classrooms and repairs at Mooncoin, prefabs for county schools, and a staffroom and toilets at Ballyhale. The Department were to be pressed to make an early lodgement to the capital fund. Within a few years this sort of money was to look comparatively small. By 1974, the Bank of Ireland, which had absorbed the Hibernian Bank, was noting that an overdraft of £65,000 was very high in a tight credit situation.

Later in the same year, the bank at first refused a request for overdraft facilities up to £120,000, but was willing to concede £80,000. They might have to charge an extra half percent interest as the account had not been in credit for the requisite thirty days in the year, and they criticised the committee's practice of funding capital projects out of revenue. By the following month the bank had agreed to the £120,000 overdraft but wanted the capital funding straightened out. Department sanction for the raising of a loan from the Office of Public Works to pay for works carried out over the previous seven years eased the overdraft situation somewhat. In 1976, the CEO stated to the committee that he had got £150,000 as part of the Department grant and due to a bank strike had had to invest the money at 3% with the Nationwide Building Society. In 1977, the bank was prepared to sanction an overdraft of £225,000 if the VEC could show a letter of authorisation from the Department of Education. Inflation and the committee's building programme were beginning to show their effects. The CEO, Mr. Conway summed up for the outgoing committee just before the local elections in 1979. During their term of office the sanctioned expenditure rose from £433,000 in 1975 to £1,200,000 in 1979. Adult education class fees had risen from £5,248 to £10,549 and the enrolment of full-time students was just over 1,700. £138,076 was outstanding which had been paid out of the revenue account for capital works. The recovery of this amount by way of a local loan fund grant had been set in motion but had not as yet been processed by the department. At this time the VEC offices were moved out of the City school and Cashel House on the Kells Road was rented as office accommodation. At the end of 1980, this was costing £5,781 per annum, following the award of an arbitrator agreed by the committee and the owners of the property.[131]

The school in Graignamanagh was host to two interesting ventures, an outdoor pursuits centre and a summer season youth hostel. In early 1977, a seminar on outdoor pursuits was held there and the Irish Canoeing Union and experts on outdoor pursuits from County Cork VEC gave an induction weekend. The VEC considered a report on the event and decided to appoint a teacher with expertise in the area of outdoor pursuits to a position in the Graignamanagh Vocational School. By September Kevin Higgins had been appointed and in October the VEC decided to fund four teachers to attend weekend courses at Tigh Linn in Wicklow, with a view to becoming leaders in outdoor pursuits. Early in the following year Cospóir, the National Sports Council, decided to give a two thirds grant to cover capital expenditure at Graignamanagh. In 1980, An Óige (The Irish Youth Hostel Association) asked the VEC to lease the Graignamanagh school to them to be used as a youth hostel while the school was closed during the summer holidays. Sixteen bunk beds would be provided and the hostel would close well before the re-opening of the school in September. The CEO was authorised to negotiate a leasing fee of £50 to £100. In October, An Óige reported to the VEC on the success of the hostel and requested a lease for the coming summer. The committee agreed in principle. [132]

In December 1980 Proinsias Ó Drisceoil was appointed Arts Education Organiser for the South Eastern Region. Though based in Kilkenny, this was a joint venture with other VECs in the region. In February, the CEO informed the meeting of County Kilkenny VEC that he was involved in setting up an arts advisory sub-committee but had not yet had a reply from other neighbouring committees. When Mr. George Vaughan was mentioned as a County Kilkenny representative, Dean Harvey objected that Mr. Vaughan was involved in a split in an arts venture in Kilkenny City. The CEO strongly defended Mr. Vaughan, who had been appointed as a teacher and not as representing any outside body.[133]

Since 1939, the press had been excluded from meetings of County Kilkenny VEC. The original ban arose from a controversy over the VEC's purchase of some bentwood chairs of foreign manufacture when the old model school had been refurbished as the City Vocational School. It was a time of vigorous promotion of Irish manufacture and the level of criticism in the *Kilkenny People* rankled with members at the time, with the result that they voted to exclude the press from all future meetings of the committee. In 1942, newly elected member Jack Leahy, supported by J.P. Pattison, proposed the re-admission of the press. The motion was lost by nine votes to six. When the question of the legality of the ban was raised at the next meeting, the committee decided to get the opinion of their legal adviser. Mr. J. Harte gave his opinion that the VEC had the right to exclude the press if they wished. In 1947, Mr. C.J. Kenealy, the proprietor of the *Kilkenny Journal*, wrote to the committee asking that the press be admitted. A motion to accede to his request was defeated by ten votes to two. A proposal in 1966 was also unsuccessful. Finally in March 1981, Cllr. Jack Murphy, the sponsor of the 1966 motion, proposed "that the local press be invited to attend meetings of this committee". Cllr. Margaret Tynan seconded. Opinion was divided and Cllr. Dick Dowling proposed an amendment "that the local Press be invited to attend four quarterly meetings of the VEC each year". The voting was tied at four votes each way, and the Chairman, Cllr. John Holohan gave his casting vote in favour of the amendment. A special meeting was called to work out how this decision was to be implemented.

Members worried about the highlighting of what the minutes call "newsy" items at the expense of the solid work of the VEC. They instanced the sorry state of school buildings at the time - a matter over which the committee or its officers had little control, being dependent on state finance. There was also discussion of the sort of items which might appear on the agenda for these meetings, with a determination that the agenda should not be an "artificial" one, but with some members anxious that restraint should be shown in putting down notices of motions designed to catch the public eye. Cllr. Meade proposed that, "VEC meetings to be covered by the press would be the ordinary monthly meetings of February, April, July, October". The *Kilkenny People*, the *Kilkenny Standard* and the *Munster Express* were to be invited to the July meeting. When the CEO approached the press informally, he was told that it was National Union of Journalists (NUJ) policy not to attend unless reporters were to be admitted to all meetings of the committee. At the beginning of the September meeting, the Chairman was able to welcome representatives of both local papers. At the end of the meeting, the representative of the *Kilkenny People*, Mr. Dermot Healy, was congratulated by all the members on his training of the Offaly team, which had recently won the All-Ireland Hurling Final.[134] The exclusion had lasted three days short of forty-two years.

Drawing by Robbie O'Keeffe of Slieverue
Vocational School

Students pictured with their teacher Vincent
Kelly in Slieverue Vocational School Woodwork
Room 1985

Thomastown Vocational School Leinster Colleges Junior Camogie Champions 1975
Back row: Kathleen Drea, Alice Kerwan, Hazel Dimond, Máiread Lee, Helen O'Carroll,
Helena Power, Mary Kelly, Margaret Farrell, Dana O'Neill
Front row: Laura Lee, Anne Roche, Nellie Shanahan (Captain), Olive Galway, Joan Lanigan,
Mary Aylward, Bríd Farrell. Missing from the photo is Carol Caulfield.

CHAPTER 8

The Impact of Free Second Level Education

By the start of the 1980s it was apparent to the County Kilkenny VEC, as to their colleagues in other counties, that while the provision of free secondary education had had its successes it had brought problems in the matter of educational provision, in the matter of accommodation and staffing, and in the matter of finance.

The original proposal had been to provide free second-level education to the age of sixteen, but the intervening years had seen an increasing demand from parents for education to Leaving Certificate level. Schools in the vocational sector which didn't cater for this demand would soon find themselves competing unsuccessfully for students with the secondary schools which had traditionally provided instruction to Intermediate Certificate level, with a follow-on to Leaving Certificate.

The increased numbers in Vocational Schools were initially catered for by the erection of prefabricated classrooms. After a very few years it was evident that these structures had a limited life, and when kept in use beyond their time, gave rise to extremely expensive maintenance, or provided very sub-standard working conditions for staff and students. The increase in staff in the schools for which County Kilkenny VEC had responsibility was noticeable in the 1970s, but the worsening economic conditions of the following decade led to a worsening of the pupil/teacher ratio and to severe cutbacks in staffing.

Financial cutbacks affected the schools in other areas besides teacher numbers. Administrative staffing came under pressure. School budgets had to be cut in the context of reduced grants from the Department of Education to the VEC. School building projects were subject to very great delays altogether out of the control of the VEC. Overdrafts and end-of-year deficits became commonplace, with late payments of monies due causing trouble with the banks.

The troubled decade opened with an obvious need for new schools or new permanent extensions at Thomastown, Graignamanagh, Mooncoin, Slieverue, and Johnstown. Kilkenny City Vocational School had begun working in their new building, even if the official opening was some years in the future. Castlecomer presented a particular problem with the local Presentation Convent Secondary School and the Vocational School competing for students, and the likelihood that there were only enough in the catchment area to sustain one school.

The former Vocational School in Castlecomer now houses an enterprise centre.

Slieverue Vocational School
Mrs. Rita O'Shea(centre front) pictured with the first Secretarial Class in 1978.

Slieverue Vocational School Staff 1980
Back L to R: Fr. Paschal Moore, Aidan McCarthy, Vincent Kelly, John O'Callaghan, Deputy Principal, Teddy O'Regan(R.I.P.), Jim Walsh, Principal, PJ O'Doherty, Johnny Walsh, Robbie O'Keeffe.
Front L to R: Rosario Walsh, Teresa Connolly, Eleanor Parks, Marion Fox, Bernadette Fitzgerald, Eileen Moyles.

Members of the cast from 1976 School Play at Kilkenny City Vocational School.

Slieverue Vocational School
Christmas Play 1980.

Thomastown

Thomastown had already suffered great delay since the project was agreed in 1975. The bill of quantities had been lodged with the Department in September 1980, but in the following February, Deputy Gibbons passed on the Minister's reply to his query on the project that "it is not possible at this stage to indicate when a contract may be placed or when building work may commence". A huge public meeting in Thomastown was attended by VEC members who reported to their committee that there was great frustration and extreme annoyance evident among the attendance. In a press statement the VEC deplored the five years of "intolerable dilatoriness" on the part of the Department, and pointed out that they themselves were faced with the problem of maintaining the temporary accommodation out of very limited resources. The conditions endured by the staff and the 350 students were intolerable. In 1958 three permanent classrooms were built and there were now in addition thirteen prefabs. They warned that from March public protests were planned in Thomastown and they were facing the prospect of a series of one-day teachers' strikes in the county. The public outcry seemed to have some effect because, by April, permission to put the building to tender had been received. A further delay was caused by the failure of the builder who submitted the lowest tender to provide a surety bond. The next lowest bid was from P. Cantwell and Sons of Kilkenny and in June the committee agreed to award the contract. Difficulties caused by the contract price being £30,000 above the limit set by the Department seem to have been resolved, because in December, the first sod on the site was cut by Bishop Forristal, who had succeeded Dr. Birch as Bishop of Ossory earlier that year. The Craft School at Grennan Mill was officially opened in April and its Director, Mr. George Vaughan brought the VEC members on a tour of the facility after the ceremony.[135]

Formerly known as Pilsworths' Mill the building now housed an attractive exhibition gallery, pottery room, printing/design/weaving room and art metal workshop. Mr. Pat Henderson, Managing Director of Kilkenny Design Workshops performed the official opening. He said that following the establishment of the Design Workshops in Kilkenny, many crafts people and artists had made their home in the area and opened studios of their own. Others were attracted there until the region "boasts more real craftsmen per square mile than anywhere else in Ireland. What makes Grennan Mill special is that the Vocational Education Committee seized upon this pool of talent and found a practical way of turning it to good effect".

The CEO, Mr. Brendan Conway paid tribute to the outstanding work of the Principal of Thomastown VS, Mr. Pat Cronin. Among those present was the former Principal of the school, Mr. Luke Murtagh, CEO of North Tipperary VEC.

The instructors included a number of part-time craftspeople as well as full-time staff of the VEC. Pottery was taught by Niall Harper and Roger Walker, Printing by George Vaughan, the Director, Weaving by Eilish O'Hare, Art Metalwork by Peter O'Donovan, Business Studies by Pat Cronin, Rush-Work and Patchwork by

Chrissie Keating, Candle-Making by Lex Hyde, and Technical Drawing by Joe Mackey.[136]

The main school buildings at Thomastown were opened by the Minister for Education, Mrs. Gemma Hussey on 15th November 1985, although the complex had been in operation for two years at that stage. The growth from a three-room, forty pupil school began in 1968, with the putting up of four prefabs, and later the school at one time had thirteen prefabs, and a converted bicycle shed doing duty as an office. The new building had eight general purpose classrooms, an assembly hall, library, and rooms for science, home economics, metalwork, drawing, woodwork and art. Already it had outgrown its capacity of 375 students with 450 on rolls. This necessitated the retention of some of the prefabs. As well as the Principal, Mr. Pat Cronin, and the Vice-Principal, Mr. Tim O'Mahony there were twenty-five full-time teachers and two part-time. Before arriving at the main building to cut the tape, the Minister visited Grennan Mill Craft Centre, and Grennan Equestrian Centre, both parts of the Thomastown Vocational School.

The Minister, in her remarks praised the commitment and dedication of the parents, who had raised £13,000 to buy sports fields for the school. Bishop Laurence Forristal, a native of the parish of Thomastown said:

> The great joy today for any native of this parish is to see a post-primary school of this nature here in Thomastown. Until the first school was opened in 1958, the nearest post-primary school of any kind was in Kilkenny - ten miles away. In those pre-tech days the majority of those who went to primary school here never went any further. The loss to the country and the community was enormous.[137]

A phased building programme for County Kilkenny

In the same year the committee was forced to confront serious accommodation problems at Slieverue where a building had collapsed, necessitating the provision of prefabs, and at Graignamanagh and Johnstown where prefabs had been adversely commented on by the committee's architect. At Ballyhale the VEC provided, out of its own meagre resources, temporary accommodation which the Department had refused to provide during the previous year. With protests coming in from Boards of Management, the committee asked the architect in June to prepare drawings to back up a proposal on a phased building programme for the county. This was to be submitted to the building unit of the Department of Education. The December meeting heard a report of a meeting in the Department on the last day of the previous month, where the proposed building programme was presented.

The Department side wanted projected enrolment figures for Johnstown which already had 294 students. They stressed that they would have to take account of a proposed school in Freshford to replace the Mill Hill Fathers' Secondary School which had closed. A decision on Mooncoin would take account of the Waterford City centres' closeness to Mooncoin. They offered a 200 student school for Ballyhale. The VEC felt that this was too low as the current enrolment was 197, but would accept the proposal if there were to be provision for a further extension if necessary. Even though a substantial increase in student numbers had taken place in Graignamanagh, the Department were not prepared to sanction a Leaving Certificate programme on the evidence of one year's figures. They also hinted that the proposed provision of a new primary school in the area would have relevance. The Department was aware of the growth of numbers at Slieverue where enrolment had reached 158, but Ferrybank Convent would be a factor in any decision affecting the area.

On the Castlecomer proposal, the committee side was reminded that they had refused to provide technical education to the community of Castlecomer when they ended the facilities provided to the secondary school pupils to study Woodwork and Metalwork at the Vocational School. They had no authority to offer the Leaving Certificate course as they were doing at present. There was pressure from the Presentation Convent for the provision of new buildings, and it was obvious that numbers required that the two schools develop a joint policy.[138]

As well as the Intermediate and Leaving Certificate courses, Castlecomer Vocational School was offering a Secretarial course and was running a one-year course in conjunction with CERT which prepared students for entry to one or other of the Regional Technical College courses connected with the hotel and catering industry. This was a very successful course - in 1983 sixteen of the eighteen students were offered places in RTC courses. The Secretarial course was losing students to Carlow Regional Technical College because European Social Fund grants were available there but not at the Vocational School. In early 1982, the CEO discussed with the staff of the school and with the Teachers' Union of Ireland the possibility of setting up a Community College with the co-operation of the Presentation Convent Secondary School. At a meeting in the Department in May of that year, officials made the points that from the previous September no students from the secondary school were accepted at the Vocational School for technical subjects, that Senior Cycle classes had commenced in the Vocational School without Department approval, and that the convent school had a strong case for a new school allowing for the provision of technical subjects.

Castlecomer Community School

The CEO, Brendan Conway met the staff of the Vocational School who declared that their preferred option was a Community College. Their second choice would be a Community School. The principle difference between the two types of institution would be that the community college would be under the administration of the VEC, while the Community School would be independent with its own Board of Management. Mr. Conway then met Sr. Ita, Mother Provincial of the Presentation Order. She agreed to put the community college option to the staff of the secondary school. They rejected the idea and expressed a preference for the idea of a Community School. At a meeting with the Department on April 29th, the VEC were asked to consider a Community School with a Board of Management consisting of three representatives of the VEC, three representatives of the religious, two elected parents, and two teacher representatives. The Vocational School had at that time 123 students while the convent had 387. A building project would be brought forward. The VEC's interest in the Secretarial and CERT courses and in adult education would be protected. Existing permanent whole-time Vocational School staff would be absorbed into the staff of the Community School and posts of Principal and Vice-Principal would be by open competition.

When these terms were put to the VEC at the May meeting, they adopted a resolution, "that County Kilkenny Vocational Education Committee regards a Community School at Castlecomer as an acceptable proposal for further discussion, and proposes that such discussion be commenced by a meeting of the Board of Management of Castlecomer Vocational School at which all members of the teaching staff of the school be invited to attend". By the following month, with no encouragement from the Department to maintain the Vocational School, with no movement on the Senior Cycle issue, and with no apparent prospect that a decent building would emerge as a Community School, the committee decided "that no commitment be made at this stage for or against the proposed Community School". In July the CEO informed the committee that there were eight students enrolled for the second year of the Leaving Certificate course and that there were no first-year applicants. The committee decided to ask the Department to recognise the eight as valid entrants to the leaving certificate in 1983, on the basis that the Senior Cycle course would be ended and negotiation take place on rationalisation of educational provision in Castlecomer. The Department proved willing to accept this if the proposition were made in writing, and this was done by letter on June 28th.[139]

The phased building programme

At the July meeting in 1982 the Chairman Cllr. John Holohan and the CEO reported on a meeting they had had with the Assistant Secretary of the Department of Education, the Principal Officer of the Planning Section and the Principal Officer of the Teachers' Section on the question of the phased building programme proposed by the VEC. The Department undertook to make a proposal for a 200 student school at Ballyhale within weeks. They conceded that a new school was required at Mooncoin. They proposed to provide a school for 200 at Slieverue in close proximity to Waterford City but this would not mean that County Kilkenny VEC wouldn't have to provide for a new Vocational School or Community College if the school-going population increased with the provision of new housing on the Kilkenny side of the river Suir. The Department's architect would visit Johnstown which now had over 300 students. The Department was still against sanctioning a Snior Cycle at Graignamanagh but the VEC was to submit a comprehensive memo on lack of capacity at Thomastown, transport costs to Thomastown and the impact on the town of Graignamanagh of closing their Vocational School. When the sanction for the course was announced at the September meeting the minutes record that "Mr. Phelan, on behalf of the Board of Management of Graignamanagh VS expressed the gratitude of that body to God, VEC representatives, and the Department of Education in approximately that order of priority". One suspects that the turn of phrase was Brendan Conway's, that minutes at that period were read aloud rather than taken as read, and that the members got as much satisfaction from the hearing as the CEO did from the delivery. At the same meeting the word from the Department was that Mooncoin would get a new school, that schedules of accommodation for major extensions were agreed for Ballyhale and Slieverue, and that there was the possibility of a new school at Johnstown.

Before the next meeting, there was a General Election, in which Seamus Pattison was re-elected and another committee member, Dick Dowling was elected a deputy for the first time. It was announced that from the following January a new method of financing building projects would commence. The Department of Education Building Unit rather than the Office of Public Works would be the funding agency and there was a promise that the Department would ensure that committees would be kept in funds three months in advance. Time would tell otherwise.[140]

In 1981, Mr. Tom Hunt, a member of the committee, was elected President of the Teachers' Union of Ireland, a full-time position in which he served for two years. He was replaced as TUI representative on the VEC by Mr. Billy Burke of the KVCS.

With such an ambitious building programme, the appointment of design teams for the various projects became urgent. In November 1982 applications were sought for architects, quantity surveyors, structural engineers and heating engineers to fill the places on several design teams. There were lots of applications to be considered in the following month, including one from Colm Ó Cochláin who noted that his application was without prejudice to the fact that he regarded himself as already appointed architect to the various projects, as he had carried out feasibility studies and prepared sketch plans for submission to the committee and the Department of Education.

Design teams were appointed for Ballyhale and Johnstown. Mr. Ó Cochláin was to be the architect for both, Mr. V. Drum was to be quantity surveyor and the structural engineer was to be J.B. Barry Consultants. No design teams were appointed for Mooncoin or Slieverue pending legal opinion.
Ballyhale staff protested at the grave deterioration in their buildings and at the difficulties they experienced in bad weather. Graignamanagh needed at least three classrooms because of their increased enrolment. The VEC decided to survey the Thomastown prefabs with the idea of relocating some of them when the new building there was completed. When the VEC eventually, in late 1984, sought tenders for taking down the prefabs and relocating some of them at Graignamanagh, the cost was estimated at £9,000.

The committee's legal advice was that the claim by Mr. Ó Cochláin was not sustained but in January 1983, he was appointed architect for the building projects at Mooncoin and Slieverue, with Malachy Walsh and Partners as consulting engineers in both. At Mooncoin, Mulcahy, McDonagh and Partners were to be the quantity surveyors, with Con Shanley and Partner to perform the same function at Slieverue.

Freshford versus Johnstown

The proposed secondary school at Freshford was causing problems. The campaign seemed to be affecting enrolment at Johnstown and possibly at Kilkenny. A public meeting at Freshford, attended by two of the VEC members was told that the committee was not opposed to the school. At the next committee meeting the CEO said that he had written to the Department on the subject. The committee decided to play a passive role for the moment but wanted their own schools protected. A deputation from the Freshford group to the Department included some VEC members. In June 1983 the CEO and Chairman reported to members that they had attended a meeting on the subject. The Department wanted a VEC response to the proposal that a voluntary secondary school be founded at Freshford and in particular the implications for Johnstown Vocational School. They professed themselves unclear on the VEC position as the Freshford delegation had included some VEC members. The CEO and Chairman made their committee's position clear, but the CEO was surprised to get a phone call from the Department to say that Freshford had been sanctioned for a co-educational secondary school with a catchment of Freshford and Clontubrid primary schools. The VEC urged the Johnstown Board of Management to meet without delay to consider the situation. The result of this meeting was a demand that existing transport arrangements to Johnstown and Kilkenny be maintained. The point of this was that free transport was in general only provided to the nearest second level school, and the setting up of a catchment area for Freshford would inevitably affect enrolment in Johnstown.

In April 1984 the VEC considered the probability that in the following September enrolment in Johnstown would be sixty first-year entrants, with Freshford having twenty. There was a high pressure recruitment campaign for the Freshford project with students being sought across catchment boundaries. In the following month alarm was expressed at a plan to run a bus through Tullaroan to Freshford thus "robbing" both Johnstown and Kilkenny City.

An invitation to Mr. Creed, Minister of State at the Department of Education resulted in a special meeting of the VEC at Johnstown. The Principal of the school, representatives of the Board of Management, of the parents and of the teachers were present. The Board of Management stressed the urgency of having provision in the school for the teaching of Metalwork, and the VEC priority was the provision of a 350 pupil school in Johnstown. The meeting was joined by Mr. Creed and the two points were put to him and forcefully argued. The Minister in reply mentioned the sixty-six projects in his Department now at bill-of-quantities stage, and the possibility of amalgamation between the schools at Johnstown and Freshford. This cannot have cheered the local people very much, and at the next VEC meeting Cllr. Cavanagh expressed the fear that the teachers were so frustrated with the state of the buildings that they might even accept a change in the management structure if they thought that this would speed the building project. Before leaving the Minister viewed the buildings

An inspector from the Department visited Johnstown and made recommendations on temporary accommodation at the school, but the Department architect had turned down the proposals as too expensive for a temporary provision. A Department proposal to provide a 250 pupil school for Johnstown was greeted with dismay by the committee members, who nevertheless reluctantly accepted the proposal. The absence of consultation beforehand was deplored by members. By October although the CEO was able to report that a preliminary briefing meeting on the project had gone well, it was evident that the school already had an enrolment which made nonsense of the limit of 250. It was late in 1985 before Johnstown was allowed to proceed to stage two in the design process, and a further year before it reached stage four.[141]

A minute of July 1982 shows how acute the accommodation crisis could become. The CEO told the meeting of the incident recently when a department inspector was unable to inspect a French class at Slieverue because three basins were placed around the room collecting rainwater from a leaking roof. The inspector complained to the department's building unit but no response was reported as yet to this report.

Already the Department was talking about the possibility of a 200 pupil school for Slieverue, and by November a schedule of accommodation was being discussed. In the following May the VEC heard that Slieverue Board of Management was demanding a permanent extension and that the prefabs were deteriorating rapidly while the number of students on rolls was increasing. As already noted, part of the design team for the project was in place in early 1983 and by September Triton Engineering had been appointed to complete the team and the project was going through the planning application stage. In the following May, the CEO reported no progress on the project, but over the next two years there was some movement, so that by February of 1986, the project was awaiting clearance to go to stage four. In May the whole project was referred to the planning section of the Department, because the enrolment in the previous September was 151, while the enrolment agreed for the new building was 200. This long-drawn-out process was typical of the experience of several schools in the county at the time.[142]

Mooncoin started out on the design process at the same time as Slieverue. By May 1984 it got permission to proceed to the developed sketch stage. By September 1985 it was waiting for permission to go to Stage four and the enrolment had exceeded 250 for the first time. In February 1986 the documentation for stage four had been sent to the Department and by September Mooncoin was to go to bill of quantities stage.[143]

Ballyhale proved the most controversial of the projected extensions. As early as 1981 the VEC was faced with paying to provide prefabs which had been refused by the Department the year before. Lobbying of Deputies Aylward and Nolan led to a deputation to the VEC which wanted the committee to follow up on indications from the deputies. By year's end there was word that the Department of Education would agree to a school for 200 pupils. With the enrolment already at 197, the VEC members considered this inadequate but would accept the offer if there were provision in the plans for a further extension if needed. It took most of the next year to get a schedule of accommodation agreed by the Department. The VEC appointed a design team led by Colm Ó Cochláin as architect, with V. Drum as quantity surveyor, and J.B. Barry as structural engineer. It was some time before the heating engineer, Trident Engineering was appointed. This firm had already handled the same task at Kilkenny City and Thomastown.

In the meantime work had to continue at the old buildings. Staff protested at the grave deterioration in the buildings and outlined the difficulties posed in bad weather. Having sent a letter to the Department outlining the situation, the CEO informed his committee that so many conferences were required on the Ballyhale building project that it would be at least the end of 1983 before a start could be made. In the event, this prediction was unduly optimistic.

Early in 1984 the committee were told that there was an urgent need of buildings at Ballyhale. Their architect's and quantity surveyor's reports indicated that they considered that the Department's architect was trying to get a design result for which the Department was not prepared to pay. The Minister for Education was to be lobbied on the need for a quick start, and in the meantime the CEO estimated the cost of essential repairs to the existing prefabs at £15,000.

While the initial lobbying had been directed at a Fianna Fáil government, the Minister now, following a series of three general elections in a very short time, was part of a Fine Gael-Labour Coalition. The Minister of State with responsibility for school buildings was Mr. Creed, and in June of 1984, he visited Ballyhale to see for himself the position. A special meeting of the VEC at Ballyhale at which parents, staff and board of management were represented heard the CEO outline the various negotiations that had taken place with the Department. He said that there was no doubt in his mind that there was "dragging of feet" by the Department. Mr. Tom Hunt of the teaching staff presented a document prepared by the Parents' Association and by the Board of Management. This outlined the great difficulties in trying to conduct a school in the situation obtaining at Ballyhale. Mr. Creed replied that he saw his visit as a fact-finding event, and after viewing the condition of the school, said that he would not be in favour of spending money on temporary repairs, but would have a response to the whole issue soon. Next month Ballyhale had moved to stage three on the long road to the Promised Land.

By year's end the CEO noted that £37,000 would be needed for temporary accommodation at Ballyhale and in February of 1985 estimated that the Ballyhale project like Johnstown was at a standstill. Mr. Billy Burke, the TUI representative on the VEC demanded that a deputation, including the Principal should be seeking a meeting with the Minister. The same demand came from parents who had met with public representatives and VEC members.

In March the Department sought further proposals from the design team, especially the services engineer. This caused a certain amount of anger among committee members and the architect was asked to report on the matter. He apologised for the oversight in providing full information to the building unit of the Department. The CEO noted that the Department's request for additional information had been replied to by return of post whereas the same Department had still not replied to correspondence on the other building projects. Deputy Dowling said that the Minister of State had told him that not all correspondence was coming through the CEO's office, to which the CEO replied that it had been agreed that the technical officers of the Department would have informal discussions with their opposite numbers on the design team.

By the end of 1985 the project was at stage four, but another serious obstacle arose. There was a difficulty getting planning permission for the school as designed. A meeting with planning officials and with the County Manager seems to have been amicable, but didn't result in planning permission. The building unit of the Department wanted to know why the VEC hadn't appealed the refusal to An Bord Pleanála. The VEC considered that such an appeal would be a futile waste of time and wondered why there had been no response from the Department on providing the money needed to make the necessary changes. The difficulty seems to have been connected to the position of the site for the school. When the VEC entered into negotiations for land beside the site, the Department said that the Valuation Office would determine the price to be offered. When land was offered at £31,000, the Valuation Office wouldn't allow any more than £14,000. After considerable behind-the-scenes negotiations, the VEC asked the Department to sanction the purchase of 1.73 acres for £12,000 and the Department refused to sanction the expenditure of any more than £7,000. The negotiations for purchase were abandoned.[144]

CHAPTER 9

Hard Times

It was unfortunate that, just at the time when the VEC needed money from the Government for the provision of permanent accommodation, the country entered a period of economic difficulty. Governments of whatever hue found themselves short of tax revenue in a time of high unemployment and high inflation. As one of the "spending" departments, Education was an obvious target for cutbacks in funding.

In 1981 the finances available for vocational education in County Kilkenny were already inadequate. The VEC were aware that from autumn of that year there would be no money available for scholarships, but the CEO advised that some committees in other counties had been advised by Department officials to offer the same number of scholarships as in the previous school year. A refund of monies due from the Department eased the position somewhat, but early in 1982 there was a warning that economies must be made and that no supplementary grants would be available that year to make up any shortfall due to spending beyond the Department allocation. By April, with a cutback on the amount which the committee estimated would be needed, it was plain that it would be impossible to maintain the previous level of service. No new equipment could be purchased. Some schools had already exhausted budgets for heating and lighting. Because of the slow release of Department grants, the committee was obliged to borrow from the bank and interest payments were a major drain on finances. There was currently a deficit of £83,234.

In the matter of Adult Education Circular letter 36/82 proposed higher fees than the committee had decided. There would be a rise of a third in the cost of a ten week course and an even steeper rise in the case of a twenty week course. Additional finance from the Department that year became available. There was £35,000 for scholarships and £50,000 for school maintenance.

A newly elected government promised that the Department of Education would ensure that committees were kept in funds three months in advance. If this had happened, it would have eased the problems, but the position at the end of 1982 was that indebtedness to the banks was £350,000 as against £240,000 a year previously. There was no reply from the Department to requests for the repayment of sums overdue on building projects, and no word of a supplementary grant. In that year the interest paid on the committee's bank overdraft was £19,242. As the CEO pointed out, this was more than the over-expenditure recorded under the heading of administration.

The Teachers' Union of Ireland notified the committee that they would be staging a one-day strike in January in protest at the cutbacks. At first the

Department proposed cutting superannuation rights for teachers on strike but this decision was reversed some months later.

The committee supported a motion proposed by the TUI representative "that the Minister for Education be requested to negotiate with relevant bodies with a view to reaching an acceptable programme of adjusted financial provision for Education." He condemned the mindless way that cutbacks were being operated, with no plan evident and no objective articulated.

The teachers' fears can be understood when one considers that in County Kilkenny it looked as if five schools would lose ex-quota Vice-Principals, and three current career guidance posts would be lost. A worsening of the pupil/teacher ratio from 16.5:1 to 19:1 could cost fifteen teaching posts in the county. There were also transport limitations proposed which could affect enrolment in some schools. The Irish Vocational Education Association (IVEA) negotiated a slight amelioration in the staffing aspect of the cutbacks, with the result that schools of less than 250 pupils would lose a maximum of one teacher, and schools of less than 500 would lose two teachers at most. This still left cutbacks of 25% or more in County Kilkenny and the loss of twelve teaching posts. Members desperately seeking possible economies suggested that since the Arts Education Officer served the whole South-East area, the other committees should fund part of his salary. The CEO explained that, even if this were done, it would not give rise to replacement funds for an extra post in the county. Coming up to the summer of 1983 it was feared that some schools would not have enough money for heating after September. There were four teaching posts to be filled and two more were to be advertised on the basis that vacancies "may occur".

The committee made a joint application with St. Kieran's College for four posts under the co-operation agreement between the two schools. The Department allowed two of these. The committee, conscious of unemployment among teachers, decided that those out of a job should get first preference as examination supervisors. The teachers worst affected were part-timers. By year's end all schools in the vocational sector in County Kilkenny were substantially overspent.[145]

Coming near the end of the school year the four posts refused sanction by the Department were still in limbo. On co-operation with St. Kieran's the VEC were told that if St. Kieran's staffed-up, the four posts involved would be lost to the VEC, and if St. Kieran's forfeited the four posts, they would be available to the vocational sector. The Department suggested an appeal for an increased allocation of posts, and this was done under the headings of increased enrolment in the schools, co-operation, and special cases. The appeal was turned down. Refunds of £68,000 on capital projects and the arrival of £89,000, the outstanding portion of the amount due for the second quarter improved the committee's cash flow in July 1984, but an overdraft of a quarter of a million pounds was the best that could be hoped for. The promise of keeping the committee in funds three months in advance had obviously gone by the board, since the final part of the second quarter grant arrived in the first month of the succeeding quarter. On the staffing question, County Kilkenny VEC was officially described as having six supernumerary posts and until six teachers left the scheme, no replacement posts could be envisaged. Four teachers left the service without replacement and two additional posts were sanctioned by the Department after the summer, and this wiped out the six supernumerary posts.

There were also cutbacks in administrative staff. As a temporary measure the CEO decided to concentrate administrative staff in head office. This caused difficulties for the schools, and KCVS was particularly hard hit, with frequent demands for the restoration of a full-time secretary. With the illness of one administrative officer, the pressure on the administrative staff was considerable and the Local Government and Public Services Union was threatening industrial action.

Overall the scheme had had two dozen teaching posts lost or suppressed over a three year period, despite the fact that there were 190 pupils more enrolled at the end of 1984 than there had been three years previously.[146]

In early 1985, even after the issue of £650,000 of the quarterly grant, there was still need for an overdraft of £350,000. The CEO noted that for 1984, on an authorised allocation of £3,130,000, an over-expenditure of £73,000 had occurred. He again pointed out that interest on the committee's overdraft was an item for which the Department had the major share of responsibility and should at least pay the major share of the cost, which came to £36,447 - a not inconsiderable sum. The committee's estimate for maintenance of schools and classes suffered a 32% cut by the Department.

A new VEC took office subsequent to the local elections of that year, and although John Holohan was a member of the new committee, he was no longer a local councillor and Cllr. Mary Hilda Cavanagh was elected to the chair, a position she was to occupy for the rest of the millennium. She paid tribute to John Holohan for his many years of dedicated service. At the ordinary meeting which followed on the election, new members were quickly introduced to the real world of educational finance. The bank was refusing payment of VEC cheques, because authorisation of borrowing had not issued from the Minister's office. The committee's account was frozen until these letters were brought up to date. The Department was unhelpful on the matter.

The CEO reported that the Local Government Auditor had expressed support for the VEC, as he knew from his audit the extent of under-funding they suffered. Members were indignant that the bank, which had formerly honoured cheques when the committee was overdrawn by half a million, should now refuse to do so when the indebtedness stood at £60,000. With outgoings for the next quarter estimated at £1.3 million approximately and income projected at £0.723 million, it was resolved to seek an overdraft facility of £600,000. The next step would be Department sanction but the CEO was refused a meeting on the subject. The Bank of Ireland would agree to a credit limit of £300,000 for thirty days only. The deficit for 1985 was half that of the previous year. Obviously the VEC was adjusting to the new financial stringency. In April of 1986 the CEO reported on a meeting with the Local Government Auditor, who had conducted a review of the committee's finances over a six-year period. He laid down strict financial guidelines: a monthly review of expenditure to date at each school, under each heading should be presented to each meeting; he expected a more persistent and detailed demand for release of funds by the Department in cases where there was clear evidence of under-funding; he set out a very detailed schedule of the level of over-staffing and demanded a programme of action in getting an agreed plan worked out with the relevant sections of the Department. While understanding the members' responsibility as public representatives to maintain the best possible standards for the pupils of the schools, he offered no joy on the possibility of their being surcharged for deliberate unauthorised spending.

This latter consideration was on members' minds at the time as there was no allocation of teachers that year for co-operation between St. Kieran's and KCVS. This meant that three teachers at KCVS would be regarded as overstaffing. Members were forced to consider terminating the agreement between the two schools. The only good news was that a slight improvement in the pupil/teacher ratio had given back six posts to the scheme. On the general financial front, there was a possibility that, if the opening debit balance could be wiped out, there was a reasonable hope of staying within the limits imposed but absolutely no chance of expansion of services.

At midsummer 1986, the allocation of 2.4 posts for co-operation with St. Kieran's eased matters a little but in October the committee was arranging a joint meeting with the authorities there to discuss a possible ending of the agreement. Already, the VEC had been instructed by the Department to charge St. Kieran's for teaching hours provided, and in return had been invoiced for £6,000 in consideration of sporting facilities and the use of the gymnasium. An attempt by the CEO to get the Department to allow him to offset this against the cost of the teaching hours had failed, and the VEC was unable to meet the bill of £6,000. At the end of the year, the CEO was able to report that the financial position had improved by £145,000 over the year. The debit balance would be £242,000 as against £387,000 twelve months previously.[147]

In the first half of 1987 matters got worse with cuts of around 30% in administration and maintenance for the coming year. No additional monies would be paid that year. The adult education and literacy budget for the coming year was cut by 20%.The Minister for Education, Mary O'Rourke had laid it down as a principle that schools should remain open as a priority over other expenditure. In May the CEO set out the scale of the cutbacks. In 1986/87 the actual expenditure on administration had been £112,344, but for 1987/88 there was an allocation of only £87,726. Maintenance was cut from £264,829 to £183,121. The non-pay instruction budget of around £12,000 was cut to less than half, with a doubling of the miscellaneous provision to £61,962, but since this was less than a fifth of the total non-pay allocation, it couldn't make up for the serious cuts under the other headings. Indeed the overall position was that the committee had £50,000 or so less to spend than it had in the straitened circumstances of 1986/1987. There was one improvement: because of prompt payment of Department quarterly grants to the committee, bank interest would be less in the coming year and there was a slight improvement in interest rates.

In March 1987, Ms. Eileen Hartley who was Adult Education Organiser with County Waterford VEC was appointed to the vacant Kilkenny position. Two months later, she faced a cutback in funding for adult education and literacy classes. The already meagre budget for County Kilkenny was cut by 20% to £7,600. A sub-committee was set up to consider the effects of the cutbacks and to consider proposals from the CEO which would then be submitted to the whole committee. The sub-committee proposed that the apprentice block in KCVS should be shut down, as it wasn't being used, and that the adult education office should be located in the Ormonde Road building of KCVS, thereby saving on the rent of the building in Patrick Street where it was currently based. The proposals were accepted.

The estimates meeting in July reported that £4.7 million would be needed for the coming year. It must be remembered that the bulk of this would be teachers' salaries. These were paid by the VEC from monies received for the purpose from the Department of Education. Any delay in these payments could spell trouble for the committee's finances. [148]

After the summer break, senior officials met with the Chairperson and CEO. They issued a major warning to the committee on overstaffing. The Department proposed to monitor the committee's financial affairs on a monthly basis. The CEO and Chairperson reported back that overstaffing in some schools was alarming. There would have to be redeployment of teachers to allow a reduction of part-time teaching services. They re-iterated that teaching services to Junior Cycle students in St. Kieran's would have to cease or be paid for in full by St. Kieran's. This proposal was rejected by the committee at first but a rethink followed consideration of the probable surcharging of members and the proposal was carried. In the non-pay budget, the CEO had to report over-runs in spending on administration, instruction costs and maintenance.

The redeployment of teachers was bound to cause trouble, as it entailed some schools losing teaching hours, and would involve teachers travelling to a new school daily, or possibly sharing their teaching time between two schools. In November the VEC meeting considered developments in this area, while the Chairperson deplored the lobbying of committee members in their homes and the demonstration outside the meeting place by some young people. After a joint consultation meeting between the committee, the TUI and the Principals had registered disagreement on redeployment, the CEO sent letters to four teachers that they would be off the payroll from the following Monday. A series of meetings with TUI representatives, including the Vice-President of the Union resulted in a draft agreement which had been sent to TUI head office and the local TUI branch. A joint consultation meeting on the day before the VEC meeting had ended with the signing of the document which was now up for acceptance or rejection. A similar meeting of the TUI branch later in the week would have the same choice. The transfers affected five teachers who would have to move to other schools. For this they would get travel and subsistence allowances. With the lessening of the need for part-time teachers, the package would save a total of £653 each week on the pay element of the committee's finances.

In the following month the committee condemned the proposal to raise the pupil/teacher ratio to 20:1. This would mean the loss of several teaching positions in County Kilkenny, would increase class size and limit the subject choice available to students. It could also have the affect of shortening the student attendance week and have a serious effect on students with learning difficulties. The CEO said that Senior Cycle courses would be endangered in some schools as would Vocational Preparation and Training Programme classes.[149]

By January of 1988, the school at Castlecomer had been closed, the adult education office was transferred to Ormonde Road and there was no longer an expenditure on rent for its accommodation, and there was an under-expenditure under the heading of "miscellaneous" in the non-pay budget. All these were now being reflected in monthly accounts. The Department was putting the committee in funds by prompt payment of grants, and this had saved £30,000 in interest charges compared with 1986/87. With all these improvements the committee's deficit had been reduced from £229,000 to £145,000 over the previous year. This improvement in the financial position, of course, did not affect the cutbacks imposed by the Government. The CEO outlined the probable effects. Twelve teaching posts would be lost to the scheme, several schools would be hard-pressed to service their VPTP schemes, and in some schools the senior cycles would be endangered.

Circular Letter F/7/88 conveyed a Department decision that surplus state properties should be sold off in order to reduce the National Debt. Net proceeds of the sale of VEC properties would be paid into Vocational Education funds but a corresponding reduction in the committee's grant would be made. Three properties in County Kilkenny suggested themselves, the derelict school in Tullaroan, the old school in Callan, and the recently closed school in Castlecomer which was being used by the new Community School, but for which the committee was getting no rent.

The Department had at last made some response to the problems caused by under-funding of the VEC, which had now reached a total of £185,000. In 1987 they had paid £80,000 of this and a further gesture in the current year would restore some order to the committee's finances.

The raising of the pupil/teacher ratio would cause problems, as would the taking of early retirement by some teachers. This latter scheme would have obvious attractions for a teacher nearing the end of career, but the trouble for the VEC arose from the fact that the teaching post could be lost with the teacher, if the scheme was in the position of having full-time teachers in excess of the Department allocation. In the event, several teachers applied for early retirement and their requests were passed on to the Department.

In April the CEO advised that there would be an allocation on non-pay items of 80% of the previous year's figure - which had been a substantial reduction on the year before that. It was difficult to see where a cutback of £40,000 on non-pay expenditure could be made. At the same meeting an offer of £1,700 for the school at Tullaroan was accepted. In May the committee reluctantly decided to cut a grant which had been paid for several years to S.O.S. a sheltered workshop run by the Diocese of Ossory. The only hope for continuing this would be a special allocation from the Department to enable it to continue. There was some lobbying on this issue, but very little in the way of response with a Dáil question from Deputy Pattison producing an anodyne reply.

Grants which the VEC had paid out for VPTP and European Social Fund schemes were proving difficult to recoup. Staffing cuts looked like being six or seven. This meant that teachers filling these posts could be regarded as supernumeraries and this number of redundancies would be offered to County Kilkenny. A redundancy sub-committee was set up, consisting of members of the Selection Board. Only the most necessary part-time teachers could be used pending the outcome of the redundancy proposals. In the event the redundancy scheme was soon at a standstill and the minutes of the January 1989 meeting describe the matter as being "abysmally handled at National level".[150]

At this time considerable difficulty was caused for the committee by a shortfall of approximately £23,000 each month in the allocation for teachers' salaries. This had reached £70,000 by the end of November. However a telephone call in December gave assurance that the matter would be rectified by the end of the year. There was still no final teacher allocation at year's end. In January the CEO pointed out that the positive aspect of this was that the committee couldn't be accused of over-staffing. Five administrative staff had resigned and one was on career break since the embargo on replacements. The Local Government and Public Services Union were now demanding re-grading due to the increased workload on the remaining staff. The Department had rejected this demand the previous year, but the CEO advocated appealing the decision. It was October of 1990 before this problem, which affected all VECs, was resolved nationally.

By summer of 1989 the committee's finances were in a satisfactory condition. Funds due to the committee for several years had been released in 1988. Instead of paying interest on bank loans, the committee was in the happy position of having around £7,500 interest arising from a credit balance. A modest programme of essential repairs could be contemplated over the summer. The committee members congratulated the CEO and the administrative staff on this favourable outcome to several years of effort. In September they were notified that all teachers employed in the previous year had been sanctioned retrospectively.[151]

There were still unresolved problems with staffing. A TUI delegation to the VEC expressed dissatisfaction with the position of eligible part-time teachers. Provision of contracts to teachers was held up because of alleged over-staffing in the scheme. The VEC was sympathetic to the teachers' view, and hoped industrial action could be avoided, but the solution lay with the Department.

The Department increased the teacher allocation for 1989/90 by 7.25 whole-time teacher equivalents "as a totally exceptional measure" but insisted that in 1990/91 County Kilkenny VEC should address the problem of over-staffing, which was then of the order of 14.5 whole-time teacher equivalents. The CEO proposed that this should be done by awarding of career breaks to all applicants and a reduction in part-time teacher use by curtailing services in VPTP courses which required part-time teachers. The proposals were rejected by the meeting "which considered the curtailment of the Hairdressing Course, the Accounting Technicians Course and three Secretarial Courses as a form of suicide for the scheme".

After the summer break in 1990, the Department issued two circulars in settlement of the dispute with the Local Government and Professional Services Union. Patti Burke, the only eligible applicant was promoted to Grade Six to replace Carmel Darcy, Ann Hennessey was promoted to Grade Five and Rita Neary to Grade Four. Two Grade Three posts would be filled from existing staff but would involve relocation within the county. Thomastown would be a priority for secretarial services.[152]

The cutbacks in administration, maintenance and other non-pay items were not the only measures that had a disastrous effect on the VEC's efforts to service its schools. There were very strict limits on what the Department of Education was prepared to spend, or indeed was able to spend, on building new schools. The long struggle to get building projects sanctioned for Mooncoin, Johnstown and Ballyhale, and the slow progress through the various stages of design and planning, clearly show the impact of country-wide retrenchment on County Kilkenny. There were endless delays in replying to letters by the Department, endless requests from the Department for more information, seemingly endless changes-of-mind on the subject of school sizes. There was suspicion on the part of the VEC, and of the design teams for the schools, that all these were simply delaying tactics. There was huge pressure in the localities from staff, Parents' Associations and Boards of Management. Most of the pressure was applied to the VEC, its Chief Executive and its members, although they had no input into the real decision-making process which was centralised in the planning section and building unit of the Department of Education. Attempts at lobbying through local TDs seemed at times to be successful, but in reality often simply moved a project on from one blockage to the next blockage. There was obviously a national list of schools which were considered to be especially urgent cases, and a good deal of building was still going on around the country, but announcements that this scheme or that was "a priority", did little except devalue the word priority.

In 1987 the committee had design teams appointed for Ballyhale, Mooncoin and Johnstown, and was considering what steps should be taken after the completion of these major projects. They decided that it would be advisable to find out what the building unit's attitude would be to Slieverue and Graignamanagh. Their assumption that the three projects in hand would proceed rapidly to a conclusion was proved over sanguine.

In Ballyhale the problem was the County Council planners' refusal of planning permission unless certain changes were made to the design, and these changes would give rise to a need for more land. The refusal of the Department to sanction the latest offer of land led to a meeting at Ballyhale at which Minister of State Frank Fahey was present. The meeting sought an assurance that the £12,000 purchase price would be sanctioned by the DJ106

Opening of Johnstown Vocational School 1996
Cllr. Mary Hilda Cavanagh, Mr. Seamus Pattison TD, Mr. Brendan Conway CEO,
Ms. Niamh Breathnach Minister for Education, Bishop Laurence Forristal.

Staff on first day in new school in Johnstown 1996
(Back Row L to R) Martin Gleeson, Paddy Broderick, Jim O'Grady, Michael Killeen, John Cahill, Martin Fahey,
Jim Ryan, Donal McCloskey, Michael Butler, Breda Manton, Chris Greene Principal, Angela Conroy.
(Front Row L to R) Patsy Costello, Mary Hyland, Margaret Rochford, Sr. Ursula, Mary Ryan.

Slieverue Vocational School -Opening of Extension on 1998
L to R: Mr. Seamus Patterson; Mr. Rodger Curran, CEO County Kilkenny VEC; Mrs Mary Hilda Kavanagh, Chairperson, County Kilkenny VEC; Mr. John O'Callaghan, Principal; Mr. Dick Dowling.

Official Opening of Grennan College by Ms. Gemma Hussey, Minister for Education in 1986
The "state of the art" new school was built on the site of the original school and consists of two science labs, a home economics room, an engineering room, a woodwork room, an art room, eight general purposes rooms, a computer room, offices and a canteen.

Johnstown Vocational School Musicians perform at the opening of Johnstown Vocational School in 1996.
L to R: Willie Cahill, Nicholas Carroll, Joe Cahill, Declan Carroll.

Department, and an undertaking was given to this effect. Some disquiet was expressed by VEC members that this meeting had not been arranged through the Board of Management or through the VEC.

While all this was going on, Ballyhale VS had to stay in operation and urgent repairs to windows were needed, a capital expenditure which would have to be sanctioned by the Department at a time when it was cutting VEC allocations heavily. At the beginning of 1989, the CEO reported that there had been no movement whatsoever on the school building project. Repairs to windows would cost £15,000, and he was afraid that this heavy capital expenditure, if sanctioned, would delay the major extension to the school which they had sought for so long. Later in the year, he told the meeting that he hoped to have the urgent repairs done over the Easter holidays. In March, after Mr. Devereux the Principal withdrew land in his ownership from the market, a public meeting was scheduled for the village. The VEC decided to announce what was called "a worthy budget for temporary repairs" but not to depart from their intention to provide a new building.

When the meeting was held, it was decided to ask the Minister to receive a deputation, but by April it was evident that the deputation didn't get the commitment sought. Mr. Devereux had failed to get a land-owner with property near the school to consider selling, and he himself was prepared to consider offering a reduced portion of his own land. The VEC decided to see if the Department would sanction this latest offer.

At the June meeting members were indignant that at a meeting in Ballyragget the Minister had produced the impression that he was trying to get the VEC to abandon Ballyhale. They stressed that this was the opposite of their policy and that delays on the project were not their doing. All this was in the heat of a general election.

After the summer the CEO was able to assure the committee that repairs costing £35,000 had been completed at Ballyhale. A year later the parents were again demanding action on the proposed new building. In 1990 and 1991 the intake of first-years into Ballyhale VS was very high, but there was still no action on the extension of the site. Indeed hopes rose with a press report quoting Cllr. J. Brett as saying that Minister Fahey had given the go-ahead for purchase, but the CEO hadn't received any written confirmation of this, and a month later told the first meeting of his newly elected committee that he had got no reply from the Department to a request for such confirmation. At this stage it was ten years since the Department had first announced that if favoured a 200 pupil school at Ballyhale and the design team had been in place since 1982.[153]

CHAPTER 10

A New Building Programme

Mooncoin

Mooncoin didn't have any difficulties with the site, and in the beginning the project seemed to be proceeding in an orderly fashion, but the familiar pattern of delay soon established itself. In June of 1987 the VEC meeting heard that a delegation which they had hoped would be received by the Minister would not now be met. In April 1988 it was obvious that there was great anger in Mooncoin at the state of the school and at the delay in starting building. A delegation to the Minister was assured that building would commence as soon as funds were available to her Department. In November, a letter from the staff of the school expressed extreme frustration with physical conditions in the school. The VEC, helpless in the face of Department inaction held the December meeting in Mooncoin as a gesture of solidarity with the community. After the meeting, the members met the parents, an occasion at which they anticipated "intense interrogation". In the event the members were pleased with the tone of the meeting and felt that the local community was aware of the VEC support for a new school at Mooncoin.

Enrolment was up at the school that year, but despite assurance from the Minister that the school would be built, the planning section had written to parish priests in the school catchment area, seeking numbers of baptisms up to 1988. During the election campaign of 1989, Deputy Liam Aylward had produced a fax message from the Minister to the Parents' Association, saying that the project was a priority and would go ahead as soon as finances allowed. In September there was still no word except that Cllr. Meade had heard that it was in the queue of projects soon to be financed. In January 1989, the VEC meeting heard that word was expected later in the month. When word did come, it was to the effect that the planning section wanted to reduce pupil places at the proposed Mooncoin school. The VEC was vehemently opposed to this. A year and a half later, in September 1990, they heard that £1.3 million had been allocated to the project. This would require a reduction in provision. Following negotiations with the design team, the CEO said that there would be diminished area provision and a saving on materials. In November the word was that the Minister had sanctioned the project to go to tender, but no written notice had issued because of a typist's strike, and no action was possible until a written notice was received. The letter issued on 13th December 1990. Tenders were invited in January, and in February the committee recommended the tender of P. and M. Cantwell to the building unit of the Department. In July, the newly elected VEC was told that the building unit was seeking further information on this tender and had not yet sanctioned the firm recommended by the VEC in March.[154]

Throughout 1991 frustration at the delays was expressed by the local community at a public meeting where a campaign of protest was mooted. When the VEC learned that the Department quantity surveyor continued to seek reductions in site works and special costs, there was considerable anger and the minutes record that "the meeting felt this was a cynical exercise in delaying signing of the contract". The design team saw the process of seeking reductions in costs and having the results vetted by a series of officials before the project would go to the Minister as merely delaying tactics. The TUI was so frustrated by the delays in three projects that they notified the CEO of one-day strikes planned for Mooncoin, Johnstown and Ballyhale. At a joint consultation meeting with the union, the VEC side pointed out that there was a new Minister of Education who would need time to settle in to his new responsibilities and that, since the VEC was still preparing a reply to a request for information, the Department could claim an excuse for the current delay. The TUI refused to accept these points as valid, and strikes would commence on 9th November. Members expressed sympathy with the teachers' point of view and the union side acknowledged that their quarrel was ultimately with the Department. In December a Mooncoin delegation to the Minister, Mr. Noel Davern TD was accompanied by the CEO and Chairperson of the VEC and they reported back that they were hopeful of a response by the Minister by the end of January. In the event, the Minister's letter announcing that the project would start was received in April. The contract was signed in May, and work commenced in June. By year's end the work was described as being three weeks ahead of schedule.

The main complaint with the process was that the Department was reluctant to fund landscaping and tarmac, and was very slow to give a decision, even when the builder looked like leaving the site in the absence of such decisions. The builders and sub-contractors were left waiting for the final payment of monies due and when all accounts were finally settled, the VEC found that the £7,000 they had spent on tarmac was not refundable. The school was occupied in January of 1995 and officially opened on 28th January by the Minister of State at the Department of Education. It was thirteen years since the Department had conceded the necessity of providing a new school at Mooncoin.[155]

The *Kilkenny People* reported the opening:

> The new state-of-the-art five-class school boasts an engineering room, a building construction room, a technical drawing room, a science room, a science demonstration hall, a home economics room, a computer studies room as well as a general purposes room which doubles up as a P.E. hall.

The school was blessed in an ecumenical service by Bishop Laurence Forristal and Bishop Noel Willoughby. Tributes were paid to Mr. Tom Walsh, Principal and his staff who had successfully maintained attendance against a backdrop of completely inadequate conditions, including dry rot in the prefabs. The long campaign for better facilities was "backed by a forceful and resourceful Parents' Association".

Minister of State, Liam Aylward who opened the school recognised the hard work of the local people and the VEC. He said that Mooncoin had had a Vocational School since 1935. At that time it offered three subjects - Rural Science, Woodwork and Home Economics. Now it had eighteen teachers besides the Principal. In the new building 210 students were offered fourteen subjects to Leaving Certificate level and beyond. He congratulated the CEO, Brendan Conway and the VEC Chairperson, Cllr. Mary Hilda Cavanagh who had "worked tirelessly with officials of the Department of Education to build the school".

Mrs. Cavanagh in her address paid special tribute to two former Principals of the school who were present Mr. James McDwyer and Mr. James Doran. "These sprightly men of interesting age are an affirmation that pioneering work in education and the public service are indeed an agent for eternal youth". She paid tribute to Brendan Conway whose "commitment to the promotion of rural schools has been an inspiration to all of us". She commended the work of the Board of Management members, her fellow VEC members and the Principal of the school who had presented the case for the new school over many difficult years. She finished with a tribute to Deputy Aylward whose support and advice at local level was treasured and gratefully acknowledged his role in the final stages of getting the project cleared and contracts signed.[156]

Johnstown

Johnstown's project proceeded at the familiar departmental leisurely pace until May 1987 when the VEC received a letter from the Department listing what the minutes describe as a litany of inadequacies in mechanical and electrical plans. The project could not proceed to bill of quantities stage until the matter had been resolved. In June the Department raised the matter of how to conduct the school while the building project was going on. Their preferred solution was to put the students in relocated prefabs, but the committee members considered this very costly. In September, the CEO outlined a plan to relocate the school to the old National School building in Urlingford, a few miles from Johnstown. The building unit saw the merit of this proposal, but sanction had to be obtained from the finance section.

In September 1988, the imminent closure of the secondary school at Freshford relieved Johnstown of a competing centre, and resulted in an increased enrolment. It was decided to re-activate the campaign for a 350 pupil school. The necessity for an enlarged school was put to the Minister, Mary O'Rourke at a meeting arranged by Deputy Aylward and Senator Lanigan. The Chairperson and CEO were present and were told that the project was to move on from stage four and that the Minister would review the figures. In November word was received that there would be provision for 400 pupils and that written confirmation would issue shortly. The schedule of accommodation for this figure was received in December.

Layouts were agreed and detailed drawings prepared, and everything seemed to be going well until February 1990 when the Department informed the committee through Deputy Aylward that they couldn't process the Johnstown case until the design team replied to their letter setting out requirements. When the CEO inquired of the design team why they hadn't replied, they told him that no such letter had been received by them. "An unhappy performance on the Department's part" is how the minutes describe the contretemps. A requirement by Kilkenny County Council Planning Department that there should be increased car-parking at the new school would bring the project outside the architect's cost limits. Cllrs. Cavanagh and Murphy were to raise the matter with the County Manager. In November, word came from the Department that they were revising the pupil accommodation downwards. This would cause further delay. In December there was agreement to proceed on the basis of 300 pupils, and the refurbishment of the old building in Urlingford was sanctioned as soon as a long-term lease of the building had been effected. Drawings for stage four were prepared and acknowledged in April 1991.[157]

In Johnstown, as in Mooncoin, 1991 was a year of frustrating delay. The Department of Education building unit found the stage four application "inadequate". The architect had to put in a fortnight's work to prepare a reply. Two months later, the necessary sanction to proceed was given to the design team. They hoped to have stage five documentation ready by March 1992. In May the bill of quantities was sent to the Department and four months later, comments of the Department experts set the design team to work on a reply. Small wonder that in November the VEC were informed of anger in the community at the delay. At year's end a letter from the Minister of State advised that Johnstown was on the priority list for commencement in 1993 and the building unit advised that it would be in order for the committee to advertise for contractors for inclusion on a selected tender list.

Early in 1993 the CEO placed advertisements for contractors and builders who might wish to be placed on a list of suitable firms to tender for the project. He stressed to the members of the VEC that this was not a sanction to go to tender. Twenty-five construction firms replied and ten were recommended to the Department. Following a deputation to the Minister for Education, invitation of tenders from the selected list was sanctioned. It was year's end before the winning tender was accepted and work commenced early in 1994. The new building was occupied in September, but the question of the old school building caused some anxiety. The committee would prefer to demolish it, considering that it took from the appearance of the new school. It was March of 1995 before the Department agreed to the demolition.[158]

The official opening of the school, under its new title, "Coláiste Mhuire" took place on the 31st May 1996. The *Kilkenny People* reported the event:

The official opening of Coláiste Mhuire in Johnstown by Education Minister Niamh Bhreathnach marked the culmination of a fourteen-year campaign to provide a new school for the area. But the joyful event was tinged with sadness due to the absence of the school's architect, Kilkenny man Colm Ó Cochláin, who died last December". The Minister pointed out that the school bore witness to the architect's great talents.

The Education Minister particularly noted the development of the school's post-Leaving certificate courses, which include a pre-nursing and child care s tudies course run in conjunction with St. Canice's Hospital. She paid tribute to parents and local representatives for their role in securing the new school. Coláiste Mhuire boasts state-of-the-art equipment and facilities, including modern metalwork and senior engineering departments and a large cafeteria Enrolment at the school which serves five parishes has reached 350 with a teaching staff of twenty-two, compared to an enrolment of twenty pupils in 1952 and 250 pupils in 1975.

The Principal Christopher Greene recalled the long fight, including strike action, for the new school. The former Principal, John Walsh who had opened the old school in 1952 was present to hear Ms. Mary Hilda Cavanagh pay tribute to his diligence as he "travelled by sturdy bicycle to assemble the first enrolments. The method of enrolment at that point was the method known to all of us politicians - door to door canvass". Cllr. Cavanagh, of course was present not only in her capacity as VEC Chairperson, but also as a member of the Board of Management and as a Johnstown woman.[159]

Graignamanagh

While the major building projects at Johnstown and Mooncoin occupied so much of the committee's time, there were serious problems elsewhere. For some time it had been obvious that the buildings at Graignamanagh were inadequate, and the VEC had been sounding out the Department building unit on the possibility of doing something about the problem. It was a great shock to members to be told in December of 1991 that the Department was refusing to sanction Mr. Sean Buckley as Principal, citing as the reason "amalgamation of Graignamanagh". A month later they had no further word on the threatened amalgamation, but when Cllr. Michael Fenlon complained of the dilapidation of the buildings, the CEO said that it might be better to spend say £50,000 and make the school secure for five years rather than wait around for sanction for a building project. In February of 1992 a case was submitted to the building unit. The by now familiar delay in replying meant that it was three months before the CEO was able to report that forms applying for temporary repairs had been submitted to the building unit. A month later the situation in the school had worsened: three prefabs had to be vacated permanently as dangerous. An official of the building unit visited the school and recognised the need for replacements for the three prefabs vacated. It was too late however to expect action before September.[160]

In September the VEC meeting was told that the repair job was to go to tender, and as a reminder that the school had been working efficiently despite all its physical problems, the CEO was able to point to good Leaving Certificate results, including nine adult ladies who had sat the English and History examinations. All were successful and one lady got an A in each subject. By January of 1993 the repairs were in hand. Their completion did not, of course, solve all the problems with old and outdated accommodation. In October Cllr. Fenlon reported a major leak, with tender for repairing it coming to £3,750. In January he proposed a motion, seconded by Monsignor Ml. Ryan and adopted unanimously: "that this committee deems as unacceptable the present state of dilapidation at each of Graignamanagh and Slieverue schools".[161]

The roof problems at Graignamanagh proved to be of major proportions, and there was no hope that Co. Kilkenny VEC could fund them out of ordinary non-pay grants, and so they decided to seek a new building for the school. The Department agreed to a meeting but the planning section questioned the need for a permanent building at Graignamanagh. When the meeting was held the VEC representatives suggested a building project which would cost £400,000. The standard delay in replying left parents outraged. In February of 1995 the Department announced that it was willing to concede temporary accommodation. The VEC accepted this as an interim solution, but stated that a new building was still their aim. This left the committee and the Graignamanagh parents at odds and led to a public meeting in the town with the slogan - "Save Our School". A visit to Graignamanagh by the Minister for Education, Niamh Bhreathnach T.D. didn't produce any joy for the parents. A parents' delegation to the VEC in July pointed out that conditions were appalling and that children were reluctant to go to school in winter weather and sit in wet clothes. The CEO pointed out that the Department letter of 20/4/95 had offered temporary accommodation, but this had been rejected by parents and teachers. The committee's architect had prepared drawings and layout to meet the requirements of the parents and teachers and this had been forwarded to the department building unit. They had requested further information on proposed costs. He pointed out that the Minister had said repeatedly on her visit to the school: "I am not going to close this school." He again urged the acceptance of the interim offer from the Department but said that the campaign for a permanent building must be sustained. In December a delegation from the town told a VEC meeting that the temperature on one day had been eight degrees Celsius, and on another nine degrees - far below the fifteen degrees considered a minimum comfortable temperature in a school room.[162]

Coláiste Pobail Osraí

In 1989 the VEC was approached by the Bord Bainistíochta of Gaelscoil Osraí. This was a successful primary school where all subjects were taught through the medium of Irish, and where Irish was the language of communication between teachers and pupils and among pupils. As the initial intake of pupils came near the age of entry to second-level schooling, the parents were naturally anxious that their children should continue their education through the medium of Irish. They asked the help of the VEC in setting up the projected school, and in June of 1989 the VEC appointed Proinsias Ó Drisceoil, the Arts Education Organiser to be the committee's representative in discussions.

The ambitious decision to try and have the school operational by September of 1991 was pursued over the intervening two years. The possibility of providing a site for the school at the Ormonde Road premises was considered but the parents pressed for the refurbishment of a building which had formerly been part of St. Joseph's Orphanage on the Waterford Road. A meeting with the Minister for Education in April of 1991 led to the school being sanctioned in August and to its opening for business in September with twelve pupils.

The Principal of Kilkenny City Vocational School had supplied a list of those staff who would be willing to teach through the medium of Irish and over the summer of 1991, the teachers involved volunteered to do an in-service course on teaching through Irish. They also got together with the parents of the prospective students. Cáit Bean Uí Chionnaith became Acting Múinteoir i bhFeighil when the school started operations in September and when the appointment of a permanent Múinteoir i bhFeighil was sanctioned in October, the position was advertised and Cáit Bean Uí Chionnaith was appointed with a Grade A post allowance. The school was referred to as an "Aonad Neamhspleách" or Independent Unit attached to Kilkenny City Vocational School. The official opening was on 27th March 1992, and already the VEC heard from the Chairperson of the excellent morale of staff and pupils and the spirit of co-operation with parents. [163]

100 Years of Vocational Education in County Kilkenny

Alt ar oscailt na scoile 1991
Article on the Opening of the
school in 1991

Dea-scéala don Ghaeilge i gCill Chainnigh

ÓCÁID mhór stairiúil ab ea an 3 Meán Fómhair do Chathair Chill Chainnigh agus do lucht taeaíochta na Gaeilge ar an dtaobh sin tíre, mar ar an lá sin osclaíodh Coláiste Pobail Osraí — Scoil dara leibhéil lánGhaelach, den chéad uair.

Aonad neamhspleách is ea an scoil atá faoi choimirce Coiste Ghairmoideachais Cho. Chill Chainnigh. Tá an scoil nua lonnaithe i bhfoirgneamh breá ar Bhóthar Phort Láirge, ar le Clochar Naomh Íosaf é go dtí le déanaí. Forbairt ar

Ghaeilscoil Osraí í an scoil nua.

Tugann an scoil nua lán-Ghaelach seo deis agus rogha dóibh siúd a bhfuil suim acu sa Ghaeilge i gCill Chainnigh agus sa dúthaigh mórthimpeall, a gcuid oideachais dara-leibhéil a fháil trí mheán na Gaeilge.

Dáréag dalta atá sa scoil idir bhuachaillí agus chailíní — tosach beag, b'fhéidir, ach tosach maith, mar sin féin. Mar a deir an seanfhocal 'Bailíonn brobh beart', agus tiocfaidh fás agus forbairt ar an scoil de

réir mar a thiocfaidh daltaí na Gaelscoile ar aghaidh. Ar ndóigh fáilteofar roimh dhaltaí ó bhunscoileanna eile sa dúthaigh chomh maith.

Cinneadh

Tá Cáit Uí Chionnaith agus a foireann teagaisc díogfraiseach lánchinnte go ndeamach (deineadh) an cinneadh ceart nuair a thug an tAire Oideachais cead an scoil a oscailt. Cloisfear a lán eile faoi Cholásite Pobail Osraí sa todhchaí.

An Chéad Bord Bainistoichta
Back Row(from left:)
Aodán Ó Ruairc,
Cathnia Ó Muircheartaigh,
Councillor Richard Dowling,
Seán Ó hArgáin,
Front Row(from left:)
Máire Uí Dhiarmada,
Máire Bhreathnach,
Tony Patterson,
Poilín Uí Leannáin,
Madailín Mhic Chana.

Mr. Liam Aylward T.D.
casting his hand print in the
Millennium Monument in
Mooncoin Vocational School
1999.

112

CHAPTER 11

More Recent Developments

Kilkenny City Vocational School and St. Kieran's College

Kilkenny City Vocational School had experienced a drop in enrolment over the 1980s and in September of 1991, Mr. Billy Burke, the TUI representative on the VEC stated that his Union considered that the co-operation which had existed between St. Kieran's College and the City Vocational School had worked to the disadvantage of the latter. In particular the TUI claimed that the formal agreement of 1978 had not been observed and they asked the VEC to discontinue an agreement which had caused a major drop in enrolment in the Vocational School. The joint management committee of the complex at New Street were to meet on September 30th and the VEC decided that subsequent to that meeting there would be a joint consultation meeting of VEC and TUI and that the matter would then be considered at a full VEC meeting.

A report from the joint management committee of the extension at New Street recommended the VEC to maintain the agreement, at least for the remainder of its term of office. In support of this recommendation they adduced the following arguments: the fact of the building's existence in all likelihood conferred a right of access by present and future pupils of both schools; the severance of the agreement would cost a reduction of 3.5 whole-time teacher equivalents from that year's allocation under the heading of co-operation; to sever the agreement would probably cause the eventual loss of Senior Cycle in KVCS.

In reply to the report, Mr. Burke expressed his disappointment and said that his Union would shortly consider the matter at a branch meeting. At the next VEC meeting the members were told that the TUI would cease co-operation with St. Kieran's College from the first of January 1992. The initial action would affect first year students of St. Kieran's. A joint consultation meeting with the TUI failed to produce any improvement in the situation and the agreement sub-committee met. This committee consisted of the CEO and Chairman of the VEC and the President of St. Kieran's. The VEC side notified St. Kieran's officially of the TUI decision and said that the VEC at its October meeting had decided to maintain the current policy of making the Vocational School building available to all St. Kieran's students who wished to avail of the technical subjects.

In reporting on the two meetings, the Chairperson Cllr. Cavanagh pointed out to VEC members that if Kilkenny City Vocational School confined their teaching to students of their own enrolment, there would be fewer doing the leaving certificate than in Graignamanagh VS, the number of teachers needed to service the co-operation would be eroded, the VEC would be in breach of the co-operation agreement for the first time, and they could be said to be in breach of their obligation under the 1930 act to provide courses of instruction in the nature of technical education.

In reply, Mr. Burke said that the first demand on VEC resources should be the welfare of their own staff and students, that the TUI foresaw a decline in enrolment to the point where teachers' jobs would go in a few years' time, and they feared that the VEC wished to close their school.

The CEO said that the VEC would be anxious to see the school providing a service which they, and only they, were in a position to provide. He foresaw the possibility of providing second chance education, the probability of a need for teachers to service the needs of Coláiste Pobail Osraí as it expanded, and the opportunities which would be provided by VPTP and VTOS schemes.

Mr. Burke asked for a joint consultation meeting and the CEO said he didn't see the point with the threat of strike hanging over their heads. Mr. Burke said that following consultation with branch officers of his union, the CEO would have a letter before they withdrew services affecting St. Kieran's first years. The action would involve two teachers and involve three hours weekly.

The Chairman reported to the February meeting that she, Cllr. Dowling and the CEO had had an informal meeting with some of the senior teachers and they were told that the agreement was not at all working on the ground as had been the previously accepted view. Cllr. Cavanagh had consulted Bishop Forristal at short notice and there were to be further discussions. In the light of this the TUI agreed to postpone action with effect from January 27. In the event the industrial action was not resumed and the teachers in the city school agreed to continue the co-operation on condition that there would be an agreed policy on openings and closings and a synchronised plan for house examinations. [164]

The Ballyhale Problem

While the first few years of the 1990s saw movement on the building projects at Mooncoin and Johnstown, Ballyhale again proved difficult. In 1992 the Board of Management there was so despairing of the possibility of solving the site difficulties that they wanted to try to acquire a completely new site beside Ballyhale Village, whereas the existing school was nearer to Knocktopher. The Minister of State at the Department of Education and the Assistant Secretary of the Department visited the school. Reluctant to abandon the existing permanent buildings for a greenfield site, the Minister of State offered a feasibility study on provision of a pre-cast building to replace the prefabs. The Principal, staff, CEO and eventually the VEC members supported the proposal on condition that the pre-cast building would be in place for September 1993.

Three months later the minutes of the VEC meeting record that "an ominous and chilling silence obtained" in regard to the Ballyhale situation and the expected Department response. However, in January 1993, a letter arrived from the Minister of State saying that Ballyhale had been included in the 1993 Post-Primary allocation for accommodation over two phases. In February sanction to advertise for a list of competent builders was received, and clearance was awaited from the valuation office for the purchase of a site. By June the purchase of the site had been completed, although members had reservations over the price. However "the brutal fact was that the land had to be acquired if the project were to proceed". Planning permission was received and tenders for phase one were due in September. The committee's deadline had already passed, and the lowest tender needed to be modified to bring the project within budget. In December the Department's permission to start work was received. Phase one was not a major project and the clerk of works appointed for the Johnstown building travelled to Ballyhale twice weekly for the short duration of the project. Phase one finished in July 1994 and already phase two was being planned, with a revised schedule to accommodate 300 pupils. This would necessitate 600m² more than the previous proposal, hardly surprising considering that the enrolment was already fast approaching 300.[165]

When the refurbished school opened in September, it soon became apparent that the building in fact provided less accommodation than before construction commenced. A quick start to phase two would have helped, but this didn't happen. A meeting in the Department agreed phase two accommodation of 1,305 m² and the design team was to submit a detailed site report. However, in December, the VEC members were informed of chaos at the school and the discontent of teachers, students and parents. To cover the shortfall in permanent accommodation the VEC was hiring prefabs and these were enormously expensive and none too popular locally. Over the summer the problem of acquiring a wayleave for the disposal of effluent arose. Eventually, rather than purchase a wayleave from a neighbouring landowner, it was decided to re-align the new building. This of course caused further delay in drawing up plans and having them approved.

Press and radio coverage of the poor conditions endured by Ballyhale students led to a special meeting of the County Kilkenny VEC. Members felt that the committee was being presented in a very bad light, that delays caused in the Department were being laid at the door of the VEC, and that there was little appreciation of the fact that, in the matter of the provision of new buildings, the VEC did not have its own sources of finance and was dependent on monies being voted by the government, and sanctioned by the Department of Education. The Chairperson, Cllr. Cavanagh reminded the meeting that a parent had stated on the "Morning Ireland" programme on RTE Radio One that the VEC had demolished a full school and replaced it with half a school. This was bound to mislead the public, she said, and was essentially untrue. The press was present at the special meeting in October 1995, as were parents from the school with observer status without the right to speak.

VEC members had been the recipients of a series of phone calls from parents and some expressed unease at this development. The CEO said that the VEC had been sceptical from the very beginning of the project, but had been forced to accept the only offer the Department building unit was prepared to make in 1992/93. With phase one completed, the committee's design team would need as much as six to seven weeks to prepare plans to move phase two of the project through stages one to seven, and if the time for Departmental responses were to be factored in, then it could be three years before the project was completed. Since the particular target of the parents' anger was the use of prefabs, he suggested moving pupils temporarily to other VEC schools which had spare rooms. This was not popular with members, and Deputy Pattison suggested that a meeting with parents would help. This was seconded by Cllr. Maher and a sub-committee was nominated to meet with parent and teacher representatives. The VEC representatives were to be the CEO, the Chairperson, Deputy Pattison, and Cllrs. Fennelly, Dowling and Ireland. Mr. Burke stated in his role as TUI representative that his union had notified the VEC of a strike of teachers at Ballyhale to take place on November 9th, and the following week also. [166]

In the charged atmosphere that surrounded the Ballyhale project it was extremely unfortunate that a Hairdressing course at the school had to be terminated. The Department wanted twenty students as a minimum for such a course and the school had six first years and six second years. The CEO terminated the first year course, in the hope that the six prospective students could be accommodated at Waterford in a similar course. In joint consultation with the TUI it emerged that the Department of Education teachers' section had told the Assistant General Secretary of the union that a favourable view would be taken of an appeal for an additional teacher to maintain the hairdressing course. A proposal from Cllrs. Fennelly and Dowling to make such an appeal was adopted. The minutes recorded this as a decision to appeal also a number of other similar courses which had been refused consideration in previous years, but an amendment at a subsequent meeting clarified the position - an appeal of the Ballyhale decision alone was intended.

A suggestion by Mr. Montayne of the building unit that the design team was responsible for the delays was refuted at the November meeting, but the statement by the Minister that Ballyhale was top of the list was welcomed as was the very significant offer from Mr. Montayne to telescope several stages of the planning process. By December stages three and four had been sanctioned on completion of the documentation for stage two. The design team could have these stages completed by the end of March. The disposal of effluent could be simplified by connection to the proposed Knocktopher Sewage Scheme and the County Council notified the committee that this scheme would take two years to complete. A local contribution of £25,000 would be levied on the VEC. Provision for this or alternatively the cost of a Puraflow system would have to be made in the estimates.[167]

At the January meeting of the VEC, Brendan Conway gave notice of his intention to retire in the coming September and the committee had to start the process of finding a successor. The Department would not however sanction a permanent appointment until the discussions on the white paper on education had finished and until a report had been received from the Commission on School

Accommodation in relation to the rationalisation of VECs. In the event his successor was to spend over a year as acting CEO before the white paper debate was ended with a change of government. In the meantime, Mr. Conway's last few months in office were eventful enough.

Some progress was made on the Ballyhale project. Planning application documentation was submitted to Kilkenny County Council in January, but alternative plans had to be submitted for sewage disposal. The public sewage scheme which was proposed for Knocktopher might or might not be ready in time for the school to connect to it. The VEC had to present alternative plans for this connection or for the Puraflow system mooted earlier. Word in March that money for the project was being budgeted for by the building unit of the Department caused some relief, but the County Council Planning Department demanded that a strip of land would have to be got to extend the school entrance in accordance with traffic regulations and in conformity with the County Development Plan. The land was acquired from Mr. Rice but the delay in getting planning permission caused a corresponding delay in submitting papers for stage three and four to the Department building unit. By July the papers were with the building unit and a Department architect had been assigned but there was no reply on the permission to proceed to stage five.[168]

Tributes to Brendan Conway

At the July meeting tributes were paid to Brendan Conway for his outstanding work over twenty-three years. His tenure of the office of CEO of County Kilkenny VEC saw huge changes in the scope of the education offered by Vocational Schools, a great increase in the number of students in the system, with a corresponding increase in the teaching staff, and the administrative personnel. When he attended his first meeting on the 7th May 1973, he was faced with expanding from a group of small schools offering continuation education, Domestic Economy, Secretarial classes, Woodwork and Metalwork. On the 23rd of July 1996, two hundred and eighty-eight meetings later, he left his successor a vastly different group of schools. They were very much bigger, offered a much wider range of subjects, had more students and teachers, and had a thriving Post Leaving Certificate and Adult Education section. New schools had opened at Kilkenny City, Mooncoin, Thomastown and Johnstown. The joint venture between Kilkenny City Vocational School and St. Kieran's College was for its day a ground-breaking initiative. An Equestrian Centre at Grennan in Thomastown and a Craft School at Grennan Mill owed a lot to his enthusiastic support. He had helped in no small way in the establishing of a Community School in Castlecomer, and facilitated the setting up of Coláiste Pobail Osraí to provide second-level education through the medium of the Irish language. He had seen the appointment of an Arts Education Organiser, and had established Post Leaving certificate courses, and Vocational Preparation and Training courses. In the middle years of his term of office he had dealt with the horrendous cut-backs of the 1980s and managed to keep his schools in operation in a very tight budgetary situation. His out-of-hours work was equally diverse and productive as a member of the Kilkenny Arts Week Committee, as a member of the Equitation Committee of Bord na gCapall, as a member and Cospóir and President of Aontas. As a loyal Clare man with a good command of Irish, he had often attended Scoil Merriman in his native county and was instrumental in attracting Scoil Gheimhridh Merriman to his adopted one.

The Chairperson said that she had related to the outgoing CEO as Chairperson and friend for the past 11 years and wished to record that he was a person of huge achievement. He had established many Courses and particularly he would be noted for the varied VPTP and PLC Courses which he had innovated with School Principals. He had spearheaded School Buildings at Kilkenny City, Thomastown, Castlecomer Community School, Mooncoin and Johnstown in that sequence. Also the donkey work for Ballyhale and Graignamanagh had been started by Mr. Conway. In his work as President of Aontas and as a Member of Cospóir, he had a national reputation.

Cllr. Dowling saw in the CEO a man who was always looking ahead and planning courses and developments in Schools which would benefit the young people. He referred to Mr. Conway's penchant for Adult Education and noted particularly the founding of "Éigse Sliabh Rua" as a personal initiative of the CEO. Tributes were paid by Cllr. Tomás Ó Dubhshláine, speaking in Irish, by Mons. Michael Ryan and by Deputy Seamus Pattison.

Mr. Rodger Curran CEO

Before taking up his appointment as Chief Executive Officer of County Kilkenny VEC, Mr. Rodger Curran had been Principal of Cobh Community College. He came to his new position with a deep knowledge of the Vocational Education sector, and with personal experience of the benefits of the Community College model of second-level education. He was welcomed to his first meeting as Acting CEO on 10th September 1996. Among the projects which engaged his immediate attention were the bringing of the Ballyhale building project to a successful conclusion, and the conduct of negotiations regarding the proposed amalgamation of The Sacred Heart of Mary Secondary School in Ferrybank and the Vocational School in Slieverue. Of great concern was the question of staffing in the schools under the County Kilkenny VEC, with the Department of Education complaining of overstaffing in the scheme. He was also faced with the necessity of providing office accommodation as the lease on Cashel House had run out.

At his second meeting on September 29th he reported to the committee that the scheme had a fairly serious overstaffing situation, and the Department was pressing for action. Any such action could have very serious implications for teachers in the

President Mary Robinson chatting to students on her visit to Ballyhale Vocational School 1994.

Group pictured at Scoil Gheimhridh Chumann Merriman, the Cumann Merriman Winter School, held in conjunction with the Co. Kilkenny VEC Arts Education Programme in the Newpark Hotel, Kilkenny, February 1995.
Left to right:
Mr.Eoghan Ó hAnluain, UCD, An tOllamh Máirín Nic Dhonnchadha, Dublin Institute for Advanced Studies, Mr. Brendan Conway, CEO, Organising Committee, Mr. Proinsias Ó Drisceoil, Arts Education Officer, Mr. David O'Sullivan, Manager, Newpark Hotel, Mr. Michael Hartnett, Poet.

Photograph taken in Butler House, Kilkenny on Thursday 5th February 1998 on the occasion of a lecture by Dr. Martin Mansergh, Special Advisor to An Taoiseach, entitled The Value of Historical Commemoration and its Role in Peace and Reconciliation, with Special Reference to 1798 and 1848. Photograph shows Dr. Mansergh (left) and Proinsias Ó Drisceoil, Director of the lecture series.

scheme and the Department would be sympathetic to appeals for a phased implementation of withdrawal. Two discussions had already taken place and further meetings regarding teachers' contracts were planned.

The next meeting heard that a timescale to regularisation was under discussion, and the CEO hoped that the adjustment could be made as painless as possible. The Public Accounts Committee of Dáil Éireann had taken an interest in the matter, following a report on overstaffing in the VEC's schools which the Comptroller and Auditor General had issued the previous April. By year's end the position had become painfully clear: the committee was to lose eight whole-time teacher equivalents. A timetable for the rationalisation process would have to be discussed with the Teachers' Union of Ireland whose members would be affected. In January of 1997, the Acting CEO was able to report that plans for meeting the strict staffing limits had been agreed with the Department of Education. Principals would have to be consulted and the TUI would be involved through the joint consultation process. Staff reductions would be necessary in some schools, though the acceptance by two teachers of transfers within the system was an early sign that the problem was solvable. Staff sharing between schools also formed part of the plan to regularise staffing levels, although late in the following year, the committee learned that the travel costs involved in staff sharing had caused an overspend in the travel budget.[169]

To deal with the need for office accommodation, a sub-committee was set up to investigate the availability of office space and, if necessary, make a decision to acquire a premises. The members were Cllr. Cavanagh, Deputy Pattison, Monsignor Ryan and Dean Lynas. In January of 1997, the members were able to congratulate the CEO on acquiring accommodation at Butler Court in Patrick Street. The premises would be leased, and some reconstruction would be necessary. As a condition of planning permission, the Borough Council required the provision of six car parking spaces. As these couldn't be provided on the site itself, the CEO appealed the decision and in May full planning permission was received. During the course of construction, dry and wet rot was discovered on the ground floor. There was a slight hold up, owing to the need to negotiate with the owners of the premises on the cost of remedying the problem, but by the end of September the acting CEO was able to assure members that the new offices were being equipped. New computer software and hardware would lead to an enhanced service to schools and centres for years ahead. Congratulations on completion of his first year in office were extended by members at the same meeting.[170]

The Ballyhale project made progress over the same period. In December of 1996, the committee was informed that permission to go to stage five had been given. Usage of the old school was to be discussed while tender documents were being prepared for the new building. By February 1996 the bill of quantities had been sent to the Department but approval to prepare the bill of quantities for the old school was still awaited. Mr. Pat Fox of the Department visited the school and by April agreement had been reached on use of the old school building for a greatly enhanced specialist provision, and approval was received to prepare a bill of quantities for this part of the project. In June approval to seek tenders was got, and in July the lowest tender proved to be that of Messrs. Cantwell. This was still outside the Department's cost limit, but discussions between the parties resulted in the signing of contracts on September the eighth and in the work commencing a week later.[171]

While the work at the school was ongoing, new temporary accommodation was arranged with Roadmaster Ltd. and land was leased from Mr. Jim Devereux and Mr. David Rice to provide a staff car park, a student circulation area, and a work and storage area for the contractors. Mr. Rice had also agreed to sell for £2,000 a strip of land to facilitate a new entrance and provide a better line of vision to the south, thereby meeting the requirements of the planning authority. Four weeks into the construction process, progress slowed because the public drainage system had not come into operation as the committee had been advised. When the public system became live, the main drainage works were quickly completed. At the December meeting the CEO was able to report "Work is ongoing on completion of foundations and ring walls, installation of floor slabs and the construction of the external and internal block walls.The foundations and rising walls are about 85% complete, floor slab 40% complete and walls about 30%. Work has commenced on the band beams and the first pour should take place on 12/13 December. Work on the roof should start after the Christmas break".

By the beginning of the school year in September 1998 the school was completed except for the usual snag list to be agreed with the builders and sub-contractors and some items which were being negotiated with the Department. Provision of paths was sanctioned and the computer room went to tender, and an extra £20,000 was provided for the metalwork room, but the Department refused to fund the leasing of the extra land. The County Kilkenny VEC had to pay this on-going annual charge from its own funds. Some items awaited sanction, outdoor hard courts and a sports field. In this latter case the community of the Carmelite Priory at Knocktopher were asked to lease land to the committee. Their policy did not allow for the leasing of land but they were willing to license the use of the field. In all the committee had acquired one-and-a-half acres of land for the use of the school. In July, the committee members were informed that planning permission fees for the project had come to £25,000. The enrolment in October of 1998 had been 313 students, making it the fourth largest of the VEC schools in the county.[172]

The school was officially opened by the Minister for Education, Mícheál Martin on October 8th 1999. The new school had a new name - "Scoil Aireagail". This referred to the nearness of the school to the Arrigle river. The word means oratory in Irish and the Principal, Mr. Tom Hunt drew a parallel between the historic ecclesiastical connections of the area and the present day close connection of his school and the nearby Priory. The *Kilkenny People* of the following Friday reported:

The new building at Scoil Aireagail includes a metalwork room, woodwork room, art room, hairdressing suite, tiered lecture room, extra classroom spaces and a new sports hall. A new home economics room, computer room and office accommodation were provided in the old school building. The high academic standard in the school was referred to by Minister Martin in his address. Speaking in Irish he said the spirit of the people was plain to be seen.

121

Refurbishment work at Graignamanagh had commenced and was well under way before Brendan Conway retired. A threat by parents to withdraw students was deferred when Deputy Pattison said that a letter from the Department was on its way. The letter from the building unit, dated 9th February 1996 sanctioned detailed drawings and specifications for prefab accommodation. Two general classrooms, one art classroom, toilets and cloakrooms were sanctioned. A letter of thanks from the Principal, staff and parents was warmly welcomed by the committee members for its courtesy. The lowest tender of £119,000 was referred to the Department and by September work was under way. In January of 1997 the work had been completed to the satisfaction of everybody and further development plans were being explored. The new facilities were officially opened by Deputy Pattison on 14th February 1997, with the name of the school being changed to "Duiske College", an acknowledgement of the part that the Abbey of Duiske (Dubh Uisce) had played in medieval Graignamanagh.

It was becoming obvious that improving economic circumstances had had a positive effect on school provision, not only in County Kilkenny, but in the country generally. The further developments at Graignamanagh took place within a few years. The first move was due solely to the enterprise of the parents, who sought matching funding for basketball and tennis courts which they proposed to provide. These hardcourt facilities were opened in September of 1998. In the first half of the following year, drawings and specifications for a home economics room were being prepared, but the end of the year saw a visit by a Department of Education Inspector and architect to several schools in the County Kilkenny scheme. Getting through the various design stages took some time, but the provision of a woodwork room, and the conversion of the existing woodwork room to a science lab and preparation area was sanctioned, together with the replacement of equipment in the Home Economics room. The removal of existing prefabs was an unwelcome consequence of the project, but replacement Portakabins were sanctioned. [173]

A make-over for Thomastown

Thomastown Vocational School had been enlarged in the 1980s, and the extension was officially opened in 1986, but ten years later both remedial work and expansion of the facilities were urgent necessities. The VEC architect, John Taylor attended a meeting of the committee in November 1996 and gave a run down on projects in hand and on possible future undertakings. In Thomastown, remedial works were essential and he promised to prepare a development plan for the new year. Over the holidays leaks and window draughts were dealt with. The heating was inadequate and a full survey was needed. This was undertaken with Department approval. At the same time plans were almost ready for works at the Craft School at Grennan Mill. About this time the decision was taken to change the name of the main school to "Grennan College". This left all three components with the name Grennan in the title, Grennan College, Grennan Mill and Grennan Equestrian Centre.

Over the summer of 1997 the report of the architect was submitted to the Department, and its urgency was underlined by the collapse of the old art room during the holidays. This necessitated the hire of a replacement. Repairs to the roof were sanctioned at a cost of £121,500 to re-cover the entire roof including insulation, and replace the existing roof lights with insulated upstands. Committee members commented on the necessity to replace the original work so comparatively soon after its completion, but commended the progress to date on the repairs. Work on the windows and doors was sanctioned and permission got to go to tender for an upgrade to the entrance and grounds.

Following a visit from the department's building inspector and architect, permission was got in late 1999 to seek tenders for a heating upgrade. In early 2000 the building unit of the Department of Education asked the VEC to put together a design team to prepare plans and costings for a new woodwork/building construction room, new staff room and art room, refurbishment of the science room, work on the existing tennis court and provision of a new one. Taylor and Freyer were appointed architects, with Noel Lawlor as mechanical and electrical consultant, Hayes and Higgins as structural engineers and McGarry and Associates as quantity surveyors.

In November the Department intimated that they were in favour of a more comprehensive development to include improvement of the home economics room, refurbishment of the toilets and the main entrance, and provision of an indoor gymnasium. It took some time to go through the various design stages, but by the time the permission to go to stage four/five was got in summer of 2002, the estimated cost of the works proposed was £619,384. The extended and refurbished school was officially opened by Minister for Education Mary Hanafin in May 2005.[174]

The *Kilkenny People* reported:

One of the county's most progressive secondary schools celebrated a £1 million refurbishment programme on Monday with Education Minister Mary Hanafin. The former teacher said she was mightily impressed with the facilities but even more taken by the commitment of the teachers, 350 pupils and parents at Grennan College, Thomastown where, she told the *Kilkenny People*, all were involved in maintaining a proud tradition in education.

Maintaining a balance between the old and the new, knowing what to throw out and what to keep, can give rise at times to all sorts of dilemmas. I'm delighted that you seem to have been able to strike that balance, giving you now, within the original walls, bright, airy, spacious rooms that are equipped and decorated to 21st century standards, said the Minister.

As well as functioning in the normal way as a regular VEC post-primary school, Grennan College offers Post Leaving Certificate (PLC) courses in Business Studies, Equestrian studies and Gardening/Horticulture, she noted. It is uplifting to visit an area that is so well known for its creativity - not only in hurling but in arts and crafts, and to see the school reflect this local culture, I note that such activity stretches beyond second level and that your Post

Leaving Certificate courses and the whole array of evening classes reflect and respond to local needs and traditions, said the Minister.

A student at Grennan Mill Craft School, Deirdre Harte, presented the Minister with a hand-tufted rug which she made herself. She was welcomed to the school by the Chairman of the Board of Management, Cllr Dixie Doyle and was also greeted by the Principal, Willie Norton, teacher Angela Downey and Parents' Council Chairman, Larry Stapleton.

Bishop Laurence Forristal and Rev. Barbara Fryday performed an eloquent ecumenical prayer service to bless the work, with the school choir, aided by a number of local musicians also performing.

Principal Norton said a new chapter in the life of Grennan College had begun after the work, which included an upgrading of the science laboratory, demonstration room, home economics room, arts and crafts room and woodwork/ construction/ technical drawing room. All the rooms were redesigned and re-equipped. He reminded the Minister that the school had an application lodged with her Department for a sports and leisure complex and thanked all associated with the project, including the Board of Management, Parents' Association, VEC Chief Executive Officer Rodger Curran, Architect John Taylor, Building contractors PHD and Site Foreman Tom Doyle.[175]

CHAPTER 12

Slieverue and Ferrybank Amalgamation

The proposed amalgamation of Ferrybank Convent Secondary School and Slieverue Vocational School would have to be carefully managed to preserve enrolment at both schools until a new building was complete. The state of the existing prefabs at Slieverue was of great concern to the VEC and it was a relief to get permission in March 1997 to go to tender for replacements. Some delay occurred in processing the planning application, but by the end of the year the work was complete and the units handed over. The Department was favourable to the amalgamation project and the VEC urged the teachers' section "not to make any reduction in staffing levels at either of the two schools earmarked for amalgamation into the new Community School in the Ferrybank area". In March the VEC held its monthly meeting at Slieverue. The Principal John O' Callaghan welcomed them and expressed his thanks and then reported on the amalgamation. The main problem was that the gymnasium proposed for the new school was less than full size and, if they wanted a full-size one, there would have to be a local contribution of £200,000. The meeting appointed its three trustees for the new school: the CEO, Chairperson of County Kilkenny VEC, and Chairperson of the Board of Management of the school. [176]

On the 7th September 1998 the monthly meeting of County Kilkenny VEC considered a letter of momentous import from the trustees of Sacred Heart of Mary Secondary School in Ferrybank. The Chairperson said that the Sisters of the Sacred Heart of Mary had decided to opt for a Community College, under VEC auspices, rather than the Community School model which had been the option under discussion up to that time. She said that County Kilkenny VEC had a proud tradition of service in education and their schools had served the people of County Kilkenny very well for many years and that their emphasis on the whole person had impressed her.

The CEO said that once the Department of Education had accepted County Kilkenny VEC as the clients in this new situation, the project could go ahead. Within weeks word was received that the change of designation to Community College was approved by the Department. The buildings would have a total floor space of 4,200 m^2 and the dispute over the size of the gym would be the subject of a meeting with the Minister. Discussions between the VEC and the Sisters resulted in the name "Abbey Community College" being chosen for the proposed school. Following the model agreement for such schools, the two parties drew up an Instrument of Management and Articles of Management. These were circulated to teachers in Ferrybank who were members of the Association of Secondary Teachers of Ireland and to the Slieverue staff who were with the Teachers Union of Ireland.

Official Opening of Abbey Community College 2002
From left: Mr. D. Dowling, Chairperson B.O.M, Mr. J. McGuinness TD, Mr. R. Curran
C.E.O, County Kilkenny VEC, Mrs M.H. Kavanagh, Chairperson, County Kilkenny VEC,
Mr. L. Aylward TD, Mr. T. Lanigan, Principal, Mr. E. Power, Deputy Principal,
Mr. M. Woods TD, Minister for Education and Science, Mr. M. Cullen TD,
Sr. R. Lenihan, S.H.M., Mr. B. Kenneally TD.

Ms. Patti Burke on the occasion of her retirement 2000
From left: Rodger Curran, Chief Executive Officer, Liam Aylward TD, Chairperson of
County Kilkenny VEC, Ms. Patti Burke and Cllr. Mary H. Cavanagh, Deputy Chairperson
of County Kilkenny VEC.

In the process of amalgamation, it would be necessary to reassure the existing staffs that their positions were not under threat. All permanent members of staff at Ferrybank and Slieverue were to be given the right to opt into the new college, and the position of non-permanent staff was to be the subject of negotiation with the Department of Education when curricular needs were identified. The position of Principal was to be advertised. In March 1999, the VEC members were shown a three-dimensional model of the proposed school. The total area was now increased to 4,443m² not including external areas, and the cost was estimated to be £3.65 million. [177]

Invitations to tender were published and an application for planning permission made to both Kilkenny County Council and Waterford Corporation - a reminder that the school would be within walking distance of the Bridge of Waterford. Even though no agreement had been reached on the question of the size of the gymnasium to be provided, the planning application was for the full-size unit. The Principal of Sacred Heart of Mary School wrote to the VEC urging that it was essential that the Department of Education should transfer the Slieverue catchment area to the new school. Waterford City was in the position that no school had an exclusive catchment area, including Ferrybank on the Kilkenny side of the river Suir. Instead, transport was provided to the city from the joint catchment area and parents were free to enrol their children in the school of their choice. Slieverue had an exclusive catchment area, and County Kilkenny VEC supported the Sisters in their urging the Department that this should transfer to the Community College.

The sisters wanted to be able to sell the old school building by September of the following year and were anxious that no delay should take place, and the design team hoped to have a contractor chosen and on site by September 1999. When the tenders were opened they were above the Department's limit, and even more calamitous was the withdrawal of the lowest bidder from the process. A new contract notice was issued and firms were given fifteen days to reply. Five were to be shortlisted and negotiations were to be conducted with the lowest bidder. The delay would push the completion date back to April 2001. This negotiated tendering process was brought to the attention of Claudio Romanini of the European Union Commission, but was found to be consistent with EU directives. Negotiations were complete by February and Department approval followed, with contracts being signed on 2nd May 2000.[178]

By the time the ceremonial cutting of the first sod happened on 30th. May the contractor was already on site and working. The main contractor was Clancy Construction of Drangan, Co. Tipperary. The contract was for a fixed sum of £4,914,037 including VAT. Suir Engineering, Mooncoin were to look after the mechanical and electrical element of the job, Duggan Systems Ltd. had the sub-contract for doors and windows.

In September of 2000 the amalgamated school was due to open, but although work was progressing satisfactorily on the site, there was no possibility of the building being ready that year. It was necessary to use the existing buildings in

Slieverue and Ferrybank to accommodate pupils and to bus some classes to and fro. The secondary school building had been sold and approval to lease it back on a caretaker agreement was got from the Department. In general the Department proved generous in allowing for extra provisions. They wouldn't fund the cost of fencing or floodlighting for the all-weather play areas but agreed to fund the builders' work on these items. A request to install data points throughout the school was refused but the necessary trunking would be installed at the construction stage, so that, with the proper infrastructure in place, data points could be installed easily later. These would be of great importance for the networking of computers and the provision of broadband.

Some delays were caused by difficulties which the contractor had with the bricklayers and unusually inclement weather early in 2001 and the discovery of a wet area near the foundations caused further slowing down of progress. The builder requested an extension of the deadline for completion, but the CEO refused. However by May, Mr. Clancy assured the VEC that the delay was outside his control and it was agreed that the practical rooms, engineering, woodwork and art would be handed over in September, with the rest of the building to be available after the mid-term break in late October and early November. In the intervening period, the builder would facilitate the equipping and furnishing of the building. The fitted furniture contract was to cost £129,736.98, excluding VAT. The builder was as good as his word and the practical rooms were handed over in time, and a safe passage provided to ensure students could get from the old buildings still in use to the new rooms. When the rest of the school population moved in after the mid-term break, there was still some work to be done on the gymnasium, on landscaping, tarmac for parking spaces and access routes, and there were some snag list items to be looked after.[179]

The building at Slieverue was now no longer required for classes. An undertaking had been given by the former CEO and his committee that, in the event of school closure, the parish would be given first option on the lease of the building. The Pastoral Council of Slieverue parish leased the building from the VEC, with provision made in the contract for the its use by the VEC should the need arise, and that, if the Council should fail in its duty to maintain the building, or should itself disband, the old school should be returned to the VEC. A field behind the school was offered to the Pastoral Council for use as a cemetery at a cost of £10,000.

Abbey Community College Opening

Abbey Community College was officially opened by the Minister for Education, Dr. Michael Woods, TD on Monday 22nd April 2002. The *Kilkenny People* reported on the official opening referred to Mr. Rodger Curran, CEO of Kilkenny VEC as saying that "Building a sense of self esteem, instilling confidence and making a difference, are three of the fundamentals for the success of any secondary school".

Over £9 million has been spent on the Abbey Community College, Ferrybank, on the edge of Waterford city. The opening marks the end of a six year merger process between two schools now closed, Slieverue Vocational School and the Sacred Heart of Mary Secondary School.

The facilities are superb, there are two fully equipped computer rooms.There are special rooms for woodwork, metalwork, technical graphics, home economics, multimedia, language, art and design, physics, chemistry and biology laboratories with a demonstration room. And the physical health of the students is also assured with a full size gymnasium, all-weather hockey pitch, basketball court, soccer, hurling and Gaelic football pitches.

There is a link with the old Sacred Heart Convent. The stained glass in the prayer room was taken from that the old convent church. The crests of the old schools which merged to form that of the new school, are on the front of the new building along with the new crest and the VEC emblem. There are 400 students attending the school which will be able to cater for up to 600 pupils. There are 32 teachers and the Principal is Mr. Tommy Lanigan. The school is built on a 15 acre site on Abbey Road, on the Kilkenny side of the river.

In his address, CEO of County Kilkenny VEC, Mr Rodger Curran, praised all those associated with the project including architects, Jim Coady and Associates; quantity surveyors, Nolan Ryan Partnership; Fearon O'Neill, structural engineers; mechanical electrical consultants, Building Design Partnership. He praised the contractors, Clancy Construction and in particular Pat Clancy, John O'Shaughnessey, Paddy Leahy and site foreman, Paddy Cavanagh. He said all in the school were to be congratulated for the work already done to develop a positive disciplinary climate and to facilitate student and parent involvement. He encouraged all to strive for the best that is possible and above all to develop a warm, caring and respecting environment that encourages all to belong.

School Principal, Mr Tommy Lanigan, thanked everyone connected with the school for their patience and dedication. He had a special word for the former Principal of Slieverue Vocatlonal School, Mr John O'Callaghan, and the former Principal of the Sacred Heart Secondary School, Sr. Catherine Dunne.
"They took the risks at the coalface, they built on the idea, they accepted and promoted the vision", he said. He also asked the pupils to look around them and see all those who had gathered in the school for the opening who were committed to their welfare and future to help make their world a better one. "We have learned much about what we can do to enable our students prepare for adult and working life, how, by working to create a warm and caring environment, we can truly make a difference for them", Mr Lanigan said.

The work carried out by the Amalgamation Steering Committee was alluded to by the Chairperson of the VEC, Cllr. Mary Hilda Cavanagh. "They made every possible effort to ensure the fears, anxieties, concerns and expectations of all those affected were respected, examined and where possible resolved", she said.

The Chairman of the school Board of Management, Cllr. Dick Dowling paid tribute to the former CEO of the VEC, Mr. Brendan Conway for seeing the opportunity to amalgamate the two schools. He made the point that proper resources were still needed to deal with learning difficulties and early school leavers.

The changed economic climate in Ireland must be seen as in part responsible for the improvement in the VEC's schools during the nineties and after. Successive governments - A Fianna Fáil and Labour Coalition, A Fine Gael, Labour and Democratic Left Coalition, A Fianna Fáil and Progressive Democrat Coalition - can also claim credit, as can the civil servants in the Department of Education. But the hard work and persistence of the County Kilkenny Vocational Committee under both Brendan Conway and Rodger Curran should be acknowledged. The series of refurbishments of schools tells its own story - Mooncoin 1995, Johnstown 1996 and Duiske 1996 and 2004, Slieverue 1998, Ballyhale 1999 and 2001 the roof of Ormonde College was replaced during the 1999/2000 school year, Thomastown 2002 and 2005. Above all, the creation of the brand new Abbey Community College in 2002, and its growth since then is a heartening endorsement of the value of the system of management represented by the VECs around the country. There are other schools requiring action and other plans to be fulfilled, perhaps unforseen challenges, but the Vocatonal Education system seems more than capable of any tasks before it.

CHAPTER 13

The People

For the most part this account of County Kilkenny VEC has been based on the minute books of the committee, with occasional recourse to newspaper reports and official documents. As one goes through these sources, it becomes obvious that there is a lot more to the vocational education system. One element that seldom intrudes in the minutes is the personal. The following interviews are an attempt to give some idea of that human element. The interviewees are a very small selection of the hundreds of people, teachers, caretakers, administrative staff and CEOs who made the whole system work.

Whereas teachers in primary schools come from the colleges of education, and secondary teachers come in the main from the universities, vocational teachers have traditionally come from a much more varied range of third level institutions. The universities have provided a proportion, but woodwork and metalwork teachers and teachers of domestic economy have taken a different path, and a no less demanding one.

All the teachers interviewed are now retired, and so have had experience of the vocational education system when it was still geared to the group certificate, with a strong emphasis on practical subjects. Most started in schools of which Graignamanagh would be a typical example - four teachers in a four room school catering for Woodwork, Commerce, Home Economics and continuation subjects. All saw the dramatic changes resulting from free education, free school transport and the resulting growth in enrolment in the vocational sector. All experienced the change from Group Certificate to Intermediate Certificate, later replaced by the Junior Certificate, with students staying in the schools for three years at the very least, and many going on to sit the Leaving Certificate examination after five years.

In the course of the interviews, all were asked about their experience of night classes, an almost defining characteristic of the vocational system in its early years. This aspect of the work gets very little mention in the minutes of the committee, mainly because it was run by individual schools and seldom required committee decisions. Peadar Madden, Principal in Castlecomer did keep a list of the classes run in the school and under its auspices from 1951 to 1985. Most night classes were held in the school building on Kilkenny Road, but out-centres were used intermittently at Clogh, Conahy, Ballyragget, Ballyouskill, Freshford, Muckalee, Moneenroe, and Coon. On a number of occasions classes in Art, Woodwork, Mechanical Drawing and Metalwork were provided for students of the local convent school, which had a co-operation arrangement with Castlecomer Vocational School.

In the early years night classes were mostly taught by the teaching staff of the school in subjects such as Woodwork, Commerce, Cookery, Dressmaking, Irish, Arts and Crafts, Domestic Economy, Typing and Shorthand. Towards the end of the period, there was a greater reliance on classes conducted by people outside the staff. Subjects such as Karate, Tractor Maintenance, Guitar Playing, Computers, the Law and You, Horticulture, Learning to play Golf and Cordon Bleu Cookery reflected the fact that night classes were no longer a compulsory part of a vocational teacher's duties.

Ormonde College still has a list of bookings of school classrooms and the school hall from 1957 to 1961. It gives a good idea of the range of after-hours activities in the school apart from the night classes. Many local societies used the facilities of the school for meetings, debates, lectures and film shows. Charges were modest: in 1958 groups were charged two shillings and sixpence per hour, five shillings for a two-hour meeting and seven shillings and sixpence for the very occasional three-hour meeting. Societies listed included the Irish Countrywomen's Association, the Young Farmers' Club, The Kilkenny Archaeological Society, Ossory Players, The Kilkenny Literary Society, The Kilkenny Arts Society, An Réalt, The Blood Transfusion Service, Kilkenny Bridge Club, Civil Defence and the Horticultural Society. The importance to the local community of the availability of such a reasonably priced venue for lectures, debates and meetings can be imagined. All the other Vocational Schools in the county provided similar facilities in their own communities, and one can appreciate the feelings of those communities when they perceived any possible move to close a school.

The people interviewed are: Brendan Conway, teacher of Irish and other subjects, later Principal in Sundrive Road in Dublin, and CEO of County Kilkenny Vocational Education Committee; Canice Ryan, caretaker of Kilkenny City Vocational School and of Ormonde College; Rita Neary, school secretary, and later an administrator in head-office at Seville Lodge; Peadar Madden, woodwork teacher, and Principal of Castlecomer Vocational School; Teresa Buggy, home economics teacher and later Co-ordinator of Post Leaving Certificate courses at Ormonde College; Christy McGrath, metalwork teacher in Castlecomer Vocational School and later in Castlecomer Community School. As to why they were picked rather than the many others with equally interesting stories, they were all personally known to the interviewer for many years.

Brendan Conway

I was born in Feakle, County Clare in 1932. As the second
son of a middling sized farm, I was always destined for off-
farm enterprise of some sort and so I was encouraged to
take my school days very seriously.

In Feakle school we were blessed at that time by the work
of an inspirational "master" - Sean Harrington. He was a marvellous teacher who
had taught us Latin - five declensions of nouns by the end of our stay at primary
school. Of some thirty-two students in my seventh class, just six had no chance to
progress to secondary school.

In my case that was St. Flannan's College. For me that was an emigration from
Feakle to distant Ennis - seventeen miles away. In those times it was very seldom
you could afford a car to take you to places. We travelled quite often by bicycle as
young lads and in a pony and trap in a more sedate way. I was delivered to St.
Flannan's as a boarder by pony and trap with my luggage. I was leaving on the third
of September and I wasn't allowed home until the eighteenth of December. Then,
as now, St. Flannan's was a hurling nursery and I made my way on to the college
team. St. Flannan's were the reigning All-Ireland Colleges champions that time. I
reached the senior team in my third year, and in my fourth and fifth years. There
was a value added to being on the hurling team because, for hurlers and footballers
representing the college, there was an extra meal per day so you would have
murdered your neighbour for a place on the team.

I played in three Harty Cup finals. The Harty cup was the trophy for the Munster
Colleges Hurling Championship. We won one and were beaten in two. In my final
year we were beaten off the field by Thurles CBS.

That performance in turn gave me access to the Clare county minor team on
which I figured in two defeats at Munster Final level - heartbreak then, as for many
years after, for Clare hurling folk. It was another thirty-two years before Clare won
their first minor title. However I had two Munster colleges medals and one all-
Ireland colleges medal when we beat Roscrea.

After leaving certificate, and four years at third level, I had a B.A. degree and H.
Dip. in Education from UCD. At that stage I had a life-changing educational
experience in the shape of one month's challenging course in Indreabh·n, County
Galway where many of us were prepared for a qualification as Irish teachers in
Vocational Schools.

I now had the Teastas Timire Gaeilge, and that qualification opened up to me a
career in the vocational teaching sector where previously my sights were set on a
secondary school teaching career.

In 1955 I was appointed to County Carlow VEC as teacher of Irish (day and
evening classes) and located in Carlow Town. One of the conditions of appointment

was to re-establish an adult evening class tré Ghaeilge. There was a heading in the paper a week later "Clare Hurler appointed to Carlow". As a result I was visited in the school by a GAA officer. He asked me to play for Carlow. I said "I'm involved in the club at home". He said "We'll play you under any name you like. Is there anything we could do to help you?" I said I was looking for people for a night class. "When is the night class enrolling?" and in an amusing utilisation off-field of my hurling fame, I assembled on Tuesday nights a fine Irish adult class which by the following Sunday was the Carlow Town Hurling team with their teacher fielding under a false name. I can say that was my introduction to Adult Education which has been a life-long preoccupation of mine ever since.

By 1957 I was teaching in Kevin Street in Dublin where I met the flower of the vocational students from schools around the country who were motivated to keep their English, Irish and general studies in step with their technical studies while they qualified as technicians in the ESB, Post Office and so on. The encounter with these students affirmed the necessity to maintain programmes of adult education as a prerequisite to advancement in technical careers.

By 1967 the City of Dublin VEC was expanding and three new schools were opened in one year, one in Sundrive Road, one in Whitehall, and one in Mount Street. So there were interviews for three appointments as headmasters on the one day. I won appointment as a Headmaster to the newly established school at Sundrive Road. It was a time of celebration of the fiftieth anniversary of 1916, and I named our school Pearse Post-Primary School. Today, as Pearse College it continues to serve a wide diet of second-chance and lifelong learning to our own and newly arrived citizens from all across the European Union.

I led our young teaching staff and a community unfamiliar with second-level education to adopt the principle that education can and does lead to economic success in one's career - which in the late 1960s, 1970s was necessarily an imposed conviction.

In 1969 as a sideline, I became the Shaw Trust Organiser. Mrs. Shaw was George Bernard Shaw's widow and she left £139,000 to the Irish nation. With the interest from that, the Government established a body called Foras Éireann, and the part-time post of organiser with an income of £500 a year which was half as much as a full-time job. I did that job from 1969 to 1973. What it did for me was to put me in contact with people like James Delahunty here in Kilkenny and Charles Acton and so on. We provided lectures all over the country in literature, music - all sorts of things. I did that job from 1969 to 1973.

In 1973 I was appointed as CEO to County Kilkenny VEC and settled here with a growing family and I have stayed ever since. Free education and the challenge it offered was only then being addressed. Kilkenny City was the only centre of leaving certificate programmes and to that centre students were transported daily from outlying schools - Ballyhale, Thomastown, Graignamanagh, Castlecomer and Johnstown. Gradually, over a period of four or five years, the leaving certificate programme became available at all of the above mentioned centres, together with Mooncoin and Slieverue which to that point had geared their students to further studies in Waterford City.

Of course the Department of Education were not always enthusiastic about the irresponsible (as they would and did say) expansion of the vocational system. The committee and the headmasters and teachers rightly sought the full fruits of free education for their own communities and it is gratifying to note that full post-primary education in all of our schools is now a 'given'.

In all schools of the county there was an ambition to have a significant Vocational Preparation course as it was in the tradition of vocational education to promote such courses. Consequently we worked together with national agencies (long before FETAC legitimised the efforts) and saw the arrival of such courses as equestrian science, craft courses, hairdressing, tourism and catering courses. All of these courses had a relevance to people's needs and led to very valuable employment for young people in their own home places. Many of these courses continue to thrive and I do think that is the greatest endorsement of their value. I can honestly say that without the backing of the committee over the years and the inspired dedication of headmasters, these courses would not have come into being.

Outside work I was involved in a lot of things. In 1973 one of our own teachers, George Vaughan, David Lee, the organist in Canice's Cathedral, and Mrs. Peggy Butler asked me to attend a meeting they were having where they outlined their plan for the first Kilkenny Arts Week. I told them that I'd give them two hundred pounds of Shaw Trust money. I had held on to the position of organiser with the Shaw Trust for about a year after I moved to Kilkenny. I became financial chairman of Kilkenny Arts Week. I suppose I had contacts - I knew Charles Acton, the music critic of the *Irish Times*. In a way he was like the Broadway Critics. If he wasn't on your side, you were gone. He provided a lot of publicity and he used come and stay here in Kilkenny for the Arts Week. Year after year we met the very best of artists. From the nature of the post of CEO, allied to an interest in cultural affairs, I have had a very rewarding involvement in the promotion of events like Kilkenny Arts Week, Éigse Sliabh Rua and more recently Kilkenny Celtic Festival. I have always seen such events as an extension of the adult education vision and certainly these events do bring an enrichment to life in our county.

It has been an interesting journey and I do believe I exploited the challenge which the post of Chief Executive Officer of the VEC offers to the unwary.

Canice Ryan

I came to the Vocational School on the sixteenth of March 1970, thirty-seven years ago.

This was Céard Scoil na Cathrach then, before the New Street building went up.

The first morning I came here, I was shown the boiler house and what had to be done. You were told to come in sprucely dressed. The first morning I came in at six o' clock. You'd do that every second morning to start the old boiler. I came in and went home to my breakfast at nine o'clock and I had to throw off what I was wearing to clean it.

The fuel was sea coal and coke, so you really were dirty. And you went up and down to that boiler every three quarters of an hour with two buckets of coal. You'd have to rake it out in the morning and set it. You'd often get rapped on your knuckles here because if the draught was going the wrong way, and you know yourself that could happen on a wet morning, you'd be told that you couldn't have been here at six, and sure you could be here at four o'clock and it would have made no difference. The heat wouldn't be right. We had old-fashioned cast iron radiators and they're still here, and I tell you they were the best radiators of all. It's still the same piping. In my own office there I had no radiator, but I had the pipe running through, and when we got a new Principal, I got a radiator.

The other days I'd come in the morning at ten or five to eight and open up the building and get it going and make sure everything was working all right. It's the same now. You'd have students coming in around that time. I'd be slagging them - try and brighten their day up as they walk across the yard. Some would be on busses nowadays, and more parents would be heading for work and they'd be dropping off their kids. And I'd hate to have them left on the road on a wet morning or especially winter time. I'd be looking out while I'd be opening up the whole place. I'd be keeping an eye on things, and then teachers would be coming in - they'd be on rotas for early morning duties.

School would be up and running at nine o' clock and I'd head on out to the yards and of course the garden would be my pride and joy - I'd stay there for ever. The garden we have here at Ormonde is all more or less to the front. Two nice big squares of grass, rose beds. You have four rose beds, the rest is in shrubs. About five or six roses are left out of the first batch were ever sowed. I don't know who sowed them but I sowed all the rest and of course I sowed all the plants.

We used to go for a lot of annuals here. We had some lovely bedding plants here one time but it got very expensive and there was a bit of a tightening up. We have leylandii, maples, dwarf leylandii, cherry trees, dwarf weeping willow, weeping birch and pyracantha trees. These are huge trees. I have the other pyrancantha growing against the wall. The big trees have a lovely blossom and then they have a massive load of berries later on. Funny enough, the last few years the birds leave them alone - I don't know if it's the milder winters or not.

Grass clippings are no problem. I have a compost heap in a corner under the leylandii here and I keep burying the stuff there. The weeds grow over it so that you don't know what's under it this time of the year. There's compost there for years. It could be open any time now. There would be layers built up - clippings of bushes, grass from mowing the lawn. It all goes back on the soil, I'd dig it in.

I got interested in the garden when I was still in school. A neighbour of ours used to work at Scott-Dove's on the Castlecomer Road. It's where the Newpark Hotel is now. She said they were looking for a young fellow to do a bit of work after school hours. So I went along there and was taken on. The gardener was Harold Reade, who use to live up on Green's Hill. I learned an awful lot from working with him in the garden.

There's always a little bit of maintenance to be done - maybe a lock on a door and what we did a lot of one time was putting in glass if it got broken. You'd have to hack out the old stuff, the old hard stuff, the hard putty, and I'm telling you it was hard. Then you had to fit in the glass, and maybe discover it was a little bit off. Do you take a bit out of the frame or get a bit taken off the glass?

In the old days the night classes were very, very busy. All classes were filled. You'd come back here on enrolment night there'd be a queue out the gate down as far as the old Presbyterian Church. When we were ready to open up, I'd be handed a heap of forms and I'd dish them out for people to sign in for whatever class they wanted to take. You had a lot of the practical subjects. The manual typewriter was a great take. You had Carpentry, Woodwork, Motor Mechanics at night - very very successful. There was Cookery, Sewing, all filled. There were some languages - German, French and Spanish. In the earlier days the teaching was done by some of the teachers here that had to fill in some hours at night. That was part of their time table, but nowadays it's all outsiders that come in. Classes would start the end of September, right up to Christmas. Then they'd enrol again for another session up to Easter, so that you'd have two sessions in the year.

Here in the grounds we have part of the old city wall of Kilkenny. The main part is the Talbot Tower. I took a great interest in it and I still have an interest. In 1970 we started clearing off all around Talbot Tower, and we got it all ready, everything prepared for the people responsible at the time to point the stone and look after it, and at that time it was a golden opportunity then if they had to do it then it wouldn't be as bad as it is today. . I remember around seventy-five a group of students won a national award for a project on that. Bernard Costello was teaching here and he was in An Taisce, He had a group of students working on it - They pulled ivy and so on. In 1989, I came in here one morning and the stairs of the Talbot Tower had fallen down. It was all a hullabaloo. They were going to do this that and the other and nothing happened. I took it up myself in the late nineties. The county manager came over to me and said they were going to do something, and he got all the stuff cut away. But now the wall will have to be taken down. It can't be repaired. Since yesterday, we had a crowd down from Dublin. They were taking pictures and they have a surveyor there. There are quotes going in to the Corporation for demolishing the wall and numbering the stones so that it can be rebuilt

We had apprentices here, fitter turners from Bord Na Móna, motor mechanics from the local garages, and we had the woodwork apprentices from the building trade - some on day release. The Bord Na Móna lads were on block release. They spent three months here. They'd be from all over the country and they'd stay in digs in Kilkenny and that meant a few pounds for the local people out of it. They'd be older than the rest of the students. They'd be first year apprentices, maybe second year in a garage. Maybe I shouldn't say this but when the apprentices would be passing through the yard, where you had six hundred and thirty students, somebody's elbow would hit off somebody, and the late Paddy Fahey and myself would be left with some little job to be done, but in general they got on very well together. It was a great school. The staff in those days were brilliant. It was electric here in those days. Everybody knew what they had to do and they went off and did their job. The only thing you'd be afraid to say around here was "have you time for a pint?" because if you said that you'd be picked up straight away.

That was a photograph was taken in 1996 with the leaving cert projects under Mr. Murt Flanagan. I was very interested in it - always interested in timber. I went in this day and I said to Murt "I'll have to test this chair, sit down in it." Murt being a decent man made sure I had a glass in my hand - with nothing in it, and then he took my photograph. And that photo was shown to Fiona O'Sullivan, and she grabbed it and the next thing it appeared on the wall in a frame.

I always had an interest in woodturning. I said I'd take it up when I retired, but in 1994, 1995 and 1996 I was delighted I had the opportunity of holding the All-Ireland Seminar for Woodturners here in Ormonde College, and I was the only person that held it for three years in succession. There was a lot of work involved but there was some team of lads - they were brilliant. I spent a lot of time watching this lad and that lad turning pieces. And I always remember I was watching somebody and this big hand came on my shoulder. It was the secretary of the South-East wood turners. An he said to me "I've been watching you for some time and you look like a lad that's fierce interested in woodturning.
I said "I'm going to do it when I retire."

"No he says you're going to do it straight away." And he got me involved. So I attended a workshop with Tom Dunlop in New Ross. One thing - don't ever think you know it all, because I certainly walked into it. I was there looking, and I couldn't see very well, so I walked around until I was right behind Tom demonstrating something. And Tom said "Is that yourself Ken? Will you hand me the skew" says he. I hadn't a clue what a skew was but I hit a lad on the arm and I said "you're nearer to it than I am."

There are twenty two members of SIPTU working for the VEC in County Kilkenny. I took a great interest in Trade Union affairs and I've been shop steward since 1973. I'm also joint chair of the local working group set up under the LPWG, the partnership agreement between the Government, employers and unions.

Rita Neary

I was educated in the Presentation Primary and Secondary School in Kilkenny. The Secondary School was situated where Superquinn now stands. After my Leaving Cert. I went to the Secretarial Course in the City Vocational School. Evelyn O'Hea was the person in charge at that time. At the end of the year there was an advertisement in the paper for a job with County Kilkenny VEC which we were all encouraged to apply for. There was a shorthand exam and a typing exam. We had manual typewriters at that time - it all sounds like a hundred years ago now but it was all manual at that time. After the exam a number of people were called for interview. At the time the interview board consisted of the CEO, the Chairperson of the VEC and various other members. The interview was in English and a couple of sentences through Irish. I was notified shortly after that I had got the job and about six or seven of us started work at the same time. Of the original six or seven there are only two of us still here. We were all assigned to schools. This was relatively new at the time because most schools did not have school secretaries up to then. Kilkenny City did have a school secretary but they were a big school at that time. I started working between two schools, Castlecomer where Peadar Madden was Principal and Dan Butler, Vice-Principal and City Vocational School where Sean Dignan was Principal and Moyra McCarthy, Vice-Principal. Ann Hennessy was working in the office in Kilkenny City Vocational School at this time as well - she had been there a number of years at this time. At one time the VEC Head Office was based in the City School. I did two days in Kilkenny and three in Comer. There was a big difference between the two schools as they were so different in size. There is a lot of work to be done in Schools. Dealing with the post, answering correspondence, typing exams, letters for the Principal, accounts, dealing with students, parents, salespeople, etc. You could even be called on for first aid. You could also be taking minutes at minutes - in Castlecomer I took the minutes at the Board of Management Meetings. I also helped the students in Kilkenny City with their annual school magazine.

It was hard work on a manual typewriter, but then we graduated to an electric typewriter. Imagine the joy of self correcting. No more Tippex. This was a great improvement similar to when we went from electric typewriter to computer. When the No Name Club started in Kilkenny I typed up the minutes.

In the beginning when exams had to be typed I had to cut a stencil which people now would never even have heard tell of - this was also done for grants and for anything which required a large number of copies. The Gestetner machine was great in its day but the stencil could tear and you would get destroyed with the ink if you were not careful. The photocopier was seldom used as it was very costly at that time. It was heaven to use the photocopier - so simple and clean. Telephone systems improved as well. In Castlecomer for a long time they only had a coin box. In Kilkenny you could transfer calls to the Principal and Vice Principal - really modern. Nowadays a lot of schools have intercom systems.

I spent several years between the Schools which I enjoyed. Eventually a vacancy arose in Head Office and I applied. I left Castlecomer at this stage and now was working between Kilkenny City Vocational School and Head Office. After a year or two a full time vacancy arose in Head Office. I got the job which was a promotion for me and I now worked full time in Head Office. The Office was in Cashel House, Kells Road. It was an old building but lovely to work in. It had lovely big airy rooms. Brendan Conway was the CEO and would have bought the building and restored it but the money was not there at the time. We moved to Butler Court in 1997 and Seville Lodge in 2002. Butler Court was lovely but just too small as the VEC grew. There are now fourteen working in Seville Lodge which is a big increase on when we were in Cashel House. At that time there was Carmel Darcy, Patti Burke, Bernadette Hughes, Ann Hennessy and myself. For a long time there was a ban on staffing in the public service so that when Carmel and Ann left there were only three of us. Bernadette and I are the only ones left of the five that worked in Cashel House when I started.

Moving up to Seville Lodge gave us a lot more room and also the option of hiring rooms if needed and of course room for parking both for ourselves and callers. We have room to bring people in to discuss their business in private which is a necessity. We are divided into three sections. I am the Head of Education Support and that covers third level grants, capital, insurance, travel and school transport. We also have personnel and finance which are big areas to cover. Catriona in reception is also the CEO's personal assistant.

It is always very busy before the monthly committee meeting for all sections as reports and minutes have to be prepared. In April and May we are very busy with School Transport. Transport forms are sent to the Schools and returned to the VEC They are checked and then signed by the CEO who is also the Transport Liaison Officer. They are then sent to Bus Éireann in Waterford who issue the tickets. We deal with all second level schools for school transport. Grants start mid to end of May and really go on for the entire year. There are many different types of grant PLC, TLT and VEC. The County Council also do grants, (Higher Education Grants). It is hoped that all grants will be done by one body next year and it is in the pipeline that the VEC will be that body. The first payment is made in October and even at this stage a lot of people will not have their forms completed - the form is very long and rather difficult to complete especially for a person applying for the first time.

Auditors come for about two weeks a year for the main audit but you could have other auditors during the year - for example, if we received any grant from structural funds. Also you would have internal auditors.

The Finance section in conjunction with the CEO allocates all budgets to schools eg. main budget, transition year, plc, etc. Schools have to keep within their budget allocation.

Our work has now become more computerised. Once everything was written into books, minutes, part-time teachers, travel etc. The manual work is gone now but much the same work is done but on computer. The volume of work in each Department has increased greatly over the years. Bigger numbers in schools, more programmes under Adult Education eg. VTOS, Youthreach.

All in all I enjoy my work in County Kilkenny VEC and I hope to be here for another couple of years.

Teresa Buggy

Teresa Buggy taught in County Kilkenny Schools from 1961 to 2004, thirty-one years in Graignamanagh and twelve in Kilkenny City.

I was educated in the Presentation Primary and Secondary schools in Kilkenny. I did my Leaving Certificate examination at the age of sixteen, which meant I was too young to qualify for any training course, so I worked for a year in Woolworth's in High Street, and this was very good for me when I got to College, as I had holiday work there every Christmas and summer. After my year in Woolworth's, I did a year at St. Joseph's College of Domestic Science in Carrick-on-Suir, and then did the entrance exam for St. Catherine's College of Home Economics, Sion Hill in Blackrock, County Dublin.

I secured a place and spent three years there. The training course was hard going. We did Irish, Science, Cooking, Art, Laundry, Housewifery, Sociology and First Aid. The Principal was a Dominican nun and the staff were nuns or lay teachers. In first year we did Cookery and Science all through Irish. As I had not done science in school, it was all new to me. In Needlework and Laundry, "perfection" was the key word, and we strove to attain it. At night we had First Aid and Sociology lectures.

In second year we had to do teaching practice in a rural school, and I was assigned to Graignamanagh. In third year Tailoring, Upholstery and Crafts were added to the list of subjects. Teaching practice was in Dublin schools, for two full weeks, plus night classes in Dún Laoghaire.

In the college there was a conference of the St. Vincent de Paul Society and with them I visited poor families in the Blackrock area. There were also Irish speaking and English speaking Legion of Mary groups. I joined the Irish one. Late leave was granted once a month but for third years, key leave was allowed sometimes.

When I qualified, my first job was in Graignamanagh. It was a four teacher school offering Commerce, Woodwork, Rural Science and Home Economics. The Headmaster was Jerry Daly, with Brian Hunt teaching Woodwork and Sean Buckley taking Rural Science. The caretaker was Gerry Kavanagh. At that time the examinations were for the Group Certificate. The girls in the school did Commerce group and Home Economics group, and the boys did a manual group. I can honestly say that they were qualified to take up employment when they left.

Over the years the system changed and extra subjects such as French and Science were added to the curriculum, so more teachers were on the staff. Before long the Intermediate Certificate was introduced, and when they had done that the students went into the Kilkenny City School to do their Leaving Certificate. That continued until 1984 when the leaving cert was introduced to Graignamanagh.

During my time in Graignamanagh, I was assigned hours in Kilkenny City, Thomastown and Mooncoin Vocational Schools and in Mother of Fair Love School in Kilkenny. Facilities in Graignamanagh were excellent. As the school had only opened in 1954, the equipment was very good and the kitchen was a pleasure to work in.

In the beginning, night classes were part of our teaching hours, and over the years I taught night classes in Graignamanagh, Gowran, Paulstown, Inistioge, The Rower, Goresbridge, Kilkenny City and Durrow. For many years I took the seminarians from St. Kieran's College for Cookery classes. I also taught Cookery to students from SOS sheltered workshop.

In the earlier years the VEC provided a taxi which took me to these night classes. I had to bring the machines and equipment etc for the Dressmaking classes with me as the classes were held in parish halls or national schools. I remember in one of these schools, the ladies would light the open fire earlier in the evening and they took turns to bring in a few blocks of wood to keep the fire going. In Inistioge, I remember one lady who made her wedding dress and the bridesmaids' dresses. Could you see that happening today in the state-of-the-art dressmaking rooms?

One night in Gowran while the hall was being renovated we had to have the class in the sacristy of the church. It was a crafts class and the ladies were creating future heirlooms - doing beautiful tapestry work, German embroidery and cane work. The late Father Halley, the Parish Priest, came in to see us and said - "Musha Girl, wouldn't it be better to teach them how to darn a pair of socks".

Cookery classes at night were a great take, especially in the first term, as people would get to make, bake and decorate their Christmas cakes. The night classes were enjoyable even if it was hard going as the people attending them were there because they wanted to be and were interested in what they were doing. Wonderful exhibitions of dressmaking, crafts and woodwork done in the night classes were held each year.

Coming into Kilkenny City after thirty-one years in Graignamanagh was a big change, but I settled in very well and had twelve happy years there teaching home economics to all classes. My time was mostly spent in Ormonde College as that is where the home economics department is. I was in charge of a catering course which was NCVA accredited. This one year course was very well attended by students from Kilkenny, Carlow, Rathdowney and Durrow. On one afternoon a week I had transition year students from St. Kieran's College. Resulting from these classes several of the students took Home Economics as a subject for Leaving Certificate. They joined the Leaving Certificate class in the Vocational School for that subject. During my last four years teaching, I took a Leaving Certificate Home Economics class.

When I got an A post, I had less teaching hours. My assignment was Co-ordinator of the Post-Leaving Certificate courses at Ormonde College. The courses run at the time were Secretarial, Art, Childcare, Nursing Studies and Print Journalism. In the beginning these courses were accredited by the National Council for Vocational Awards, but now all these courses are examined by FETAC.

Christy McGrath

I started my working career as an apprentice in Carlow Sugar Factory. I was an apprentice fitter-turner and in my fifth year one of my workmates spotted an advertisement in the paper for metalwork teachers. He gave me the advertisement and I applied and got the call to go ahead for the first part of the examination. I got through the practical exam and there was a second part involving Irish, English, Maths, and after I got through that I had an interview and that was it. We trained in Ringsend in Dublin. It was basically a Vocational School with an adjunct onto it for training metalwork teachers. Now it was very basic training but good nonetheless. It was a two year course. There were sixteen of us on the course. The school in Ringsend had a metalwork room for the day pupils and a different room for the trainee teachers and they had a garage where we did garage work - assembling and dismantling engines. We did quite an extensive course actually in motor car engineering, or motor car mechanics. Basically when we started in the first year we were given a box with a whole lot of bits of an engine in it and we were given an engine block on a stand. At the end of the two years this engine had to be up and running - and it was. It was quite interesting. Apart from metalwork we had seventeen exams in our final year, including Irish , English, Maths, Physics, Chemistry, Mechanical Drawing, Engineering Drawing, Teaching Practice and Theory, Electricity. The practical metalwork exam was thirty hours spread over five days. The practical motor car engineering exam was four days. It was a totally different orientation from, say, the leaving cert which is basically an academic exam and ours was basically a practical exam to see if you had the skills to do the job first of all, and secondly if you had the ability to impart the skills and knowledge.

There was a core of teachers almost specifically for us. Some of them would have had other teaching hours with the day pupils but they were mainly concerned with us.

We did the Ceard Teastas Gaeilge in February, and the main exams were in June. For the Ceard Teastas we learned off several compositions, a page and a half of foolscap in each, and I don't think any of them came up but it didn't matter - we struggled through.

Castlecomer was the first place I taught - the only place I taught apart from one day a week in Kilkenny during my second year. I saw the advertisement in the paper, applied, posted the letter on my way to Dublin for a weekend and got the job without any interview. I just got word to say that I had it. I'd never been in Castlecomer in my life, despite the fact that I was only over the hill from it in Leighlinbridge. I got a loan of my brother's car and came up to see where it was, looked around, and got accommodation through Mrs. McCarthy, who was teaching in the Boys' School here. She had a sister who was friendly with my family at home and she used be down in Leighlinbridge. I asked her could she recommend a place to stay. She recommended Rothwell's and that's where I stayed until I got married.

I spent a week in the old school in the Workhouse. The school on the Kilkenny Road was a bit late being completed and I was up in the old place with Peadar Madden. I didn't fancy it. There was no metalwork room, and the conditions under which they worked there were very bad. The conditions in the new school were good. For its time it was reasonable enough. The heating was weak enough in the beginning and the equipment was basic - sufficient but very basic. It was very slow arriving. The benches in the metalwork room were around the walls, and there was a crate in the middle of the floor, with a lathe in it. That was the full extent of the equipment on my first day. The equipment kept coming up to possibly Easter, certainly Christmas. But if you were young and enthusiastic, you could make it work. After a year or so I had adequate equipment, and I'd have to say I was never really short of anything. I was lucky in the sense that the Principal, Peadar, was a practical teacher. He was a woodwork teacher and he understood that you can't teach a practical subject if you haven't the tools and the materials, so if I wanted stuff, unless it was a little bit off the wall, there was never any problem. We had a lathe, a drilling machine, a grinder and a forge. These were all power tools. We had a guillotine -that was hand operated. We had a welding set, and oxy-acetylene.

The students would have their own tools. The way the workshop was set up was - each student would have a vice, and we had tools boxes for each of the twenty vices. In the toolbox would be a set of files (usually three), a hammer, tri-square, rule, marking out tools like a scriber, a punch, and a dividers. At the end of class the boxes were checked to make sure the tools were still there. The way we operated was: "they're your tools while you're here, and when you leave, they have to be available for the next guy. So I'll check them at the end of the class and you check them at the start of the class, and if there's something not there, tell me and I'll sort it out". Surprisingly enough after years and years and years there wasn't a single tool missing. They wore out of course but for a long, long time I never remember anything being stolen. We had a maximum of twenty in the class because we only had twenty benches. If there was only one first-year class, which sometimes happened in the early days and again towards the end of the Vocational School in Castlecomer, that would usually mean the room was full. If you had two classes, one of them would be full, but the other mightn't be.

144

They were grand kids. It was all new to them. The school, of course, was new and most of them were coming in from country schools, which in most cases wouldn't have been as well set up as the new Vocational School. The subject was new to them and in general most kids took to it. Some of course didn't have the manual skills or didn't have the interest to develop the skills, but most kids liked the practical subjects, because there was a great freedom. In an ordinary classroom there's somebody at the top of the room, and he's doing something at the blackboard, and you're writing. You can't talk, or you couldn't then at any rate. I remember telling them the very first time "I don't mind you talking to your neighbour, provided you're working. I don't mind if you sing provided you're able to sing. Now very few of them took me up on it. I suppose they wouldn't sing, because there'd be a lot of slagging going on. A couple of them did, and I really wouldn't have minded because it was no problem. They had the freedom to walk around, to go to a drilling machine, to do something there, go into the store to get something. They found it relaxing, I think, after the sitting still.

Of course there was a different sort of discipline required. Safety training was part of the class - not an adjunct. Every time I introduced a new tool, machine or process, the safety aspect was part of the introduction. How to hold a file had a safety aspect. A lot of people curl their fingers under the end of the file. It's dangerous because if they bring it back too far, they skin their knuckles. General safety aspects are important - not running, not talking to someone when he's using a machine, because you might distract him. There are specific safety points to be observed with each specific machine or process. Safety was not something added on - it was simply part of the whole thing. It was all introduced on a very gradual basis. The first tool they used was a file. You learned how to hold it and use it and then as you went on the other hand tools were introduced, and then came the drilling machine, the first power tool you'd use and the same thing applied. I'd introduce the specific safety requirements for that particular machine. We got skinned knuckles but we never had a serious accident. We didn't have anything that couldn't be fixed with a plaster.

Some of the lads would have made a career in metalwork. In the early days, the openings for guys from a Vocational School would have been in apprenticeships mainly. They did the group certificate and there wasn't a step up from that, unless they went in to the Brothers in Kilkenny and moved to the secondary system. It was mainly oriented towards the trades so most of our lads would follow on into the trades - not necessarily into metalworking trades, but they all did woodwork as well, and they might end up as electricians, motor mechanics, carpenters, plumbers or whatever. If a lad can use woodworking tools, he can to an extent use metalwork tools as well. There's a basic skill in using tools.

My subject didn't lend itself to night classes very much. For two or three years I did it but there aren't too many people interested in learning how to make a square in metal or learning how to cut out a triangle or mark out something, so we were sort of pushing a large rock uphill on a slippery surface. We started off the first year with about ten or twelve and it deteriorated fairly quickly down to about four who kept coming. However we did a welding class and that was fairly successful. The welding classes were full mostly of farmers. They'd have a use for it. The class was from half seven to half nine, but fellows would ramble in at eight o'clock, or twenty past or half past and still expect their full two hours.

The first big change was in 1969 when we moved from group certificate to what was then intermediate cert. In my subject it meant that the practical end expanded slightly, but for the first time a written element was introduced. It wasn't any big problem because with a background in the trade, you'd know the stuff. Fellows came from Thomastown, actually, to do leaving certificate metalwork, and the theory part of that was pretty extensive. They came two days a week and that was fairly intensive. You didn't have much time for the pleasantries of life. There was a lot of up-skilling or a lot of reading to be done.

The two subjects that I taught always in the Vocational School were metalwork and maths. Occasionally, depending on manpower, I did a little bit of drawing. I taught English to first and second years for four or five years. I taught Irish for a while but they removed me from that to the satisfaction of all concerned.

We were twenty-five years in the Vocational School and from the early seventies there was "co-operation" with the Convent. The theory was that their students would come to us for our specific subjects and our students would go to them for French, some maths and business. The co-operation for one reason or another ended up with the convent students coming to us for science, woodwork, metalwork and drawing. We felt that we were providing a service to the convent and to an extent we were providing a stick to beat ourselves because our numbers were going down. The result was that the Community School was built. The first site that was picked was the Prince Grounds where the second soccer pitch is now, down beside the river. The Convent were mad anxious to get anywhere away from where they were and who could blame them. But the site was too small, the river was too near, and there was no way you could get buses down there. We opposed it and there was a little bit of bad feeling about that for a while. Then the site up beside the barracks came up and they built the school there.

It was a really smooth transition moving up there. We moved into a different building and there was a certain amount of nervousness, I'd say, on the part of both staffs. We knew our own little patch, and they knew their somewhat larger patch. They had a totally different system to ours in a number of ways, but we fitted in because there was a lot of goodwill on both sides. Both staffs gelled very well together. Each made allowances for the other.

All of our staff that wanted to moved up- all except Peadar Madden who had only a year to go to retirement. There were about nine of us. There were over twenty in the Convent, so there was a big staff of thirty-three or four. We never had a staff-room in the Vocational School - we had our tea in the kitchen. If we had to meet, we met in Peadar's office, but we had a fine big staff room in the new place.

It was a new experience for us - in the vocational system we had someone in Kilkenny that we knew - we knew the CEO and some of the committee members and we were dealing with local people to an extent. We knew our immediate boss, who was the CEO. He'd be out in the school and you could talk to him or ring him up. When we moved into the Community School system, immediately we were divorced from the VEC and our immediate "boss" was the Department of Education which was some unknown body up there in Dublin that nobody knew anything about. If there was a difficulty with the VEC, you could talk to someone. If you have a difficulty with the Department of Education, what do you do? For the first time as well, we had a Board of Management and we didn't quite know how that was going to operate, but I wasn't too worried about that because my wife Margaret was on it.

Peadar Madden

I was trained as a woodwork teacher. We had a fairly big workshop in Kinsale, my home town and the boss used often invite me up to give a hand doing something. I was attending the Vocational School there at the same time. He had the contract for all the joinery, windows, doors, desks and everything. He had a couple of men working with him. One day he said to me "Did you ever think of making up your mind, Peadar, to become a woodwork teacher?" I said I had thought about it. "Well, says he, you should write off to the Department. There was an ad in the paper yesterday about it." I did write off to An Roinn Oideachais at Coláiste Chaoimhghin. They told me that in about three weeks time there would be a national competition in English, Irish, Maths and Technical Drawing and all sorts of things. The result of that would stand for the filling of the course for woodwork teachers. I got back the details and I attended the examination which was held in The Sharman Crawford in Cork and it lasted for two days. 'Twas very stiff but I was able for it and I got the result a couple of weeks later stating that I had done well and that I was invited to attend a two year course in the College of Technology in Bolton Street in Dublin. I went there and enjoyed it even though it was hard as hell. There were twenty of us on the course. There were aircraft technicians, metalwork teachers and accountants on other courses. There was great attention given to English, Irish, Technical Drawing and Science of all sorts, We had to do some metalwork as well even though that strictly speaking wasn't in our department. Every Tuesday we had teaching practice. When we'd go in on Tuesday morning we were afraid to look at the board in the hall, because it would say at eleven o' clock Mr. Peadar Madden will give a talk on, say, How the County of Sligo is run by the County Council. You'd only get about two days to get it ready. We'd go down to the library to prepare it. I remember well, there was a fellow in digs with me, and it was a frequent thing for me to wake up in the middle of the night with a very strong smell of tobacco. He smoked a pipe in bed and, of course, also when he was doing his studies he smoked his pipe. On a couple of occasions I had to say "Con would you mind putting out that God damn pipe?" But it would be the same the following night, because that was the way he was comfortable preparing for the following day. We went around to other schools on teaching practice. Generally speaking it was fairly comfortable, but now and then you might be asked to speak on something for which you had no advance notice. Sometimes we had to teach Woodwork. We were usually dumped (as one of the lads used to say) at Gardiner Street for the first session.

I always had a great interest in Irish. For a couple of years I was going to the Vocational School in Kinsale, and the Headmaster, Mícheál Ó Conaill, was a teacher of Irish and he was a great man. One of his techniques was to tell us an interesting story, maybe about Finn McCool, always in English. Then he would translate it into Irish and he would put the salient points on the board and we would take that down and our job then was to write an essay for the coming week. I got into the use of Irish, and my mother, God rest her, used to say "It's good that you speak a bit of Irish in front of the lads (my brothers and sisters) and encourage them". I used do that but I had an interest in Irish and I'd put it down to the headmaster that I had. While I was on the training course, we had to attend the Coláiste Gaeilge in Carraroe, so I improved my Irish there.

I started teaching here. I applied for two jobs, one in Galway and one in County Kilkenny. I got both of them on the same day, but I said Kilkenny was nearer to Cork. I had an appointment with the Doc - Doctor Walsh - and he met me inside in his office on the Ormonde Road. He had a grand chat with me, mostly in English but a little bit in Irish now and then. He was sizing me up, I knew by him. Then says he "Did you ever hear of a place called Coon". I said no. "Well" says he, "From today on you'll be hearing a lot about it because that's where you'll be working." He drove me up one day and introduced me to the Headmaster, Phil Dunne who was a grand man, but didn't like bending the rules and regulations of the Department at all. There were four of us altogether and four classrooms.

I was living in Rothwells' in Barrack Street in Castlecomer and the weather was often wet and windy and stormy. I used get on my bike and cycle up to Coon. In the meantime Mick Walsh of Coon would send down his taxi and collect five or six students in Castlecomer to bring them up to Coon Vocational School. They passed the teacher, of course, on the way and all the windows would be wound down and there'd be a great cheer. I'd arrive in Coon, maybe twenty minutes later soaked to the skin in many cases. I said to Phil one day - we were great friends really - "Is there any chance that on the very wet mornings you'd permit me to come in the school car, And I will pay you whatever it is?"

"Well, he says there's nothing in the Department's regulations, Peadar, concerning that". He was a great man for standing by the Department. He never permitted me to go in the taxi. I persisted in getting drowned. It was quite a trip out to Coon, about six miles, and a huge climb up the Spa Hill, and when you'd get over the hill and then down to the end of the slope, you were in for another climb. I was fit then of course. I was playing rugby at that time and that helped.

We had to teach night classes as well. I taught woodwork to up to twenty people at night. One man might want to make a little table, another a jewellery box. Some only wanted to learn to draw. That was difficult because you were trying to teach

148

drawing during a noisy woodwork session. In the beginning we'd do the basic joints, halving joint, the various dovetail joints, mortise and tenon. At the end of a two hour session, each student would be expected to have one complete joint. And then in order to ensure that they weren't getting bored we would now and then move away from the joints and give them a little project to do.

I taught about two years in Coon. I was moved by Doc Walsh to Castlecomer. He said I was to get the place ready, because Castlecomer was re-opening in September. It had been closed for a number of years. That had everything to do with Canon MacNamara's attitude to vocational education. He described our school one time as a godless institution, although the curate at a later mass urged people to send their children to the technical school. It affected our attendance in the beginning. The school was in the old workhouse building. They never did it up for us - we had to do it up ourselves. The workhouse was difficult but the male teachers were great at doing whatever had to be done. For heating we had a stove in the middle of the room with a flue going right up through the ceiling and that gave us some degree of heat. The caretaker would light it in the morning.

When I re-opened the old technical school in Castlecomer in 1951, it was decided to have night classes. I got posters printed in the *Kilkenny People* office and cycled to all the outlying national schools and churches when I was finished my day's teaching, and delivered the posters. There was no extra pay for that of course and no cycle allowance either. Later, when we moved into the new school, we had night classes there and also in Moneenroe, Conahy, Clogh and Ballyragget.

It was a big change when we moved down to the Kilkenny Road. We had six grand comfortable rooms and all sorts of up-to-date equipment with twenty benches for woodwork and the same for metalwork. In the science area, they updated our equipment very much. We got a gymnasium built behind the school as well. Fair dues to Eddie Gibson, he was the man who got that. I remember going in to the office when he was CEO and he got on to the Department. "Oh, says he, before I hang up, I want to mention about this gymnasium you've been promising us for so many years". And your man was inclined to shut him down, but he says "you can shut me down if you like, but it's started anyway. We started the foundation last week". And nobody stopped us.

We had a very good heating system in the new school. We had some trouble in the beginning, but it turned out very satisfactorily. We had a good number of teachers, an increase in staff and also in numbers. People began to see that the "Tech." was going ahead. Sometimes we had a fifty-fifty divide between girls and boys, sometimes more of one or the other. A lot of them came in from the country on bikes, and later on the free transport on the buses helped our numbers. Free education made a difference as well. The group cert was our well-known, well established exam and there were some great results from it. That was a two-year course, and when the inter cert came in there were a lot of complaints. Some of our pupils were saying it was too difficult, but they adjusted to it.

Altogether, I was Principal of Castlecomer Vocational School for thirty-seven years from the re-opening in 1951 until 1988.

The following tribute to Peter Brennan, who taught for many years in Kilkenny City Vocational School, is a timely reminder of an important figure in the cultural life of Kilkenny from the 1940s to the 1960s. The collection of paintings referred to by Michael O'Dwyer was housed for many years in the school until the art gallery in Kilkenny Castle was opened.

Peter J. Brennan ANCA 1916-1995
by Michael O'Dwyer

Peter Brennan was born in Glasthule, a suburb of Dun Laoghaire in 1916. He was a student at the National College of Art in Dublin for seven years, graduating in 1939. He had won the Taylor Scholarship for sculpture a number of times at the College. After graduation, he became an art teacher at the Kilkenny City Technical School. His teaching duties were shared with Carlow VEC which he travelled to on his motorcycle.

Peter became aware that a craft based education would be more suitable for his students so he spent his holiday times in Carrigaline Pottery in County Cork making models for casting and learning the basics of throwing pots. Peter had a very big influence not only on his students in Kilkenny but on a wider public also. Evening classes were held where mature students learned pottery as well as painting. Exhibitions of his own and of his students' paintings were held in the Technical School a few times during the year.

Another artist, George Pennefeather, came to live in Kilkenny from 1940-1946. George was a native of Cork. He and his wife lived in a caravan on the Freshford Road. The Pennefeathers were attracted by the old streets, lanes and fine stone buildings of Kilkenny. Peter and George worked together in Kilkenny, putting on exhibitions of their own work and also the work of other well-known Irish artists. The Kilkenny Art Gallery Society was founded in 1943 and by the time George left Kilkenny in 1946, the basis of a Municipal collection had already been formed. The *Kilkenny People* newspaper gave publicity to these exhibitions. In October 1943 the paper reported that there were thirty paintings on exhibition and members of the public purchased many of them.

In 1944 Peter made plans with art dealer Victor Waddington to set up a studio for the making of pottery. An old grain store in the Bull Ring in Parliament Street (opposite Rothe House) became the Ring Ceramic Studios in 1945. Originally all the production was sold through the Waddington Galleries in Dublin. All manner of pottery making was used to produce a hard, fired earthenware sometimes in white clay from Cahir in County Tipperary and in red clay from Carlow. All were glazed with commercial glazes. In October 1945 an exhibition of Peter Brennan's pottery and that of some of his pupils was held in the window of E.J. Delehanty's shop in High Street.

John ffrench came to work with Peter Brennan in the Ring Pottery in Kilkenny in 1956. Together they turned out an interesting range of Irish ceramics. An exhibition of almost two hundred and fifty items including vases, bowls and jars was held at Switzers, Grafton Street, Dublin. Two thousand tankards were manufactured by Peter for the first Kilkenny Beer Festival. John ffrench did not remain in Kilkenny. Peter also left in the late 1960's. Both became very successful potters.

When we see the later developments such as the Kilkenny Workshops and the thriving craft scene in and around the county it can be appreciated that Peter Brennan did much to initiate the growth of this movement. The enlightened outlook of the VEC in appointing such an enterprising and talented artist to the staff of the City Technical School should be recognised and appreciated.

A minute for December 1943 notes Peter's request for £90 to buy secondhand pottery equipment and by the following April permission to spend £60 had been agreed. It should be noted that this was a considerable amount of money at the time, and the sourcing of the equipment cannot have been easy during the Second World War. It points up Peter Brennan's determination, and the readiness of Dr. Walsh as CEO and of the committee to advance the arts.

Miss Margaret Walsh

Dunnamaggin Vocational School was one of three one-teacher Vocational Schools in County Kilkenny. The following account of the school and its only teacher, Miss Margaret Walsh was written by Seán Ó Coistealbha and is taken from 'Dunnamaggin, The History of Saint Leonard's National School'. Edited by Michael O'Dwyer. Published by Dunnamaggin Board of Management 2005.

Among the earliest Vocational Schools opened in County Kilkenny was the Dunnamaggin school in 1933. In its 34 years of existence the school made a very significant contribution to education in Dunnamaggin and neighbouring parishes.

The VEC meeting of 12th December 1932 reported that Fr. O'Keeffe P.P. had a renovated room available to accommodate a Domestic Economy Course. (The old National School building in Baurscuab was vacated in 1929 and no doubt the Parish Priest was anxious to put the building to good use). On the 13th November 1933, the minutes relate that the Parish Priest had converted the old schoolroom into "a fine room suitable for Vocational Education Courses". The school had been re-floored, new windows inserted, wainscoting fixed, the roof newly ceiled inside, the outer walls dashed and chutes fixed. The minutes further relate, "Seventeen girl students are in regular attendance 22 hours per week and are determined to attend the whole year's course". The committee's permission was sought to purchase a range, an iron water container and to erect a shed of corrugated iron sheets and wood. There was a proposal also to distemper the inside walls and paint the woodwork. A rent of £10 per annum had been agreed between Fr. O'Keeffe and the CEO.

In 1933 Miss Margaret Walsh was appointed as a domestic economy teacher to the newly opened school. She became the school's only full time teacher and played a central role in the story of the school. She was born in Ahenny, County Tipperary in 1901. The eldest of a large family, Miss Walsh graduated from Aberystwyth University, Wales. Following her return to Ireland, it seems that she spent a short time teaching in Ramsgrange, County Wexford and in County Louth.

The school enrolled girls between the ages of 14 to 16. The number of years spent by students in the school varied from one to three years but for many years it operated on the basis of a two year cycle. To appreciate the importance of the school to the locality, one must remember that for financial reasons, second level education was beyond the reach of the majority of the Irish population. The advent of the vocational schools was an attempt to widen the educational opportunities to the public. In addition, some parents felt that the emphasis on the practical subjects in the Vocational Schools was more suited to the needs of their children. The Dunnamaggin school attracted pupils from Windgap, Hugginstown, Knocktopher, Thomastown and of course from Dunnamaggin Parish. For many years its annual average enrolment was approximately 20 pupils.

The emphasis was on domestic science ie. cookery, needlework, crafts, personal hygiene and housekeeping. Pupils competed in county competitions e.g. cookery and had some notable successes One of the first assignments of the new student was to make an apron, which also served, as a school uniform. Past pupils vividly recall Miss Walsh's insistence on the highest standard of cleanliness and hygiene, though, in the absence of running water, the school relied on an outside pump. Cleaning and scrubbing of tables and furnishings and cooking the dinner became part of the daily routine. Pupils paid for foodstuffs and clothing materials used in class, though costs were kept to a minimum.

The school curriculum was not restricted to Domestic Science Subjects. English, Irish and History were also taught. Fr. Reidy and later Fr. Raftice took religion classes twice a week and the pupils also sat for exams in Religion. Miss Walsh taught most of the subjects but Irish was taught by Mr. Bric from Callan for a time. The pupils took the Group Certificate and the results and inspectors' reports are a testament to the quality of the training the pupils received. On completion of their education in Dunnamaggin, some pupils received scholarships to Ramsgrange School, County Wexford. This school provided training in poultry and farm household management i.e. training in tasks that were seen as part of the work of the farming housewife.

Some of the girls competed in the County Sports and camogie was played in a field at the back of the Baurscuab school. However, Miss Walsh's practical strategy for compensating for the lack of proper heating in the school might not meet with the unanimous approval of today's teenagers! On cold winter mornings a brisk march in the school vicinity was organised and supervised by Miss Walsh, though many pupils did not lack for physical exercise as they cycled considerable distances to school.

A timber prefab/chalet was built about 1959 in Baurscuab. This building became known as the "O'Keeffe Centre": named after Canon Edward O'Keeffe, Parish Priest of Dunnamaggin 1922-1967. The old School at Baurscuab was demolished and the pupils moved into the new building. However the new Vocational School in Ballyhale, which opened in 1959, began to affect enrolment in Dunnamaggin. Ballyhale's facilities and range of teaching staff ensured that it became the popular Vocational School in the area. When the Dunnamaggin School closed in 1967, Miss Walsh had taught in the school for its entire lifespan of 34 years. She was in her ninetieth year when she died in   1990.

Reflecting on their years in Dunnamaggin Vocational School, past pupils acknowledge the quality of the education they received. "Anything Miss Walsh taught, you remembered", is a comment frequently heard from them. There was a strict code of behaviour. Pupils left the school with a thorough training in household management, a sound education and an appreciation of Miss Walsh's singleminded dedication to duty.

References

1 Kilkenny Journal, 14/05/1902 and 22/9/02

2 Third Annual Report of the County Kilkenny Joint Technical Instruction Committee, (Session 1907 - 1908), Kilkenny 1909

3 A New Dictionary Of Irish History From 1800, D.J. Hickey and J.E. Doherty, Dublin, 2003, p. 318

4 Addendum to the minutes of the meeting held 14th December 1931. This is a printed account of a meeting with John Marcus O'Sullivan, Minister of Education. It is pasted into the minute book of Kilkenny Vocational Committee for that year. The report was presented by V. Rev. Canon Staunton, president of St. Kieran's College, and later Bishop of Ferns.

5 Irish Educational Documents, ¡ine Hyland and Kenneth Milne, Dublin 1992. Page 3 et seq.

6 Minute Book 9/6/'19, 16/06/'19, 14/07/'19 , 03/09/'19, 13/10/'19, 10/11/'19, 8/12/'19, and Jim Maher, lecture given at Rothe House, April 2006

7 The Irish Republic, Macardle, Dublin, 1951, p. 325

8 Minutes 10/5/'20

9 Minutes 25/10/'20, 14/03/'21

10 Minutes 13/2/'22 and 09/5/'22

11 Idem.

12 Minutes 14/5/'23

13 Minutes 7/8/'23

14 Minutes, 8/10/'23, 13/10/'23, 10/11/'23

15 Minutes, 21/7/'24

16 Minutes 13/12/'26

17 Minutes 14/12/'26, Kilkenny People, 15/11/'24

18 JTIC minutes 17/5/'26 and 14/6/'26

19 Irish Educational Documents, ¡ine Hyland and Kenneth Milne, Dublin 1992. Page 3 et seq.

20 Minute Book of County Kilkenny VEC , 10/10/'32, 11/6/'34, 10/9/'34

21 Minute Book 13/11/'33 and Kilkenny Journal 18/11/'33

22 Minute Book 11/6/'34

23 Minute Book 17/9/'34

24 Minute Book 17/1/'38

25 Minute Book, 23/1/'35, 11/2/'35, 11/3/'35, 8/4/'35, 11/6/'35, 14/8/'35, 14/11/'35, 12/10/'35, 23/12/'36

26 Minutes 23/3/'39

27 Minutes 17/4/'39,12/6/'39, 10/7/'39, 18/7/'39

28 Kilkenny People 13/1/1940

29 Minutes 22/9/58, 9/2/57

30 Irish Educational Documents, Vol II, page 216

31 Irish Educational Documents, Vol. II, p. 221, 222

32 Minutes 1/12/'30, 12/1/'31, 13/4/31

33 Minutes 14/3/'31, 8/6/'31,11/1/'32, and insert opposite minute of Inaugural Meeting 3/11/'30

34 Minutes 12/1/'31, 9/3/'31, 8/2/'32, 14/3/32, 11/7/'32, 14/11/'32, 12/12/'32

35 St. Leonard's N.S. Dunnamaggin, Appendix 9/quoting minutes 13/11/'33

36 Minutes 9/1/'33, 13/1/'33, 13/2/'33, 8/5/'33, 9/10/'33

37 Information supplied by Mr. Jim Cooke, who is engaged in preparing a history of the I.V.E.A.

38 Minutes 12/2/'34, 11/6/'34

39 Minutes 12/3/'34, 14/5/'34, 10/9/'34, 8/10/'34

40 Minutes 14/1/'35, 23/1/'35, 11/3/'35, 13/5/'35, 1/6/'35, 5/7/'35, 16/8/'35, 11/11/'35

41 Minutes 20/1/'36, 10/2/'36, 9/3/'36

42 Minutes 9/5/'38 and 10/10/'38

43 Minutes 16/1/'39

44 Minutes 3/4/'40

45 Minutes 8/2/'37, 10/5/'37, 28/7/'37, 11/10/'37, 17/1/'38, 14/2/'38, 14/3/'38, 13/6/'38, 12/12/'38, 5/5/'39, 12/6/'39.

46 Minutes 18/9/'39, 5/11/41, 13/10/43

47 Minutes 12/3/'45, 11/3/'46 and 11/11/'46

48 Minutes, 9/1/'41, 3/12/'41

49 Minutes, 5/10/'42, 10/11/'43, 13/3/'44, 5/5/'44, 12/6/'44, 10/7/'44, 9/10/'44, 12/2/'45

50 Minutes 7/5/'41 and 7/6/'43

51 Minutes 13/1/'43

52 Minutes 4/2/'42, 1/4/'42, 11/11/'42

53 Minutes 11/11/'42 and 5/7/'43

54 Minutes 3/12/'41 and 4/2/'42

55 Minutes 14/7/'42, 15/1/'45, 12/3/'45

56 Minutes 6/12/'43 and 10/7/'44

57 Minutes 14/1/'46 and 14/10/'46

58 Minutes 10/2/'47, 10/11/'47, 19/1/'48, 7/2/'48, 8/3/'48

59 Minutes 14/6/'48,11/10/'48, 21/2/'49, 14/11/'49, 16/1/'50, ?/2/'50, 8/5/'50

60 Minutes 12/3/'51, 9/4/'51, 8/10/'51, 9/6/'52

61 Minutes 14/11/'49, 16/1/'50, 8/5/'50, 7/7/'50, 21/7/'50, 16/10/'50, 12/2/'51, 9/4/'51, 13/7/'53, 12/10/'53

62 Minutes 10/2/'47, 9/5/'49, 10/11/'50, 11/12/'50, 4/6/'51

63 Minutes 12/4/'48, 11/10/'48, 21/2/'49, 21/7/'50, 16/10/'50, 11/10/'50, 11/12/'50, 9/4/'51, 9/7/'51

64 Minutes 14/1/'52, 10/3/'52, 10/11/'52, 24/11/'52, 9/3/'53, 8/6/'53

65 Minutes 11/5/'53, 12/6/54, 20/9/'54,

66 Minutes 12/3/'51, 8/10/'51, 11/2/'52,10/11/'52, 9/3/'53, 9/11/'53

67 Minutes 3/4/'50, 7/7/'50, 16/10/'50, 15/1/'51, 12/3/'51, 9/7/'51, 8/10/'51, 9/6/'52, 14/7/'52, 13/10/'52, 9/2/'53, 9/3/'53, 11/5/'53, 10/5/'54, 19/7/'54, 14/2/'55

68 Minutes 10/10/'49, 14/11/'49, 9/3/'53, 13/7/'53, 12/10/'53, 12/6/54, 8/11/'54

69 Minutes 8/2/'54

70 Minutes 13/12/'48, 14/3/'49, 4/6/'51, 10/3/'52, 8/4/'52, 9/6/'52, 14/7/'52, 13/10/'52, 10/1/'55, 14/11/'55, 11/6/'56, 20/6/'56, 9/7/'56, 17/7/'56, 10/12/'56, 11/3/'57,

71 Minutes 11/3/'57, 14/10'57

72 Minutes 14/10/'57, 10/2/'58, 10/3/'58, 9/6/'58, 13/10/'58, 12/1/'59, 17/5/'59, 7/8/'59, 11/4/60

73 Minutes 14/2/55, 14/3/55

74 Minutes 14/11/55, 14/5/56, 11/11/57, 2/6/59, 17/7/59

75 Minutes 12/5/58, 10/11/58, 9/2/59, 9/3/59, 2/6/59, 17/7/59

76 Minutes 14/12/59, 18/1/60, 24/3/60, 14/7/60, 3/10/60, 14/11/60, 1/12/60, 31/7/61, 9/10/61, 8/1/62, 9/4/62, 17/7/62

77 Minutes 8/1/62, 12/2/62, 20/2/62, 9/4/62, 17/7/62

78 Minutes 12/3/62, 9/4/62,

79 Minutes 8/4/63, 21/5/63, 10/6, 8/7/63

80 Minutes 21/5/63 and 10/5/65

81 Minutes 11/3/63

82 Minutes 23/7/63

83 Minutes 12/12/63, 24/1/64, 24/3/64, 8/6/64, 12/10/64, 20/10/64, 14/8/65, 13/9/65, 8/11/65

84 Letter quoted in Irish Educational Documents, Part II, ¡ine Hyland and Kenneth Milne, Dublin 1992

85 Minutes 24/1/66, 14/2/66, inserts in minute book 21/2/66, 24/3/66

86 Minutes 12/4/48, 9/5/49, 10/11/58, 13/6/60

87 Minutes 10/7/61

88 Minutes 8/3/48, 14/6/48, 9/2/53

89 The Kilkenny Debates, Proinsias " Drisceoil, in Unfinished Ireland, Ed. Chris Agee, Belfast 2003, Minutes 11/2/57

90 Minutes 13/1/47, 10/2/47, 14/4/47, 14/7/47

91 Minutes 11/09/33, 5/7/33, 16/8/33, 10/3/47, 14/4/47, 7/2/48, 10/9/62

92 Minutes 16/5/66, 13/6/66, 11/7/66, 6/9/66

93 Minutes 13/2/67

94 Minutes 11/7/66, 10/10/66, 13/2/67, 8/5/67, 12/6/67, 9/10/67,16/11/67, 30/9/68, 15/4/69, 14/7/69, 14/12/70, 21/9/712, 11/10/71, 13/12/71, 19/9/72, 13/11/72

95 Minutes 6/9/66, 1010/66, 9/1/67, 13/2/67, 10/4/67, 12/6/67, 31/7/67

96 Minutes 10/4/67, 31/7/67, 4/8/67

97 Minutes 1/9/67, 11/9/67, 9/10/67

98 Minutes 16/11/67

99 Minutes 16/11/67, 1/12/67, 10/6/68, 9/9/68, 30/9/68, 14/10/68, 10/2/69, 12/5/69, 10/11/69, 12/1/70, 18/6/70, 13/7/70, 4/9/70, 12/10/70

100 Minutes 11/7/66, 6/9/66, 8/5/67, 16/11/67, 5/1/68, 8/7/68, 14/7/69, 14/9/70

101 Minutes 31/7/67, 4/8/67

102 Minutes 10/11/69, 9/3/70, 11/1/71

103 Minutes 12/10/70, 9/11/70, 11/1/71, 12/7/71, 19/9/72

104 Minutes 10/2/69, 10/3/69, 31/3/69

105 Minutes 14/7/69,

106 Minutes 9/12/69, 11/5/70, 20/4/71, 14/6/71

107 Minutes 13/7/70, 4/9/70

108 Minutes 14/6/71, 17/4/72, 6/7/72

109 Minutes 14/6/71, 14/2/72, 10/4/72, 17/4/72, 8/5/72, 28/7/72, 12/3/73

110 Minutes 11/5/72, 12/3/73

111 Minutes 7/5/73, 12/6/73, 29/6/73, 10/9/73, 11/2/74, 13/5/74, 8/7/74

112 Minutes 29/6/73, 16/7/73, 10/9/73, 19/9/73, 3/12/73, 23/1/74

113 Minutes 11/2/74, 6/5/74, 8/7/74, 19/9/74, 13/1/75

114 Minutes 9/12/74, 10/2/75, 7/4/75, 9/12/75, 19/1/76, 17/2/76, 8/3/76, 11/6/76, 19/7/76, 13/9/76, 4/10/76, 14/12/76, 18/1/77, 14/2/77, 4/4/77, 2/5/77, 4/7/77, 13/9/77, 3/10/77

115 Minutes 13/2/78, 14/3/78, 18/4/78

116 Minutes 17/10/78, 9/11/78, 13/3/79, 8/5/79, 1/6/79, 2/7/79, 23/7/79, 3/9/79, 2/10/79, 5/11/79, 3/12/79

117 Minutes 16/4/80, 5/5/80, 17/7/80, 9/9/80, 5/1/81, 19/3/81, 6/4/81

118 Minutes 6/7/81, 5/9/81, 2/11/81, 3/5/82, 11/1/83, 2/7/84, 11/9/84

119 15/9/81, 2/11/81

120 Kilkenny People newspaper, October 26, 1984

121 Minutes 12/5/74, 14/10/74, 12/5/75, 9/12/75, 8/3/76, 3/5/76, 13/9/76, 10/11/76, 13/9/76, 10/11/76, 13/9/77, 3/10/77, 7/11/77, 12/12/77, 14/3/78, 11/7/78, 12/9/78, 17/10/78, 12/12/78, 1/6/79, 4/2/80, 4/3/80, 16/4/80, 10/6/80, 5/1/81

122 Minutes 8/5/72, 28/6/72, 12/2/73, 10/4/73, 7/5/73, 11/2/74

123 Minutes 10/6/74, 3/5/76, 19/7/76, 14/12/76, 14/3/77, 4/4/77

124 Minutes 3/5/76, 11/6/76, 14/8/78, 16/5/78, 6/6/78, 11/7/78, 9/11/78, 9/01/78, 2/4/79, 5/11/79, 16/4/80, 10/6/80, 9/9/80, 5/1/81, 2/2/81

125 Irish Educational Documents Volume II, P. 242 - 246, ¡ine Hyland and Kenneth Milne, Dublin 1992

126 Minutes 10/6/74, 8/7/74, 19/9/74, 13/1/75, 10/2/75, 7/4/75, 9/12/75, 19/1/76, 17/2/76, 8/3/76

127 Minutes 3/5/76, 10/11/76

128 Minutes 18/4/78, 9/5/78, 6/6/78, 10/10/78, 12/12/78

129 Minutes 7/11/77, 22/11/77, 20/12/77,16/1/78, 27/2/78, 14/3/78

130 Minutes 5/11/79, 19/5/81, 2/6/81, 15/9/81, 2/11/81, 10/3/82, 8/12/86, 9/3/87, 11/5/87, 15/11/88, 8/5/89, 11/5/90, 19/7/91, 10/2/92, 14/9/92 and scrapbook of cuttings kept in Adult Education Office, Ormonde Road, Kilkenny

131 Minutes 8/5/72, 10/9/73, 11/2/74, 11/11/74, 9/12/74, 16/9/75, 9/12/75, 13/9/76, 14/2/77, 9/12/80

132 Minutes: outdoor pursuits - 14/3/77, 2/5/77, 13/9/77, 3/10/77, 18/4/78, 4/3/80; hostel -16/4/80, 6/10/80

133 Minutes 3/12/79, 4/2/80

134 Minutes 18/9/39, 9/9/42, 5/10/42, 11/11/42, 11/12/42, 10/2/47, 14/4/47, 11/11/66, 4/3/81, 19/3/81, 6/7/81, 15/9/81

135 Minutes 18/2/81, 6/4/81, 19/5/81, 2/6/81, 6/6/81, 15/9/81, 15/12/81

136 The Kilkenny People, Friday April 9, 1982

137 The Kilkenny People, Friday October 25, 1985

138 Minutes 2/6/81, 6/6/81, 13/10/81, 7/12/81

139 Minutes 7/12/81, 3/5/82, 14/5/82, 8/6/82, 5/7/82

140 Minutes 5/7/82, 14/9/82, 9/11/82, 6/12/82

141 Minutes 7/12/81, 14/9/82, 9/11/82, 7/2/83, 12/4/83, 10/5/83, 14/6/83, 12/7/83, 13/9/83, 10/1/84, 8/3/84, 13/3/84, 7/5/84, 12/6/84, 2/7/84, 23/10/84, 18/9/86

142 Minutes: 8/6/82, 14/9/82, 9/11/82, 10/5/83, 13/9/83, 3/10/83, 14/2/84, 12/6/84, 10/2/86, 12/5/86

143 Minutes 7/5/84, 9/9/85, 10/2/86, 18/9/86

144 Minutes 19/5/81, 6/6/81, 13/10/81, 7/12/81, 14/9/82, 9/11/82, 6/12/82, 11/1/83, 7/2/83, 12/7/83, 12/2/84, 13/3/84, 7/5/84, 19/6/84, 2/7/84, 11/12/84, 4/2/85, 4/3/85, 1/4/85, 11/6/85, 9/9/85, 10/2/86, 10/3/86, 14/4/86, 12/5/86, 18/9/86, 13/10/86, 8/12/86

145 Minutes: 19/5/81, 6/6/81, 9/2/82, 5/4/82, 5/7/82, 4/10/82, 6/12/82, 25/1/83, 7/2/83, 8/3/83, 12/4/83, 10/5/83, 14/6/83, 13/9/83, 3/10/83, 5/12/83

146 Minutes: 12/6/84, 2/7/84, 11/9/84, 23/10/84, 11/12/84

147 Minutes: 8/1/85, 4/2/85, 4/3/85, 22/7/85, 9/9/85, 14/10/85, 13/1/86, 10/3/86, 14/4/86, 12/5/86, 9/6/86, 14/7/86, 18/9/86, 13/10/86, 3/11/86, 18/12/86

148 Minutes: 13/4/87, 11/5/87, 16/6/87, 13/7/87

149 Minutes 12/10/87, 2/11/87, 12/11/87, 14/12/87

150 Minutes: 8/2/88, 14/3/88, 11/4/88, 9/5/88, 13/6/88, 14/7/88, 13/9/88, 15/11/88

151 Minutes: 12/12/88, 9/1/89, 13/3/89, 8/5/89, 18/7/89, 12/9/89, 9/10/89,

152 Minutes: 9/4/90, 5/6/90, 9/7/90, 9/10/90, 9/11/90, 13/12/90, 12/3/91

153 Minutes: 12/1/87, 9/3/87, 13/4/87, 11/5/87, 14/3/88, 9/1/89, 13/2/89, 13/3/89, 10/4/89, 8/5/89, 20/6/89, 12/9/89, 9/10/89, 9/7/90, 19/7/91

154 Minutes: 13/4/87, 16/6/87, 11/4/88, 13/6/88, 15/11/88, 12/12/88, 9/1/89, 13/2/89, 20/6/89, 12/9/89, 5/3/90, 14/9/90, 9/11/90, 13/12/90, 12/3/91, 19/7/91

155 Minutes 23/9/91, 22/10/91, 22/11/91, 13/12/91, 10/2/92, 13/4/92, 4/5/92, 13/7/92, 8/6/92, 14/9/92, 12/10/92, 19/5/93, 22/7/93, 20/9/93, 12/12/94, 14/2/94, 14/2/94, 10/3/95

156 Kilkenny People Feb 4, 1994

157 Minutes: 11/5/87, 16/6/87, 14/9/87, 11/10/88, 15/11/88, 12/12/88, 9/1/89, 13/2/89, 8/5/89, 9/10/89, 9/2/90, 14/9/90, 9/10/90, 9/11/90, 13/12/90,

158 Minutes 23/9/91, 22/10/91, 22/11/91, 13/12/91, 8/1/92, 4/5/92, 14/9/92, 9/11/92, 10/12/92, 1/1/93, 8/2/93, 8/3/93, 8/4/93, 13/12/93, 13/6/94, 11/9/94, 10/3/95

159 Kilkenny People, 7th June 1996

160 Minutes 13/12/91, 8/1/92, 10/2/92, 13/4/92, 4/5/92, 8/6/92, 13/7/92

161 Minutes 14/9/92, 10/12/92, 1/1/93, 11/10/93, 8/11/93, 10/1/94

162 Minutes 11/3/94, 13/6/94, 19/90/94, 10/10/94, 12/12/94, 13/2/95, 10/3/95, 5/5/95, 20/7/95, 11/9/95, 10/11/95, 11/12/95

163 Minutes 20/6/89, 9/10/89, 13/12/89, 16/4/91, 23/9/91, 22/10/91, 13/4/92

164 Minutes 23/9/91, 22/10/91, 22/11/91, 8/1/92, 10/2/92, 13/4/92, 4/5/92

165 Minutes 2/3/92, 13/4/92, 13/7/92, 1/1/93, 8/2/93, 8/3/93, 8/4/93, 8/6/93, 22/7/93, 20/9/93, 11/10/93, 13/12/93, 14/2/94, 6/5/94, 19/7/94

166 Minutes 11/11/94, 12/12/94, 13/2/95, 12/6/95, 20/7/95, 11/9/95, 9/10/95, 20/10/95

167 Minutes 10/11/95, 11/12/95

168 Minutes 16/1/96, 8/3/96, 12/4/96, 23/7/96

169 Minutes 25/9/96, 14/10/96, 15/11/96, 9/12/96, 13/1/97, 9/2/98, 7/9/98

170 Minutes 9/12/96, 13/1/97, 14/2/97, 14/4/97, 12/5/97, 25/7/97, 8/9/97

171 Minutes 15/11/96, 9/12/96, 14/2/97, 10/3/97, 14/4/97, 9/6/97, 16/12/97

172 Minutes 9/2/98, 7/9/98, 12/10/98, 16/12/98, 19/1/99, 12/4/99, 14/6/99, 11/10/99

173 Minutes 16/1/96, 12/2/96, 8/3/96, 12/4/96, 23/7/96, 9/12/96, 13/1/97, 14/2/97, 21/4/97, 7/9/98, 8/11/99, 14/2/2000, 9/10/00

174 Minutes 15/11/96, 9/12/96, 13/1/97, 14/2/97, 10/3/97, 14/4/97, 25/7/97, 8/9/97, 8/3/97, 8/3/99, 14/6/99, 11/10/99, 8/11/99, 13/2/2000, 13/11/00

175 The Kilkenny People May 2005

176 Minutes 14/10/96, 10/3/97, 9/6/97, 25/7/97, 15/10/97, 11/11/97, 16/12/97, 23/3/98, 8/6/98

177 Minutes 7/9/98, 9/11/98, 16/12/98, 19/1/99, 4/2/99, 8/3/99

178 Minutes: 12/4/99, 14/6/99, 8/11/99, 10/1/00, 14/2/00, 8/5/00

179 Minutes: 12/6/00, 4/9/00, 13/11/00, 11/12/00, 9/4/01, 14/5/01, 11/6/01, 10/9/01, 11/10/01, 12/11/01

157

Committee Members 2004-2009
Back Row (from left:) Cllr. Matt Doran, Cllr. William Ireland, Cllr. Pat Crotty, Mr. Tony Patterson, Mr. Sean Treacy, Mr. Rodger Curran, Chief Executive Officer, Mons. Michael Ryan, Mr. Gerard Dowling, Cllr. Pat O'Neill, Ms. Joan Murphy, Cllr. Dixie Doyle, Cllr. Maurice Shortall.
Front Row (from left:) Ms. Peg Barry, Cllr. Marie Fitzpatrick, Cllr. Mary Hilda Cavanagh, Cllr. Richard Dowling, Chairperson, Cllr. Ann Phelan, Cllr. Cora Long, Ms. Eleanor Parks, Rev. Canon Barbara Fryday.

County Kilkenny Vocational Education Committee Administrative Staff, Seville Lodge 2007
Back Row (from left:) Ms. Bernadette Hughes, Ms. Rita Neary, Mr. Martin Ryan, Ms. Catherine Barron, Ms. Triona Delaney, Mr. Colin Hamliton, Ms. Teresa Connolly, Ms. Christine Mc Grath, Ms. Mary Walton, Ms. Olive Morrissey, Ms. Marion Croke.
Front Row (from left:) Ms. Catriona Brennan, Ms. Ann Lennon, Ms. Anne Coonan, Mr. Rodger Curran (Chief Executive Officer), Ms. Fidelma Morton, Ms. Gillian Rea, Ms. Margo Roche.

CHAPTER 14

County Kilkenny Vocational Education Committee in the Modern Era

Over the years County Kilkenny VEC has continually evolved to meet the changing education needs of young people and adults. As a statutory local education authority County Kilkenny Vocational Education Committee continues to operate under the terms of the original Vocational Education Act 1930 and its subsequent amendments, most notably the VEC Amendment Act 2001 which substantially modernised the running of the VEC. The VEC is governed by a committee of elected members and run by a management team. There are 19 democratically elected VEC members, nine members are elected by the local authority and a further two by the Kilkenny Borough Council. There are two elected parents and two elected staff representatives as well as a further four sectoral interest representatives. The Management Team of the VEC led by the Chief Executive Officer comprises of an Education Team and an Administration Team each of whom has responsibility for the day-to-day operation of the organisation. Kilkenny VEC is now the largest provider of learning opportunities for young people and adults in the county.

Today, County Kilkenny VEC takes a more planned, strategic approach to the provision of its education services and published its first Education Plan in 2006. The Plan entitled *Facilitating Quality Teaching and Learning* sets out a vision and a framework for the development and enhancement of the VEC education and support services in the county. The plan is underpinned by a strategy which promotes the principles of integration and cohesion focusing on the overall development of the organisation and providing for the cross-cutting needs of the service in terms of quality enhancement and policy development. These are reflected in the culture of the organisation and give broader meaning to our day-to-day educational work. The work of County Kilkenny VEC is set within the context of its overarching vision and mission statements and is grounded in its core organisational values and principles.

VISION

The vision of County Kilkenny VEC is to be a listening and learning organisation which is vibrant, dynamic and responsive.

MISSION

The mission of County Kilkenny VEC is to be a key provider of quality, inclusive education opportunities and support services that enable young people and adults to reach their full potential and contribute in a positive and meaningful way to society.

ORGANISATIONAL VALUES AND PRINCIPLES

- To place the learner at the centre of all our work
- To provide quality services
- To promote quality teaching and learning
- To engage in building positive, respectful relationships
- To value and respect all staff and learners
- To promote a culture of openness and fairness
- To promote inclusiveness and embrace diversity
- To be responsive in our approach and promote innovation and partnership
- To be an integral part of the local community.

Kilkenny VEC provides a comprehensive range of quality education programmes and supports designed to meet the needs of young people and adults throughout the county. Over the years it has developed a range of educational provision to address the diverse and ever changing demands of learners. Today, County Kilkenny VEC runs eight second level schools, including an all Irish school, an extensive adult education service and a range of post-leaving certificate courses. It is involved in many partnership activities at local level and provides a range of educational supports to enhance the quality of its education programmes.

County Kilkenny VEC supports young people and adult learners through its four main areas of activity.

Second Level Education

Abbey Community College, Ferrybank
Coláiste Cois Siúire, Mooncoin
Cólaiste Mhuire, Johnstown
Coláiste Pobail Osraí, Kilkenny City
Duiske College, Graiguenamanagh
Grennan College, Thomastown
Kilkenny City Vocational School
Scoil Aireagail, Ballyhale

Partnership Activities

Castlecomer District Community Development
Network (CDCD)
County Development Board
Kilkenny County Childcare Committee
Kilkenny Community Action Network (KCAN)
Kilkenny Homeless Forum
Kilkenny Recreation and Sports Partnership
School Completion Programme
Social Inclusion Measures Group
RAPID
Youth Co-ordination Committee

County Kilkenny VEC

Education Services

Educational Support Services

Arts Education
Building and Development Programme
Budgetary and Financial Management
Corporate Services
Customer Services
Grants/Scholarships
Recruitment and Personnel Services
School Transport (Co-ordination)
Staff Support
Staff Training and Development
Youth Work Activities

Adult Education Service

Adult Guidance Service
Adult Literacy
Back to Education Initiative (BTEI)
Community Education
Co-operation Activities
Evening Courses/Part-time Courses
Interagency Projects
Vocational Training Opportunities (VTOS)
Youthreach

Second Level Education

County Kilkenny VEC now has responsibility for eight second-level schools. These schools are co-educational, non-denominational and non-selective at entry. They are:

- Abbey Community College, Ferrybank
- Coláiste Cois Siúire, Mooncoin
- Coláiste Mhuire, Johnstown
- Coláiste Pobail Osraí, Cill Chainnigh
- Duiske College, Graiguenamanagh
- Grennan College, Thomastown
- Kilkenny City Vocational School, Kilkenny
- Scoil Aireagail, Ballyhale

The aim of the second level schools is to provide a quality, inclusive, holistic education that will enable each individual to reach his/her full potential so that each learner may lead a fulfilling life and contribute to the development of society. The school communities strive to achieve these aims with professional, collaborative staff by offering:

- an extensive curriculum, catering for the spiritual, moral, intellectual, physical, social, personal and aesthetic development of learners
- a co-curricular education programme
- a pastoral care programme

All schools offer the Junior Certificate and Leaving Certificate Programmes and a range of Transition Year, Leaving Certificate Applied, Leaving Certificate Vocational Programme and Post-Leaving Certificate Programmes as well as an Adult Education Programme.

The schools of County Kilkenny VEC were founded as a response to local educational need and this tradition of meeting the needs of learners is ever present in the schools. The innovation and management of change is clear from the range of programmes on offer.

Partnership is also a key concept in the development of our schools and is apparent in our active Student Councils and Parent Associations. We also work in partnership with other stakeholders, particularly in the religious, youth, sport, community development and business sectors, to enhance the educational experiences of our students.

Adult Education Service

County Kilkenny VEC has a long history and tradition in the provision of adult education programmes.Through its Adult Education Service it strives to continually develop and provide a wide range of quality learning opportunities for adults throughout Kilkenny city and county. The aim of the service is to encourage, enable and support adults who wish to return to education to avail of the educational opportunities that best suit their needs.

The VEC Adult Education Service provides the following range of learning opportunities and supports:-

Adult Guidance Service
This service established in 2002 provides individuals and groups who return to education with information and guidance to assist them in making the choices which suit them best. The service strives to provide adults with access to up to date information and supports them in making informed decisions for their future learning and/or career progression.

Adult Literacy Scheme
Word Aid, Co. Kilkenny VEC Adult Literacy Scheme provides help on a confidential basis for those experiencing difficulties with reading, writing, spelling, numeracy, form-filling, letter writing and other associated tasks. Tuition is offered on a one-to-one and small group basis and the service is free of charge. Increased investment in recent years has enabled provision to be expanded so that literacy classes are now available at a network of centres throughout the county.

Back to Education Initiative (BTEI)
This initiative was introduced in 2002 and provides part-time learning opportunities for young people and adults who wish to combine a return to learning with family, work and other responsibilities. The Back to Education Initiative allows people to continue learning, obtain national certification, develop new skills and upgrade skills in line with emerging needs. Under this programme courses are available in Kilkenny City and in centres throughout the county.

Community Education Service
This service facilitates and supports community based learning in locations throughout the county. Its aim is to encourage adults to return to learning in their own local communities. The focus of the service is to provide local learning opportunities throughout the county particularly in rural and urban areas where participation rates in education have traditionally been low.

Evening Classes
A variety of self-financing courses are provided at VEC schools and centres throughout the county. These range from short, hobby and leisure courses to certificate and diploma level courses which provide recognised qualifications for career enhancement.

Vocational Training Opportunities Scheme (VTOS)
Established in 1991, this is a second chance education and training programme for adults who are long term unemployed and who wish to return to education to gain a qualification and develop their skills in a friendly, supportive learning environment. The VTOS Centre is located in Kilkenny city.

Youthreach

Kilkenny Youthreach offers a programme of second chance education for young people who have left school with few or no formal qualifications. Youthreach caters for students aged 15-20 years who have left school early and enables learners to complete examinations such as the Junior and Leaving Certificate as well as FETAC modules. The Youthreach Centre is located in Kilkenny city.

Educational Support Services

County Kilkenny VEC provides a range of education support services which complement the complex network of programmes, schools and centres within its catchment area. They include the following:

Arts Education Programme

County Kilkenny VEC hosts the Arts Education Service for the South East Region. Through the Arts Education Officer, the Arts Education Advisory Committee seeks to promote arts education in second level schools and communities through a bilingual programme. The programme covers the visual, literary and performing arts.

Grants/Scholarships

County Kilkenny VEC administers three different grant/scholarship schemes for students attending courses in further and higher education approved by the Department of Education and Science.

Youth Work Service

Since the enactment of the Youth Work Act in 2001, County Kilkenny VEC has a statutory responsibility for the development of youth work in the county. This will involve the setting out of an integrated plan for youth work programmes and services in its area.

Each year the Department of Education and Science provides a grant to County Kilkenny VEC to support the work of voluntary Youth Clubs and related organisations. Priority is given to organisations working directly with disadvantaged and marginalised young people.

School Transport

Bus Éireann operates the school transport scheme on behalf of the Department of Education and Science. The VEC liaises with Bus Éireann in the organisation of school transport for students in the post-primary schools in County Kilkenny.

Partnership Activities

As the largest provider of learning opportunities for young people and adults in the county, the VEC works in partnership with an extensive network of community and statutory partners. It regards its collaborative role within the community as a key organisational strength and is committed to playing a strategic role in the development of new and existing initiatives. It acts as a lead partner in a number of adult education, youth, sport and community based projects. In addition, staff and members of the VEC play a key representational role on a number of national fora and on almost all education and local development initiatives in County Kilkenny.

The Future

County Kilkenny VEC now caters for an average of 2,300 full-time and 3,500 part-time students annually. These students attend second level schools and centres throughout the county and participate in a broad range of learning programmes. Over the years the VEC has been able to continually expand both its programme suite and the essential supports which enhance the delivery of these. As a statutory local education authority County Kilkenny VEC must continue to play a critical role in meeting the learning needs of the local community and position itself to respond effectively to existing and emerging education needs. It must always strive to promote and develop initiatives which support teachers to teach and learners to learn. The provision of high quality teaching and learning must be at the core of its education provision. It must continue to build strategic partnership alliances and develop creative and innovative ways of working. The current educational and legislative environment within which County Kilkenny VEC operates has become increasingly complex and as a large educational body it must have the management and organisational capacity to enhance the quality of its services and embrace new opportunities.

County Kilkenny VEC is a local education authority founded on the belief that access to education is a basic right which has the potential to enhance people's lives enabling them to participate more fully in their communities and contribute to the development of a caring and just society. The challenge for the VEC going forward is to continue to strive to meet this ideal and in so doing to make a difference to the lives of the people of County Kilkenny.

Schools/Centres and Services

Adult Education Officer with VTOS Staff Team 2007-08
Back Row Left to Right: Mr. David Brydone, Mr. Anthony Ryan, Ms. Patricia O'Connor, Ms. Fiona Phelan, Ms. Bernadette O'Rourke, Ms. Sylvia Lutter, Ms. Maura Comerford, Ms. Breda Hamilton, Mr. Donal Costigan, Mr. Peter O'Carroll.
Front Row Left to Right: Ms. Siobhán Carroll, Ms. Niamh Dowling, Ms. Frances Dempsey, Ms. Eileen Curtis, Adult Education Officer, Ms. Geraldine Moran, Co-Ordinator, Ms. Catherine O'Keeffe, Ms. Charlotte Beattie, Ms. Leanne Butler Davis. Missing from photograph Ms. Frances Doyle.

A History of Adult Education in County Kilkenny VEC

The Early Years

The provision of adult education in Co. Kilkenny dates back to the setting up of the Agricultural and Technical Committees following the enactment of the Agriculture and Technical Instruction Act of 1899. The Committee as part of its technical instruction remit dealt with the setting up of night classes in various parts of the county. Even prior to the setting up of its one permanent school, the Committee employed what were called itinerant teachers to conduct night classes in various parts of the county. In the early years instruction was provided in the Irish language as well as in practical subjects such as poultry-keeping, bee-keeping, laundry and woodwork. When the Vocational Education Committee was established in 1930 following the passing of the Vocational Education Act it took over the running of the City Vocational School and night classes became a valued part of the life of the school. The Act also conferred on the VEC a statutory responsibility to provide for the educational needs of adults in County Kilkenny. This created the initial base for adult education in the county.

As vocational schools opened in centres around the county, other smaller communities benefited from the night courses provided in each area. Classes were conducted by teachers working in the vocational schools. They provided classes for younger students during the day and for adults at night. At that time many day school teachers taught two hours a night on two or three evenings a week. These classes were very well attended and excellent results were achieved. The classes

169

were a central part of the fabric of rural life in the county for many years providing adults with access to educational opportunities which would not otherwise have been available. Classes were held in the committee's schools for the most part, but centres which didn't have a vocational school were not neglected. The classes in these areas were held in national schools, parish halls and sometimes even private houses. Some centres were in better condition than others but few were ideal.

From the early 1900s the Agricultural and Technical Committee and its successor the Vocational Education Committee continued to provide adult education in the form of night classes right around the county with large annual attendances. The newspaper advertisements and brochures over the years reflect not only the changing nature of society but also the changing educational demands of adults in the county. In the earlier years classes were primarily designed to provide practical learning opportunities in subjects like domestic economy, dressmaking, shorthand and typewriting, while in latter years art, pottery, upholstery and computer classes became more popular.

Gradually day school teachers were no longer required to teach at night as part of their class contract hours and in the early 1970s some schools were able to appoint teachers with posts of responsibility for the organisation of adult education classes. Following the publication of the Murphy Report on Adult Education in 1973 there was an increasing move towards putting adult education within the VEC system on a more stable footing and in 1979 the Department of Education conferred on the VEC the right to appoint an Adult Education Organiser for the county. In November 1979 County Kilkenny VEC appointed its first Adult Education Organiser, Mr. Michael O'Neill. The new Adult Education Organiser was to be responsible for the provision and organisation of the adult education programme in the county.

The 1980s

From 1980 onwards Mr. Michael O'Neill was charged with expanding the provision of adult education. An advertisement for night classes in the autumn of 1980 listed over sixty subjects offered in various schools and out-centres - eight vocational schools and centres in Callan, Ballyragget and Kilmacow among others. In November 1980 County Kilkenny VEC and Seville Lodge Adult Education Centre ran what was referred to as an exploratory meeting to determine the extent of adult literacy difficulties in County Kilkenny and the training needs of Adult Literacy tutors. An article publicising the meeting printed in the *Kilkenny Standard* recounted some harrowing examples of the difficulties faced by those who could not read and write. By July 1981 a course consisting of four day-long sessions for adult literacy tutors was held in Kilkenny. This was sponsored by the National Adult Literacy Agency. At this point the VEC also began supporting the Éigse Sliabh Rua and Daonscoil Osraí programmes which promoted various aspects of Irish language and culture. In May 1981 Mr. Michael O'Neill submitted a report to the VEC outlining a major expansion in adult education enrolments, particularly in out-centres. Unfortunately, a month later Committee members were informed that the new Adult Education Organiser had not reached the necessary standard in Irish. The requirement was that he should have the same qualification as any vocational teacher, the Ceard Teastas Gaeilge (CTG). In an interview with a local newspaper he outlined the efforts he had made to learn Irish. Born in England, he had been working in Northern Ireland and studying Irish when he was appointed to the job of Adult Education Organiser with County Kilkenny VEC. The committee recommended to the Department of Education that his temporary contract be extended for one year, but his appeal seems to have been unsuccessful. In September 1981 Mr. O'Neill resigned his position, expressing his sense of grievance at having to do so through lack of a qualification in Irish.

On November 1st 1981 his successor, Mr. Martin F. O'Grady, took up his appointment as Adult Education Organiser for the county. At this stage a Sub-Committee on Adult Education had been set up. The Sub-Committee's remit was to provide for the educational needs of adults in the county and at this point it was recommending the setting up of part-time day classes for adults in Kilkenny, a trend which was emerging in many towns and cities throughout the country. A series of meetings organised by the Adult Education Service was held in the winter of 1985 which led to the setting up of both the Kilkenny Adult Learning Group (known subsequently as the Kilkenny Liberal Studies Group) and the Kilkenny Women's Studies Group. Both groups were interested in daytime education options and in the provision of accessible Third Level education in Kilkenny. To this end a Distance Learning Seminar was organised on 24th June 1986 to which representatives from Maynooth College, NIHE Limerick and Dublin, the Institute of Public Administration, the Open University and R.T.E. were invited. At this time also the Bennettsbridge Community Education Group was established with members pursuing a Diploma in Social Studies from Maynooth College. By September 1986 County Kilkenny VEC had forged its first links with St. Patrick's College, Maynooth and was providing a 'Taste of University Programme' through its Adult Learning Department. Each group met on a weekly basis in rooms provided by the VEC in the Ormonde Road building of the City Vocational School. In 1986 over one hundred participants enrolled on the 'Taste of University Programme' in English Literature, History and Sociology, with over seventy receiving their extra- mural certificates in November 1987.

In 1985 the first Adult Literacy and Community Education Budget was allocated to County Kilkenny VEC. Though small, it was to prove significant in the years ahead and was in effect the first direct budget to be provided for adult education. The Adult Education Organiser began inviting applications for volunteer tutors to provide help for those with reading and writing difficulties. He had also proposed to the VEC meeting in March 1986 that it would be helpful to co-ordinate the Adult Literacy Programme of the VEC and the provision in Seville Lodge Adult Education Centre which was effectively under the auspices of the Diocese of Ossory at that time. The two organisations began to recruit tutors and gave them basic training before they commenced providing confidential one-to-one tuition to members of the public who needed help. In late 1986 a part-time Literacy Organiser was appointed for one afternoon each week to begin the process of matching tutors and students. During this period night classes continued to be provided at vocational schools and out-centres. However, the range of classes on offer had changed considerably and now included Arts and Crafts, Pottery, continental languages as well as Leaving Certificate subjects, particularly English and Mathematics.

The then CEO of the VEC, Mr. Brendan Conway, had a particular interest in adult education and supported the organisation of a series of special lectures which began in 1983. The first lecture entitled 'Ireland and the Classical Tradition' was given by Professor William Bedell Stanford, Regis Professor of Greek in U.C.D. and Senior Fellow of Trinity College, on the 9th March 1983. These lectures were designed to bring scholars of national and international repute to Kilkenny. Many eminent lecturers came to Kilkenny as part of the annual 'University to the People' Lecture series run by both the Arts and Adult Education offices in subsequent years. In 1988 the CEO Mr. Brendan Conway was elected as President of Aontas for a two year period. Mr. O'Grady spent almost five years in the post of Adult Education Organiser and died tragically in a road accident on his way to an Adult Education Organisers' meeting in Portlaoise in December 1986.

In March 1987 Ms. Eileen Hartley who was Adult Education Organiser with County Waterford VEC was appointed to the vacant position in Kilkenny. In July 1987 Circular Letter F49/87 issued from the Department of Education. This instructed Vocational Education Committees to ensure that all adult education courses be self-financing except second chance courses for those with no formal education. This led to a substantial increase in night class fees and a twenty per cent decrease in the numbers attending classes. The impact was greatest in the rural areas where falling enrolments meant that the number of classes was significantly reduced. The office located in Patrick Street which had served the Adult Education Service for some years was relocated to the Ormonde Road premises of the City Vocational School. A minor relief was provided in 1988 when a Social Employment Scheme worker was allotted to the service to provide secretarial services. Despite the very difficult prevailing circumstances adult education provision continued to develop. The numbers attending classes in the City Vocational School stabilised and began to increase again. Advertisements at the time reflected a growing interest in certified courses with extra-mural Certificates in Addiction Studies and Counselling as well as a Diploma in Industrial Engineering and Social Studies on offer in Kilkenny. A Peace Studies Programme was run in Bennettsbridge in association with the Community Education Programme.

The fledging Adult Literacy and Community Education Budget was also cut back with only £7,600 provided to County Kilkenny VEC in 1987. The process of training adult literacy tutors continued during the late 1980s and this was to represent the beginnings of the Co. Kilkenny Adult Literacy Scheme which adopted the name Word Aid in 1988. As part of its activities for Literacy Awareness Raising

Week County Kilkenny Adult Literacy Scheme launched its first student publication *Second Chance* and organised a public meeting on adult literacy in Butler House on 6th May 1988. Premises were secured for the fledgling service in 1989 in Desart Hall, New Street and the hours for the part-time Literacy Organiser increased. There were approximately 30 students receiving one-to-one tuition at the end of the 1980s.

1990 - 2002

The 1990s heralded a period of significant growth and development for the Adult Education Service. In early 1991 the first allocation of twenty places was made to Co. Kilkenny VEC to run the Vocational Training Opportunities Scheme. This was the first occasion on which people in receipt of an unemployment payment could return to education without losing their benefits. Premises were secured for the programme in the Bishop Birch Training Institute on the Waterford Road and a Leaving Certificate Course was run over two years. In 1993 the allocation of places was increased to forty and a VTOS course was established in Graiguenamanagh Vocational School. Throughout the 1990s the VTOS programme continued to grow offering Leaving Certificate, Junior Certificate and National Council for Vocational Awards certificates to students. In 1999 the allocation of VTOS places to Co. Kilkenny was increased to 120 and the VTOS centre in Kilkenny was able to consolidate and develop its provision combining Leaving Certificate, City and Guilds, and FETAC Certification with the provision of programmes from Foundation Level to FETAC Level 2 standard. In more recent years the Centre has concentrated on improving the variety of learning opportunities available to students. This has included the introduction of new subject choices, acquiring additional space, developing the information technology capacity of the centre, introducing learning support, developing childcare support and providing for the information and guidance needs of its participants. By early 2000 the Centre was offering a series of courses to learners varying from a one year Leaving Certificate course, a two FETAC Level 2 Information Technology courses, a Foundation/Junior Certificate course and a Woodcarving course.

The early 1990s saw Word Aid, Kilkenny Adult Literacy Scheme continue to grow and develop. A full-time Adult Literacy Organiser was appointed in 1994 with the subsequent appointment of an Out-Reach Co-ordinator. By the end of the decade the budget for the adult literacy service had increased substantially. Tackling the literacy problem had become a national priority. In 1999 the scheme was providing one-to-one and group tuition for almost 100 students. Staff numbers increased, out-reach tuition centres were secured in Castlecomer, Callan, Urlingford and Graignamanagh. Programmes began on the Traveller Halting Sites, with Teagasc and with the National Rehabilitation Board. The Scheme began running return to learning programmes with FÁS and Kilkenny County Council. Word Aid also began to make accreditation available as an option for students as well as supporting the development of volunteers. Training programmes and supports were provided for staff and volunteers and many activities provided to encourage student participation. By early 2000 the Scheme was catering for the needs of over 400 students with 40 volunteer tutors and 26 part-time tutors. The Scheme moved to larger premises in Butler Court in 2002 and at that time began providing English language classes for asylum seekers and refugees, thus reflecting another significant change in Irish society.

The VEC in Co. Kilkenny was always interested in the promotion of all forms of adult education in the community and even prior to the allocation of a Community Education Budget in 1985 was involved in supporting many local initiatives. Throughout the 1990s the adult education programme was expanded and developed and began providing tuition hours and small grants for local voluntary and community groups throughout the county. Over the years the community education programme supported the provision of daytime and evening classes for organisations like Grow, I.C.A., Women's Groups, the Deaf Association, the National Council for the Blind, the Carer's Association, Active Retirement Groups, Family Resource Centres and the local development partnership groups like Kilkenny Community Action Network and Castlecomer District and Community Development Network. Classes have varied widely and included topics like personal development, assertiveness training, sign language, computers and art. This provided an opportunity for people throughout County Kilkenny to participate in various programmes of learning in their own local area. During this period also the Adult Education Organiser began to represent the VEC on a growing number of local groups and became involved in many programmes in partnership with other groups. In 2002 1472 students participated on community education programmes in the county. The service received a much needed boost with the appointment of a Community Education Facilitator to support the programme in 2002.

A partnership of local youth and community groups came together in 1997 to seek to address the need for the provision of alternative educational options for early school leavers. This series of meetings led to the submission of an application by the VEC for Youthreach places for County Kilkenny. The application was successful and permission to establish a 25 place Youthreach Centre was received by County Kilkenny VEC on 21st June 1998. A premises was secured for Youthreach in the Diocesan Youth Service building in Desart Hall, New Street. Staff recruitment began over the summer period and a sampling programme for early school leavers began in October 1998. The Youthreach Centre has continued to operate from Desart Hall combining a Junior and Leaving Certificate Programme for early school leavers with a personal and social development and work experience programme. The Centre has concentrated on providing a holistic learning programme by developing a wide range of learning supports, childcare support and guidance and counselling for the young people attending.

The publication of the White Paper on Adult Education *Learning for Life* in 2000 was to have a significant impact on the provision of adult education in County Kilkenny as in other VECs. It led to the development of a much expanded Adult Education Service with the appointment of a Community Education Facilitator in early 2002 and the allocation of an Adult Guidance Project in March 2002. This led to the establishment of an adult information and guidance service for the county located in premises shared with Word Aid in September 2002. An Adult Guidance Counsellor and an Information Officer were appointed to staff the service in September 2002. In addition, the VEC received its first budget allocation under the Back to Education Initiative in July 2002 and began providing certified part-time programmes for adults through its existing VTOS, Youthreach and Adult Literacy programmes and with other local groups in the county. Each has become significant in the development of the Adult Education Service in the county.

By 2002 Co. Kilkenny VEC was in receipt of significant budgets for adult education and was providing a range of programmes to meet the needs of adults in the county. The emergence of flexible forms of accreditation through the NCVA and latterly FETAC (the Further Education and Training Awards Council) meant that adults could access many more certified programmes locally. The learning needs of adult learners could be met within the context of the lifelong learning agenda set out in the White Paper on Adult Education and the priorities identified in the National Development Plan. Adult education became a significant vehicle through which to address issues of social inclusion and up-skilling in an Irish society which was changing rapidly. As a result, the elements of a new structure for the delivery of adult education at local level began to emerge. The Adult Education Service was coming of age.

VTOS Awards Night 2001

Attending the annual conference of
AONTAS 1987
(National Association of Adult
Education) in Hotel Kilkenny were
(from left) -
Mr. Proinsias Ó Drisceoil, Arts
Education Organiser;
Ms. Eileen Curtis, Adult Education
Organiser;
Ms. Mairéad Wrynn, President, Aontas
Mr. Brendan Conway, C.E.O.

Launch of *A Glitter of Hope*
– a magazine of Word Aid
students writings on the 9th
October 1992

(from left:)
Ms. Bernadette Brennan,
Mr. Brendan Conway, C.E.O.,
Mr Liam Aylward T.D.,
Mr. Noel O'Keeffe,
Ms. Mary Buckley.

Sample of VTOS Student Work

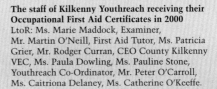

The staff of Kilkenny Youthreach receiving their Occupational First Aid Certificates in 2000
LtoR: Ms. Marie Maddock, Examiner, Mr. Martin O'Neill, First Aid Tutor, Ms. Patricia Grier, Mr. Rodger Curran, CEO County Kilkenny VEC, Ms. Paula Dowling, Ms. Pauline Stone, Youthreach Co-Ordinator, Mr. Peter O'Carroll, Ms. Caitriona Delaney, Ms. Catherine O'Keeffe.

Sr. Grainne McKelvey, Counsellor and Ms. Patricia Grier(R.I.P.) Administrator, Kilkenny Youthreach 1999

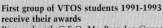

Word Aid Students get down to work.

First group of VTOS students 1991-1993 receive their awards
Pictured with C.E.O. Mr. Brendan Conway, Ms. Eileen Curtis, Adult Education Organiser and their tutors.

A group of Adult Literacy Volunteers and staff from the Adult Literacy Team

VTOS Students Leaving Certificate Construction Studies Projects 1993
Left to Right: Mr. Oliver Hennessy, Mr. John Griffin, Mr. Gerard Lanigan, Mr. Matthew Tighe, Ms. Josephine Ryan.

Tree planting ceremony to mark the launch of *Second Chance* - the first magazine of Word Aid Student writings on 6th May 1988.

Adult Education Careers Evening.

Ms. Mary Buckley, Adult Literacy Organiser and Ms. Kathie Hamilton during Adult Literacy Awareness Week 2000.

Adult Literary Organiser, Ms. Mary Buckley and Word Aid Students meet President Mary McAleese in September 1999.

Adult Guidance Staff 2007
Left to Right: Ms. Aisling Boyd, Information Officer; Ms. Mary Rose Carr, Guidance Counsellor; Bernadette O'Rourke, Guidance Counsellor/Co-Ordinator.

Community/Back to Education Staff 2007
Left to Right: Ms.Mary Butler, Back to Education Co-Ordinator, Ms. Martha Bolger, Community Education Facilitator, Ms. Patricia O'Dwyer, Administrator, Ms. Bridget Cassin, Administrator.

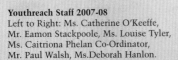

Word Aid, Co. Kilkenny Adult Literacy Scheme Staff 2007
Left to Right: Ms. Carmel Bryan, Resource Worker, Ms. Miriam Copeland, Administrator, Ms. Marion Dermody, Resource Worker, Ms. Mary Buckley, Adult Literacy Organiser.

Youthreach Staff 2007-08
Left to Right: Ms. Catherine O'Keeffe, Mr. Eamon Stackpoole, Ms. Louise Tyler, Ms. Caitriona Phelan Co-Ordinator, Mr. Paul Walsh, Ms.Deborah Hanlon.

Proinsias Ó Drisceoil
Arts Education Officer (South East)

Arts Education

To coincide with International Children Year, the Arts Council, in 1979, issued a report entitled *The Place of the Arts in Irish Education*. This report contained a complete account of the state of arts education in Ireland and recommended a large number of substantial and significant reforms.

The Department of Education, as part of its response to the issuing of the report, decided to appoint three suitably-qualified persons as Arts Education Organisers. The three appointees were to have as their areas the South-East, the North-West and the Midlands. The South-East Organiser was to be based with County Kilkenny VEC and to cover the seven VEC areas of the South-East, a formidable task.

The fact that the Minister simultaneously appointed forty-seven Adult

Education Organisers gave an initial impression that the Arts Education Organiser would operate in the Adult Education area. The precise field of education in which the Arts Education Organisers were to be deployed then became the subject of negotiations and as a result it became clear that their function would be the promotion of the Arts within the entire educational system, but with a special emphasis on schools.

In February 1980 Proinsias Ó Drisceoil took up duty as Arts Education Organiser for the South-East and he continues in that position.

It was intended that a committee be established by the seven CEOs in the region to work with the appointee, but this failed to materialise.

On appointment, The Arts Education Organiser set the following aims for his office and communicated these to the seven VECs:
(a)   promoting all art forms equally;
(b)   involving all types of school and educational institutions in his work;
(c)   bringing the Arts to those students normally without access to them;
(d)   creating institutions that would give the greatest possible opportunity
to young Arts practitioners to develop their skills.

A programme was evolved from these intentions and this programme forms the subject of the first annual report of the Arts Education Office. This was issued in 1981.

The Arts Education Office has organised innumerable Arts events and initiatives over the years and the Arts have gradually attained a mainstream place in education at all levels, as well as in the wider community.

The year 1985 might be taken as a typical example of the work done by the Arts Education Office. The annual report for that year includes reports on master classes in pottery given to students in a series of schools by Professor Frank Breneisea of Mornington College, Sioux City, Iowa; a world expert in the field; an art course for art college aspirants; an art history study weekend for adults; art, music and poetry classes for patients in St. Canice's Hospital; a slide/video service for art teachers; workshops and auditions for aspiring participants in the National Youth Theatre; two theatre-in-education tours by Graffiti Theatre-in-Education Company; an in-service course in drama for the classroom; a series of dance workshops by Barefoot Dance; organisation of Irish participation in the European Youth Theatre Encounter (where Ireland was represented with great distinction by Martina Connolly of Graignamanagh Vocational School); schools workshops by Scottish National Opera to coincide with the Wexford Opera Festival; a sustained series of school visits by poet, Eavan Boland, who worked closely with the Arts Education Office over a number of years; linked public poetry readings by Eavan Boland and Róisín Cowman; a series of *Irish Times*-sponsored creative writing workshops given by Maeve Binchy and held in Carlow, Kilkenny, Carrick-on-Suir and Waterford; master classes held during the Kilkenny Arts week; a concert of pieces on the Leaving Certificate music syllabus; a schools music workshop by Dr. Gerard Victory; a course for teachers on the creative use of Irish folksong and a series of traditional music concerts. In addition, the Arts Education Organiser served that year on a variety of boards and committees including the Music Association of Ireland, as well as acting as chairperson of the innovative Theatre Unlimited, an avant garde professional theatre company based in Kilkenny and directed by the Polish director, Maciek Reszcznski.

Public lecture series were organised by the Arts Education Office over many years, principally in Butler House, Kilkenny. For instance in 1998 the programme was as follows:

Thursday 22nd January
An Dr. Máirín Nic Eoin, St. Patrick's College, Drumcondra, Dublin:
Critical Misconceptions of the Role of Women in Irish Literature and Society.

Thursday 29tb January
John McGahern, novelist and short-story writer.
A Reading.

Thursday 5th February
Dr. Martin Mansergh, Special Advisor to An Taoiseach:
The Value of Historical Commemoration and its Role in Peace and Reconciliation,with Special Reference to 1798 and 1848.

Thursday 12th February
Professor Gabriel Lipshitz, Balilan University, Israel:
Country on the Move: Immigration and Internal Migration in Israel, 1948-1995.

Thursday 19th February
Professor Hugh Kearney, Emeritus Professor of History at the University of Pittsburgh:
Faith or Fatherland: Contesting the Memory of Daniel O'Connell.

Thursday 26tb February
Professor Roy Foster, University of Oxford:
Theme Park and Stories: History and Identity.

The advisory committee to assist the work of the Arts Education Office mooted over the years was finally established in 2002 and became the Arts Education Advisory Committee for the South East. This committee held its first meeting in the KCAT Arts Centre Callan on January 24th 2002. The meeting elected Tony Patterson as chairperson and he has been subsequently re-elected to the position each time a vacancy has arisen. The committee comprises representatives of all VECs in the South-East as well as secondary schools, community schools and the TUI, ASTI and IVEA. The committee can be credited with aiding considerably the advance of the Arts in education.

The promotion and development of the Arts in education has been identified as a long-term aim of successive Ministers for Education and the importance of the Arts

Education Office and the South East Arts Education Advisory Committee has grown accordingly.

As well as acting as a direct facilitator, the Arts Education Organiser has participated in national policy formation through membership of bodies such as Teastas, the Cultures of Ireland Group and An Coiste Téarmaíochta, through acting as an Arts Council nominee on boards such as the board of the Butler Gallery and the Watergate Theatre, through chairmanship of Graffiti Theatre-in-Education company over many years and, more recently, through membership of the board of Barnstorm theatre company.

Seirbhís dhátheangach í Seirbhís Oideachas Ealaíon na gCoistí Gairmoideachais agus bíonn áit lárnach ag an nGaeilge i ngach aon ghné d'obair agus de sheirbhís na hoifíge agus de na himeachtaí ar fad a eagraítear inti.

Arts Education
Programme Traditional
Music Workshop 2004.

Photograph taken in Butler House, Kilkenny on March 2nd 1995 on the occasion of a poetry reading given by Nobel Prize winner, Mr. Seamus Heaney as part of the County Kilkenny VEC lecture series of that year.
Left to right: Mr. Adrian Munnnelly, Director of the Arts Council, Mr. Seamus Heaney,
Mr. Brendan Conway, CEO, Ms. Marie Heaney, Mr. Proinsias Ó Drisceoil, Director of the lecture series.

A scene from Silas Marner adapted by Storytellers Theatre Company from the novel by George Eliot
This was staged at the Watergate Theatre during April 1997 and attended by all the County Kilkenny VEC schools, as well as by VTOS students.

Abbey Community College Staff 2007-08
Front: Eoin Kissane, Declan Stapleton, Robbie O'Keeffe, Tommy Lanigan (Principal),
Eugene Power (Deputy Principal), Paul Durnan, Ann-Marie Boyle, Eleanor Parks, Niamh Kenny.
Middle: John Keane, Ann Condon, Detta Cahill, Kathleen Ryan, David Costine, Cleir Tierney,
Roisin Meaney, Anita Butler, Catherine Donegan, Regina Dooley, Breda Keyes, Ellen Lynch,
Leona O'Doherty, Sr. Mary Gough, Mairead Mackey, Aidan McCarthy, Eoin McCormack, Brian Egan,
Maurice Brosnan.
Back: Ruby Jacob, Katherine O'Sullivan, Mary McCarthy, Mary Colton, Linda Aylward, Tammy Lapthorne,
Oliver Kiely, Jean Cusack, Aedín Tynan, Gerry Kelly, Matt Kenny, Mary Butler.

Abbey Community College, Ferrybank

Amalgamation

By the mid nineties rapid changes had occurred in the governance of schools throughout Ireland. The numbers of clergy directly involved in education were diminishing rapidly. In addition, many school buildings were in dire need of upgrade, since only meager capital investment had been made by the State during the previous decades. In Ferrybank, the Religious of the Sacred Heart of Mary had applied for significant capital funding for their secondary school. A French order, they had been involved in education in Ferrybank since 1879.

In 1995 the idea of an amalgamation between Slieverue VS and SHM secondary school was first mooted. It was envisioned that the strengths of both schools could be combined to provide a broad and modern education that would serve the community of the south Kilkenny and Ferrybank areas well into the 21st century. The management structure was the 'model' agreement, a nationally agreed contract of joint trusteeship between County Kilkenny VEC and the Sisters. The school would be run by a Board of Management, consisting three representatives of the VEC, three representatives of the Sisters, two staff members, two parent representatives, with the latter two groups being elected. The CEO and the Provincial were ex-officio members of the Board and Sr. Catherine Dunne, Principal, SHM school acted as non-voting secretary. This Board first met on 22nd November 1999. The members were, Mrs Mary Hilda Cavanagh, Mr. Dick Dowling, Mgr. Michael Ryan (VEC), Sr. Therese English, Mr. Michael Mullowney, Br. Denis Minehane (Trustees), Mr. Maurice Brosnan, Ms Eleanor Parks (Staff), Ms. Kathleen Phelan, Mrs. Mary Purcell (Parents). Dick Dowling was nominated as Chairman. Discussions about the planning of the new school fell on the shoulders of CEO Rodger Curran and the Sisters led by Sr. Catherine Dunne. Initially the negotiations focused on the ideal of a Community School, ie. with the VEC as partners but not managers of the school. After further negotiations it was agreed by the partners that the school would be a Community College, under the trusteeship of the Sisters and VEC but managed by the latter.

The site chosen for the new school was the 'nuns field' at the rear of the convent school. In 1998 Minister for Education, Micheál Martin, after much pressure from parents and management, agreed that the school should include a full size Sports Hall of 600m². Architects Cody and Associates, Ranelagh, Dublin were appointed to design the new building. Early in 1999 the appointed building contractors withdrew before commencement of the building and new contractors had to be sought. Clancy Construction, Drangan, Thurles were appointed following an eight month delay. This meant that the building would not be completed in time for the amalgamation date of September 2000.

The practicalities of developing a new school, staff development, school uniforms, school planning fell to a Steering Committee of the following: John O'Callaghan, Sr. Catherine (Principals), Sally Kavanagh, Siobhan O'Flaherty (staff, SHM), Aidan McCarthy, Eleanor parks (staff, Slieverue) and Rodger Curran CEO. This group met monthly over two years until the new Principal was appointed. Their constructive work and positive outlook contributed much to the success of the amalgamation. Mr. John O'Callaghan retired after 32 years service with County Kilkenny VEC while Sr. Catherine became the first full time chaplain in the new school.

The post of Principal was filled on 1 March 2000 by Mr. Tommy Lanigan, who had taught in St. Kieran's College, Kilkenny. Mr. Eugene Power was appointed Deputy Principal in May 2000, having taught in Loreto, Crumlin.

Eighty one first year students enrolled for school on 1st September 2000. The total number was 368, which included 16 adults on a Post Leaving Cert Fashion Design Level 5 course in Slieverue. There were 33 teachers and administration and caretaking staff in both centres held their posts until the new school would be completed. All First and Fifth years were based in Ferrybank. One class of Second, Third and Sixth year students remained in

Slieverue. All wood, metal and technical graphics classes were held in Slieverue. This necessitated many students being bussed from one centre to the other, at least three times a week. The Department of Education and Science paid for this service. In addition all students who attended Slieverue VS were entitled to free transport to Ferrybank for the duration of their education. Understandably, the first year proved demanding on all parties. The school operated on two sites three miles apart, buildings were in poor condition and new procedures and practices were in the development stages. Nevertheless the First Year enrolment for the following year was 78 despite a drop in primary school numbers in the area. The building contractor was unable to complete the building for September 2001 and for two months all students remained on the Ferrybank campus.

Finally the state-of-the-art building was handed over in November 2001 though building work continued on it until January 2002. Staff and students appreciated the modern building and the up-to-date facilities. The contribution of the former schools has not been forgotten. The crests of SHM Ferrybank and Slieverue VS, between the crest of County Kilkenny VEC are etched into the windows over the entrance with the Abbey Community College crest, reminders of the roots from which this new school had grown. The school colours of blue and red also reflect the former schools colours.

The design of the Abbey Community College crest incorporates the old abbey - which used to stand where this College now stands, and the ships on the river - which recall the thriving ship-building industry of the city.

The College was officially opened, by the Minister for Education Mr. Michael Woods, on 22nd April 2002 before an audience of 700 guests.

The student population burgeoned after 2002. In each of the following three years over 135 First Year students were enrolled until a cap of 116 per year was imposed as numbers increased to 615 by 2006. By then there were 44 teachers on staff. In early 2005 a formal application was made to the Department of Education and Science for an extension to increase the size to accommodate 850 students. At the time of writing waiting lists for entry extend eight years ahead.

The curriculum in the new school is broad and balanced. In addition to traditional Junior Certificate and Leaving Certificate, the school offers Transition Year, Leaving Certificate Vocational Programme and Leaving Certificate Applied. At Senior level, Irish, English, Maths, History, Geography, French, German, Physics, Chemistry, Biology, Business, Accounting, Home Economics, Construction Studies, Engineering and Technical Drawing are available to boys and girls. Music was introduced as an academic subject in 2001 and subsequently a music school was established, where students received private music tuition on campus. In its Mission Statement, Abbey Community College seeks "to educate in a reflective way with an emphasis on the development of the whole person, thereby enabling the student to participate fully in society and to live a fulfilling life". It seeks to promote values "based on the traditions, ethos and philosophy of its founding partners" and "is committed to enriching through education the lives of the people in its care and encouraging them, in turn, to bring life to others".

The first five years of the College's history provide ample evidence that this mission statement is alive and active. The management and staff have remained faithful to the traditions of both the Sacred Heart of Mary and Slieverue Vocational Schools and have moved beyond them to provide a learning environment that is second to none. Here we have an excellent 'centre for learning at the heart of the community' that will serve the south Kilkenny and greater Waterford areas for many years to come.

Students at work

Transition Year Students from Abbey Community College visit Dail Eireann 2000
Pictured with Mr. Liam Aylward MEP and teachers Robbie O'Keeffe and Eleanor Parks.

Abbey Community College 5th year LCA students present a cheque for 2,500 to Our Ladies Hospital for Sick Children, Crumlin
The money was raised from Jump for Joy in the School organised by the students. Seated from left are: Emma Daniels, Eimer Walsh, Eoghan Forristal, Martin Cahill, Crumlin Hospital, Liam Byrne and Sarah Brett
Standing from left are: Conor Flynn, Eoin Scannell, Barry Duggan, Mark Carew and Larry Kehoe.

Abbey Community College

Students from Abbey Community College fundraising for the Special Olympics 2003.

191

New Technologies: Declan Stapleton
teaches Leaving Certificate Geography
using the Interactive Whiteboard and
'slate'.

John O'Shea from
Manchester United
visits Abbey
Community College

South Leinster Juvenile C Hurling Champions 2007
Back Row(from left:) Oisin MacCaomhaoil, Bill Irish,Josh Tobin, Conal McIntyre, Denis Scully,
Kelvin Lyons, Neil Wemyss, Kevin Hurley, Sam Lawless, Damien Aherne, Dylan Haberlin, Brian Grant,
Ross Kelly, Patrick Foran, Dean Power, Aidan Sinnott, Paul Rockett.
Front Row(from left:) Conor Fripps, Darren Hickey, Ryan Dowling, Cormac Heffernan, Shay Dempsey,
Kevin MacNamara, Seamus Burtchaell, Eoin Buggy, Chrisopher Penkert, Jason Grant, PJ Roche,
Sean Duggan, Luke Walsh, Sean Byrne.

Coláiste Cois Siúire Staff 2007-08
(Seated L to R) Madge Barry, Jeanette Fitzpatrick, Shelia O'Dowd, Kathy Cronin, Susan Power, Imelda Behan, Winnie Manning, Mary Purcell, Michelle Finnegan, Caroline McCarthy.
(Back Row L to R) Kay Meany, Michael Malone, Maureen Conneely, John Kennedy, Fenton McHugh, Finola Cummins, Aisling Gannon, Doreen Griffin, Stephen O'Keeffe, Tom Walsh, Jim Ryan, Martin Gordon, Pat Grant, John Foley, Eddie O'Keeffe, Anita Dunne.

Coláiste Cois Siúire, Mooncoin

Historical Background

Mooncoin Vocational School was one of the first rural Vocational Schools in Ireland. It was built in the year 1935 after much persistence from Canon Doyle (local P.P.) and the people of the area. As the Minister for Education at that time Mr. Tom Derrig was a good friend of Canon Doyle the school went ahead fast and early. When the school was opened, there were three classrooms in it with one teacher assigned for each room. The main subjects that were taught were Woodwork, Rural Science and Domestic Science.

The main aims in setting up the school were to provide post-primary education to the rural children and also to improve agricultural knowledge especially horticulture for home growing. The purpose of this was to have educated people in the parish after leaving school which would result in an improvement in the standard of living in the area. Gardening was a compulsory subject at this time and each pupil had to spend not less than two hours each week in the garden. The fruit and vegetables grown were then used for domestic purposes in the Domestic Science room.

Night Classes for adults were set up a few years later. The men made furniture in the Woodwork classes for their own homes and the women learned new skills in Domestic Science. Thus education was not confined to the younger generation, but was for anyone who wished to avail of it. People came from as far away as Thomastown and Carrick-on-Suir.

The school was also used as the social centre for the parish. Once a year the wooden partitions between the classrooms were removed and tables were arranged for a supper and a dance later on in the evening.

In 1939, an adult discussion group for the farmers in the area was established in the school. Such topics as modern farming methods, developments in machinery and fertilisers were discussed. This led in 1943 to the establishment of a Farmer's Club in the parish and from this, in May 1944, the first national executive for the first farmers movement, afterwards called "Macra na Feirme" was formed.

After World War II the "Post War Building Boom" led to a shortage of qualified tradesmen and to counteract this a building course was set up in the school in 1950. A new woodwork room and store was built by the students that were undertaking this course and two years later a metalwork room was added. Thus the foundation was laid for trades in the building and engineering industries in the area.

A Home Garden Scheme was established whereby the students attending the school cultivated fruit and vegetables at home. There were prizes for the winners and the aim of this was for the students to expand and develop their resources at home. From this the first "Macra na Tuaithe" group was launched in the school on 14th March 1952 by the Minister for Education Mr. Sean Moylan in the presence of the Minister for Agriculture Mr. Tom Walsh.

Day school enrolments increased in numbers with the introduction of the Group and Intermediate Certificate Examinations. This allowed the children to obtain certain qualifications that were becoming necessary for jobs. There was a demand for more and more rooms as enrolments increased so pre-fabricated classrooms were introduced.

In 1978 the Leaving Certificate was introduced. During the 1980s, it was obvious that the accommodation was outdated, inadequate and dilapidated and a local campaign to provide a new school was initiated.

In 1993 the new school renamed as "Coláiste Cois Siúire" was opened by Mr. Liam Aylward, Minister for State at the Department of Education.

Leaving Certificate Class 1992

Martin Gordon, Stephen O'Keeffe, Breda
Keyes and Jim Ryan at School's Millennium
Ball December 1999

Millennium Ball December 1999
Siobhan Delahunty, Emily Synnott,
Mary Power, Peter Sutton, Ger Sutton

School Trip to London 1982

L.C.V.P. Class trip to Waterford Glass

**Erecting Millennium
Monument**
Michael Malone,
Jim Ryan,
Martin Gordon.

**Minister for Education, Mr. Paddy Cooney
visits Mooncoin Vocational School in 1986**
Mr. Frank Hogan, Parents' Association,
Mr. Paddy Cooney, Minister for Education,
Mr. Tom Walsh Principal,
Mr. Kieran Crotty, TD,
Cllr. Mary Hilda Kavanagh,
Cllr. Eamon Meade,
Cllr. Dick Dowling.

Leaving Certificate Accounting Class 2004

School Bank Officials
Eoin Crowley, Shane Walsh,
Elaine Delahunty, Elaine Kennington,
Daniel Purcell

Junior Certificate Woodwork Class 2006

196

Leinister Champions 1993 1994
Mooncoin Vocational School
Pictured after their epic struggle
with Coláiste Eanna
(Back L to R) Liam Walsh,
Michael Gordon, Alan Walsh,
Billy Ryan, Wesley Synnott,
Ciaran Dunphy, Ger Kirwan,
Eddie Mackey.
(Front L to R) Ger Maher, Lee
Kelly, Bill Gaule, Captain, (R.I.P),
Tommy Faulkner,
Laurence Dunphy,
Richard Carroll, Dick Walsh.

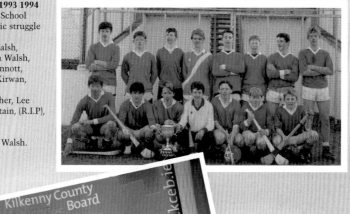

L.C.V.P. Class 2006-2007
Runners up in Kilkenny
County Enterprise Board's
Young Entrepreneurs'
Competition

The cloister area,
Coláiste Cois Siúire

School Pupils 1953-54
Back Row(from left): R. Bowe,
T. Barden(R.I.P.), J. Cuddihy, Unknown,
T O'Hara(R.I.P.), M. Walsh.

Front Row(from left): J. Byrne,
W. Walsh, R. Walsh, J. Laffan,
D. Walsh, M. Foley, I. Walsh, S. Fosksh

Coláiste Mhuire Staff 2007-08
Front Row (L to R): Valerie Bergin, Patsy Costello, Eamon Phelan, Emma Dempsey, John Cahill, Michael Killeen, Rosemary Power, Dolores Lyons, Ruth O'Brien, Gemma Dunphy, Helen Kelly, Paddy Broderick.
Middle Row (L to R): Breda Manton, Ann-Marie Ryan, Ita Doyle, Mary Sheehan, Aoife Neary, Katie Kilkenny, Angela Conroy, Mary Birch, Catherine Garrett, Jennifer Nolan, Michael Butler, Eamon Marnell, Jim O'Grady, Paddy Comerford, Tom Dollard.
Back Row (L to R): Priscilla Gleeson, Patricia Tallis, Martin Fahey, Anne Carroll, Pearl Codd, Mary Hyland, Anne-Marie Bedrani, Martin Gleeson, John Dunne, Catherine Maher, Ciara Ryan, Jennifer Cahill, Julie Gleeson, Dermot Maher, Paul O'Flynn. Missing from photograph Cathryn O'Grady.

Coláiste Mhuire, Johnstown

History of Coláiste Mhuire, Johnstown

Johnstown Vocational School opened in 1952. It had three classrooms, for Woodwork, Science, and Home Economics. Mr. Pat Taaffe was appointed Principal, Moira Moynihan, Home Economics teacher and Father Carroll taught Religion. Thirty-three students enrolled in the first year. In 1953 Mr. Taaffe returned to Kilkenny VS and Mr. John Walsh was appointed Principal.

Mr. Walsh taught Science for years and was responsible for establishing this new venture. He spent forty years working diligently for the school community. He loved the school garden and in 1978 and 1979 the school was honoured with first place in Ireland for the best-kept school garden with its wide range of shrubs and flowers.

In 1953 Mr. Bernie Ryan arrived as woodwork teacher. The increase in school numbers was slow in the early days and in 1964 there were only 65 students on the roll. In 1964 the staff included Mr. Walsh, Mr. Ryan, Mr. Sean Hennessy, Ann Carroll and Father Langton. Mr. Maurice McGrath arrived as Irish teacher in 1968 and acted as Vice-Principal up to 1980.

In the 1950s the only examination available was the Group Certificate which students sat after two years. In the late 1960s students were allowed to sit the Intermediate Certificate. The inaugural meeting of the Board of Management was held on the 13th of April 1976. The VEC representatives were Very Rev Dean

Harvey, Councillor Mary H. Cavanagh, Councillor Tom Waldron, Councillor Jack Murphy, Councillor Tom Crotty and Mr. Seamus Pattisson TD. Parent representatives were Mrs Josephine Costelloe, and Mr. Edmond Curran. School staff were represented by Mrs Margaret Rochford, Mr. Maurice McGrath, Vice-Principal, and John Walsh, Principal. Mr Conway CEO also attended. At this meeting the board recommendations to the VEC were

1. That 3 new classrooms be provided.
2. That Senior cycle education be offered.
3. That a career guidance teacher be employed.

The Leaving Certificate Examination was introduced in 1977.

After years of campaigning a new school was built in 1995 to cater for 300 students. It was officially opened by Niamh Breathnach Minister for Education in May 1996. After consultation with parents and staff it was decided to call the new school "Coláiste Mhuire". The crest for the school was designed by Art teacher Mr. Donal McCluskey. It depicts the round tower - the Steeple of Fertagh. The sports field was extended by buying extra land from John Walsh and Mrs Liston. Three new classrooms were built with parents' financial contribution in 2003. A new all weather pitch was opened in 2007. The school numbers today are 407 with over thirty teachers on staff.

The school now offers many new programmes. The Transition Year was introduced in 1996. This provides an opportunity for students to experience Leaving Certificate subjects and take part in school musicals and plays. It also offers students a chance to sample different work placements. The school also offers Post Leaving Certificate courses in Computers, Childcare and Care of the Older Person. It also provides two homework Clubs for students between 4.00 pm and 6.30 pm, with approximately sixty students availing of this service. In the last two years Music has been introduced as a subject. Our Music Teacher offers lessons to students after school each week.

Night courses are always very popular in the school. In the early days large numbers attended the very popular lectures provided by the R.D.S. Dublin. Dr Garrett Fitzgerald gave an inspiring lecture on the benefits of Ireland's entry to the E.U. in 1972. Dr Mould gave a glowing overview of Ireland with pictures taken from a heilcopter showing all our ancient monuments. Today, a wide variety of classes are offered in Wood-Turning, Upholstery, Computers, Salsa Dancing, First Aid, Aerobics, Gardening, Flower Arranging, Yoga, Interior Design, Welding, Pottery, Textiles and Digital Photography.

Sport has played a huge role in the life of our school. The school has won several Under 14 hurling titles, two Under 16 All-Ireland titles in 1987 and 1988, one Senior Hurling All-Ireland in 1982 and one Under 14 football All-Ireland in 1974. In 2005 the school reached All-Ireland hurling finals at Under 14, Under 16 and Under 18 levels. Camogie and football are also played. Famous sporting past pupils include Ger and John Henderson, Murty Kennedy, David Burke, Paddy Ryan,

Stephen Grehan and of course on the present Kilkenny Senior Hurling team, the great J.J. Delaney. PJ. Delaney is also on the Kilkenny panel.

FIRST ALL-IRELAND FOOTBALL TITLE - 1974
Johnstown Vocational School U-15 football team hold a unique record in Kilkenny. They are the only side to have won a football All-Ireland. This notable achievement was accomplished in 1974, the inaugural year of the competition, when Johnstown, who had earlier beaten teams from Edenderry, Wexford, and Athboy, defeated Galway city in Athlone. The Noresiders got a tonic start with a Joe Fogarty goal. Galway levelled the game with three points, but Jimmy Tone scored another goal for Johnstown who led at half time by 3-6 to 0-3. Johnstown only scored once in the second half, but they held out for a great 4- 6 to 1- 8 victory.

The panel and scorers were: Michael Kenny, Liam Leahy, Michael Morrissey, Michael Caesar, Maurice Burke, Ned Lennon, Michael Campion, Tom Lennon (0 - 4), John Joe Buckley, Michael Fogarty (1-1), William Guilfoyle, Tony Thornton, Jim Tone (2 - 0), Joe Neary (0 -1), Liam Moriarty, Michael Tobin, Michael Bowe, Joe Fogarty (1- 0). J. Power and Michael Bartley.

COLÁISTE MHUIRE AND THE GAA
Johnstown Vocational School has contributed much to the GAA in Johnstown and surrounding parishes. Johnstown players featured on Kilkenny teams that won the Inter-County Vocational All-Ireland five times in the 70's. In 1972 Martin Orr, Martin Kennedy and Martin Joyce were on the side that defeated Cork by 3-9 to 3-7. The following year the same three players plus John Henderson and Joe Ryan were on the team that beat North Tipperary on a score of 3-11 to 1-8. Martin Kennedy scored a magnificent 2-9 in that final.

Kilkenny again faced North Tipperary in 1975 and were victorious on a score of 3-8 to 2- 6. John Power was the star in the second half notching four points. In 1976, Kilkenny's toughest opponents were Offaly, with the game finishing level 3-7 each after extra time. Kilkenny won the replay and went on to beat Galway easily in the final by 1-15 to 1-10.

Kilkenny reached their third successive All-Ireland in 1977. On that occasion they defeated North Tipperary on a score of 2-12 to 1-10. John Moriarty was introduced in the second half and scored 2-1. John Power played a captain's role while Tom and Ned Lennon, Tony Thornton and Pierce Phelan were stars.

ALL-IRELAND SUCCESS
Johnstown became the first Kilkenny side to win the All-Ireland individual Senior Schools title when they triumphed in 1982. In Leinster, they defeated arch rivals Banagher and went on to defeat St. Brogan's, Bandon at Emly on a score of 3 -7 to 2-3. Goals in the first half by Jimmy Queally and Gerry Phelan laid the foundations for victory. Nicky Grace and Pat McEvoy added two points each and they led at half time by 2-4 to 1-2.

With the wind advantage, St. Brogan's piled on the pressure in the second half, but found Johnstown goalie and captain, David Burke in brilliant form. Jimmy Queally scored a fine goal and two points and Pat McEvoy a point. Martin Bartley (Gortnahoe) held Cork minor Tony O'Connell scoreless. Milo Phelan and 15 year old Martin McEvoy also played very well.

The team and scorers were: D. Burke, (capt), M. Bartley, J. Coady, Wm. Stanley, G. Kavanagh, M. Phelan, M. McEvoy, L. Maher, P. McEvoy (0-3), N. Grace (0-2), T. Drennan, J. Queally (2-2), G. Phelan (1-0), M. O'Gorman, P. Phelan; Subs: J. Farrell, S. Whyte, M. Sweeney.

JUNIOR ALL-IRELAND TITLES. 1987,1988
In 1987 Johnstown had their first win in the U 15 championship. In the Leinster Final they defeated old rivals, Banagher VS by 5-5 to 1-2, Michael Phelan scoring 4-1. They emerged from a rather torrid semi-final with two players suspended. In the final, they faced St. Brogan's of Bandon. Playing with the wind, the Cork boys opened impressively and hit 1-2 without reply.

Austin Cleere replied with a point but the Leesiders replied with another goal. A great goal from Cleere reduced St. Brogan's lead to four points by half time, 2-3 to 1-2. Michael Phelan pointed early in the new half, and then Cleere shot the equalising goal. From then on, Johnstown took over with points from Austin and Cyril Cleere and David Moriarty. A great late save by goalkeeper, Declan Tobin, kept St. Brogan's at bay and Johnstown won by 2 - 6 to 2 - 3.

The team in the final was: D. Tobin, D. Costigan, G. Quinlan, T. Watson, A. McEvoy, C. Cleere, J. Carroll, K. Wall, P. Murphy, A. Bartley, J. Corcoran, D. Moriarty, E. Murphy, M. Phelan, A. Cleere. Sub: R. Butler.

Johnstown retained the U-15 title the following year. They had a close game against Kilcormac (Offaly) in the Leinster Final, but held on to win by two points, 0-9 to 0-7. In the All-Ireland semi final, it was touch and go against an aggressive Scoil Ruain, (Killenaule VS). An Alan Behan goal in the 50th minute saw Johnstown through by 2-10 to 0-7. In the final Johnstown faced a handy New Inn side. The Galway lads were full of running in the early stages but the ability to grab scores when most needed helped Johnstown to a 2-13 to 1-9 win.

The team in the final was: D. Tobin, D. Anderson, D. Behan, P. Phelan, D. O'Neill, J. Carroll, A. Bartley (capt), D. Moriarty, A. McEvoy, J. Ryan, A. Cleere, B. Lonergan, Alan Behan, Adrian Behan, K. Behan.

Coláiste Mhuire Role of Honour

Hurling

Leinster Juvenile U 14 Champions: 1976, 1977, 1978, 1998, 2004.

Leinster U 16 Champions: 1987, 1988, 1991, 1992, 1997, 1998, 1999, 2002, 2005, 2007.

All-Ireland Junior Champions: 1987, 1988.

Leinster Senior Champions: 1982, 1983, 1991, 1997, 1999, 2001, 2005, 2007.

All-Ireland Senior Champions: 1982.

All-Ireland Junior Football Champions: 1974.

Camogie

Leinster Junior Champions: 1991.

Leinster Senior Champions: 1992, 1996, 1997, 1998, 2003.

Leinster Junior Camogie Champions 1991.

Leinster Senior Camogie Champions 1997 and 2003.

Senior Colleges and Vocational Champions 1992.

Johnstown Macra Na Feirme

Johnstown Macra na Feirme was founded in 1963 by Mr. John Walsh, Principal of the Vocational School, Johnstown. It originated as a Macra na Tuaithe club and developed into the present Macra na Feirme Branch, which presently is numbered among the most successful clubs in the country.

From the beginning, Macra na Tuaithe in Johnstown was very strong. Members took part in many activities at club, county and national level. One activity which proved very successful within the club was the crop project in sugar beet and potato growing. At that time, these projects were sponsored by the Irish Sugar Company and each year Johnstown won a number of first prizes. As members got older and got more involved in their family farms, Macra na Tuaithe developed into Macra na Feirme.

The first officers of the club were, Tom Hickey, Chairman, Jim Renehan as Secretary, and Paddy Ryan as Treasurer.

In the early years, educational tours were organised to places of agricultural interest, such as Bacon Factories, the Sugar Co, etc. During the winter months, lectures and night classes were run in Johnstown Vocational School. The club had its first taste of national honours when club member Michael Joyce finished second in the Young Farmer of the Year Competition. (Incidentally, the winner of the competition that year was Seamus O'Brien, Carlow, who later became National President of Macra na Feirme).

From its initiation down to the present day, the club has been blessed with members, many talented and all willing to work hard. As most will appreciate, hard work bears fruit and the achievements of this branch are no exception to the rule. Johnstown Macra was the first club in the country to organise a Building Construction Course and run useful and practical courses annually in the local Vocational School.

The club has been represented on numerous occasions at national level. It was represented on three successful Cross Country Quiz teams on RTE. Television. The Kilkenny team included three Johnstown members:- Willie Norton, Jimmy Renehan and his wife Kathleen. Willie Quaney, a former County Chairman brought All Ireland Sheep Judging honours to Johstown in 1970. Edward O'Gorman won the section Beef Judging section in 1980.

1980 also proved successful for the Farm Tasks team who won the National final of this competition in the RDS at the Spring Show. The team members were:- Richard Curran, Denis Large and Martin O'Gorman. They were coached by Willie Quaney.

The club won many more honours in various competitions at county and national level. A team consisting of Jim Renehan, Tom Hickey, Margaret Fitzpatrick and Willie Quaney brought county debating honours to the club as did the panel speaking teams of 1975 and 1976. The Panel Speaking team of 1975 were narrowly beaten by Wexford in the quarter finals of the All Ireland. Wexford subsequently went on to win the All Ireland. The team consisted of Sean Power, Denis Large, Diarmuid Broderick and Paddy Kavanagh. The two latter members of this team were also successful in the

1976 county final. The club won the Farm Plan Competition in 1978 which was run for the first time in County Kilkenny and was sponsored by the Bank of Ireland.

In 1981 the Club won the much coveted award of County Efficiency Title at Kilkenny Agricultural Show. The team members were Barbara Taylor, Mary Fitzpatrick, Mary Ryan, Maura Curran, Gretta Power, Michael Power, Ken Whitford, George Leahy, Liam Leahy, John Large, and Richard Curran.

At county level the Club supplied three County Chairmen: William Campion, William Quaney, and Sean Power. Breda Dunne served as County P.R.O.

The members of the branch have also been involved internationally. A number of members travel each year on various Macra trips to the continent and in 1976 a very successful trip was organised by the branch to Belgium and Holland. The idea for this trip originated from the fact that good fortune befell the club the previous year (1975) when they won £5,000 in the Prize Bonds. The club had two representatives on the Irish team in the European Rally - Willie Quaney, Spain 1976 and Sean Power, Italy 1977.

The Branch are also very involved socially, running a number of events each year which include a very successful field evening, question time, and dances. The annual Concert in the Premier Hall, Thurles is the main fund raising venture every year.

Board of Management Presentation to Rev. Barbara Fryday 2007
(Back Row L to R)
Cllr Pat O'Neill, Mr. Brendan O'Gorman,
Ms.Linda McEvoy, Ms.Peg Barry,
Ms. Ann Marum, Mr. Martin Gleeson.
(Front Row L to R)
Ms. Angela Conroy,
Cllr Mary Hilda Cavanagh, Chairperson,
Board of Management,
Rev. Barbara Fryday,
Mr. John Cahill, Principal.

Coláiste Mhuire Receiving Green Flag Award 2002
(from left):
Mr. Tom Dollard, School Caretaker,
Frank Murphy,
Mr. Tony Walsh, Director of
Services, Kilkenny County Council,
Cllr Mary Hilda Cavanagh,
Chairperson VEC,
Ms. Saídhbh O'Neill,
Environment Officer, Kilkenny
County Council,
Mr. R.C.Greene, Principal,
Julie Mackey,
Mrs Pearl Codd, Science Teacher.

Aerial View of Johnstown Vocational School 1980

All Ireland Vocational School Champions 1982
Back Row: Tom Phelan, Pat McEvoy, Kevin Bartley, Gerry Kavanagh, Michael O'Gorman, James Farrell, Joe Coady, William Stanley, Milo Phelan, Paul Phelan, Martin Bartley, Gerry Phelan, Patsy Murphy.
Front Row: Jim Ryan (Trainer), Tommy Drennan, Michael Sweeney, Shay Downey, Martin McEvoy, James Queally, David Burke (Captain), Nicky Grace, Sean White, Billy Molloy, Jim Brennan, John Walsh,School Principal.

Hurling Champions 1988
Back Row: Declan Tobin, David Moriarty, Damien Anderson, Pat Doyle, James Carroll, Keith Beehan, Alan Beehan, Derek Beehan, Anthony McEvoy, Adrian Beehan, Austin Cleere.
Front: Alan Grey, Brendan McEvoy, (RIP) Declan O'Neill, Paul Phelan, Alan Bartley, James Ryan, Paul Bowe, Brian Lonergan, Mervyn Queally, Thomas Dowling.

1987 Hurling Champions
Back: Nigel Dunphy, David Moriarty, Austin Cleere, Daniel Costigan, Stephen Grehan, Joseph Corcoran, Cyril Cleere, Robert Butler, Eugene Ryan, Eoin Murphy, Matthew Walsh.
Front: Peter Moriarty, Declan Tobin, Gerard Quinlan, Anthony Watson, Kevin Wall, Michael Phelan, Alan Bartley, Patrick Murphy, Anthony McEvoy, James Carroll.

1999 Leinster Senior Hurling Champions
Back: Dermot Power, Ger Power, Ger Henderson, Paul Quinlan, John O'Loughlin, James Meagher.
Middle: Donnacha Grey, Robbie Dowling, Noel Dowling, William Cahill. JJ Delaney, Sean Minogue.
Front: John Bergin, Emmett Kavanagh, Kevin Fitzpatrick, Ramie Moriarty, Kevin Power, Padraig Bergin, Anthony O'Hara.

VEC Under 14 Girls Football Champions 1999
Back: L to R Caroline Delaney, Aisling Tallis, Ann Marie Delaney, Mae Barnaville, Amanda O'Shea, Tracy Tobin, Patricia Orr, Joanne Holohan, June Fogarty
Front: L to R Sarah Bergin, Margaret Mary Marum, Siobhan Tobin, Lisa Dowling, Selina Power, Shona Power, Tara Warren, Eileen Hughes, Triona Maher, Julie Mackey.
Trainer: Dermot Maher.

Leinster Senior Colleges Camogie Champions 2003
Back Row (from left): Paddy Broderick (Trainer), Máiréad Bergin, Lisa Dowling, Julie Mackey, Lorraine Peters, Tom Dollard (Coach), Aisling Tallis, Saralee Murphy, Shona Power, Siobhan O'Hara, Trisha Orr, Selina Power, Tara Warren, Mary Sheehan (Manager)
Front Row (from left): Orla Hughes, Áine Mackey, Ashling Fitzpatrick, Marian Ryan, Mary Margaret Marum (Captain) Michelle Garrett, Eileen Hughes, Triona Meagher.

Dancers 1990
(L to R)
Melissa Dermody,
Susan Bowe,
Sharon O'Gorman.

First Place in BSc Applied Physics DCU 1999
L to R: Mr. Michael Killeen Physics Teacher, Philip Bowe, Student, Professor M. Henry DCU.

Euroscola Winners of Trip to Strasbourg 2004
Back: L to R Tom Barry, Paul Sweeney,
Kevin Hogan, Kevin Doran.
Front: L to R Christine Fogarty, Maryanne
Kavanagh, Áine Mackey.

**Mr R.C. Greene, Principal, on the
occasion of his retirement 2004**

**Transition Year Play
Wizard of Oz 2002**
James Hayde,
Frank Murphy,
Julie Mackey,
Martin Purcell.

Visit to President Mary McAleese
Back Row (from left): Valerie Bergin, Mr. McCloskey, Tom Barry, Stephen Delaney, James Tynan,
Kieran Grehan, Brian Webster, John Morrissey, Michelle Skehan, Mr. Tom Dollard.
Middle Row (from left): Maryann Kavanagh, Michael Bourke, Kevin Doran, Joe Bergin, Paul Sweeney,
Pauraic Kenny, Declan Brennan, Martin Holohan, Áine Mackey
Front Row (from left): James Dermody, Daniel Eyre, Marian Ryan, President Mary McAleese, Aisling
Fitzpatrick, Thomas Dowling, Lloyd McGree

Foireann Choláiste Pobail Osraí Meán Fómhair 2007-08
Staff of the Coláiste Pobail Osraí September 2007-08
Front row, (L-R) Síona Nic Eoin, Deirdre Dowling, Cathnia Ó Muircheartaigh, Madailín Mhic Chana, Máire Uí Shluain agus Póilín Ruane.
Back Row (L-R) - Micheál Seoige, Máire Uí Dhiarmada, Ainemáire Ní Dhóráin, Lorna Ní Ghallchobhair, Margie Wall agus Gemma Ní Bhroin.

Coláiste Pobail Osraí, Cill Chainnigh

D'oscail Coláiste Pobail Osraí, an chéad scoil chomhoideachais lán-Ghaelach, dá 13 mac léinn tosaigh ar an 3ú Meán Fómhair, 1991. Sroicheadh an lá stairiúil sin in oideachas i gCill Chainnigh tar éis idirbheartaíocht fhada, chuimsitheach, chasta agus brú idir Coiste Gairmoideachais Chontae Chill Chainnigh, an Roinn Oideachais agus Aire Oideachais an ama sin, Máire Uí Ruairc. Dream tuismitheoirí cróga, tiomnaithe, diongbháilte, a dhein formhór na h-oibre seo. Chuir na tuistí san rompu oideachas trí Ghaeilge a sholáthar ag an tarna leibhéal do na mic léinn uile ar mhian leo tairbhe a bhaint as i gCill Chainnigh. Ní foláir a chur san áireamh gurbh iadsan tuistí an chéad ghrúpa scoláirí a chuir a mbunoideachas i gcrích trí mheán na Gaeilge. Tháinig an smaoineamh ar iarbhunscoil lán-Ghaelach chun cinn ag tosach na bliana 1989 nuair a cuireadh an cheist go dúshlánach faoi bhráid thuismitheoirí Ghaelscoil Osraí gur rud nádúrtha é go bhforbródh iar-bhunscoil lán-Ghaelach ón nGaelscoil.

Tionóladh líon cruinnithe le tuismitheoirí na ndaltaí a bhí ar tí an Ghaelscoil a fhágaint an bhliain sin le freastal ar cheann de na hiarbhunscoileanna eile i gCill Chainnigh ag an am. B'iomaí duine a bhí in amhras faoin gciall a bhain le hiarbhunscoil eile a bhunú nuair a bhí rogha mhór d'iarbhunscoileanna i gCill Chainnigh cheana féin. B'é an buntáiste ba mhó a bhain leis ná go leanfadh an scoil nua leis an traidisiún a bheith toilteanach Ghaeilge a labhairt mar ghnáth theanga chumarsáide i measc na mac léinn agus múinteoirí.

Chuathas chun cainte le hiarbhunscoileanna eile, mar atá, Scoil na mBráithre Críostaí agus Meánscoil na Toirbhirte, is dá thoradh san, dheineadar sruth Gaeilge a thairiscint mar chuid de na seirbhísí a bhí acu ag an am. Thairg an Coiste

Gairmoideachais, faoi threoir an Phríomhoifigigh Fheidhmiúcháin, Breandán Ó Conbhuí, an deis scoil neamhspleách a bhunú is a d'fheidhmeodh mar scoil ar leith laistigh de struchtúr an Choiste Ghairmoideachais le soláthar foirne agus bainistíocht dá cuid féin aici. Ghlac na tuistí leis an moladh deiridh seo. Anois, bhí sé thar a bheith riachtanach go gcuirfí a leithéid d' áis ar fáil do dhaltaí a nglacfaí isteach i Meán Fómhair 1991.

Fágadh an tasc dúshlánach chun an scoil nua a chur ar bun ag dream faoi leith tuismitheoirí, ian measc Seán Ó Dulchaointigh, Eoin Ó Néill, Diarmuid Ó Druacháin, Micheál Ó Máirtín agus Réamonn Ó h-Aonghusa. Tharla sraith cruinnithe le Breandán Ó Conbhuí maidir le curaclam, soláthar foirne, rogha ábhar, múinteoirí agus láthair na scoile.

Cheap an Coiste Gairmoideachais Proinsias Ó Drisceoil mar idirghabhálaí idir an coiste bunaithe agus an Coiste Gairmoideachais féin.

Bhuail baill an ghrúpa oibre leis an Aire, Máire Uí Ruairc, nuair a thug sí cuairt ar Chaisleán an Chumair is chasadar ar a príomh státseirbhíseach ag láthair na Roinn Oideachais i mBaile Átha Cliath. Ní mór sochar a thabhairt don Aire, Máire Uí Ruairc, is do Bhreandán Ó Conbhuí as an dtacaíocht a thugadar ag an am seo.

Le deontas ón Roinn Oideachais aithníodh, roghnaíodh is athchóiríodh foirgneamh a bhí as úsáid ag láthair Sheosaimh Naofa ar Bhóthar Phort Láirge. Dhein Diarmuid Ó Druacháin suirbhéireacht air. B'é Réamonn Ó hAonghusa, go ndéana Dia trócaire air, a chuir sáriarracht isteach chun an foirgneamh seo a ullmhú do thús na scoilbhliana. Ag baint leis an obair seo bhí pluiméireacht, péinteáil, seomraí ranga a roinnt agus araile.

Bhí spéis thar na bearta ag an am seo i gcomhartha na scoile. Diarmuid Ó Druacháin a d'oibrigh air is bunaíodh é ar an seanchomhartha bóthair le h-aghaidh scoile, a d'úsaideadh na hudaráis áitiúla roimh 1950, mar atá, siombail lóchrainn le bladhm aonair. Taca an ama chéanna a línigh Diarmuid a chéad sceitse, tionóladh comhdháil Phairtí na gCoimeádach faoi cheannaireacht Bhean Thatcher i Sasana. Suimiúil go leor, bhain an chomhdháil feidhm as lóchrann le bladhm aonair. Chinn Diarmuid ar an bpointe boise go mbeadh trí lasair ag an gcomhartha do Choláiste Pobail Osraí, rud a ghlacadh d'aon ghuth. Le cabhair Eoin Uí Néill a choinnigh an dréimire, chuir Diarmuid an comhartha in airde in am don oscailt oifigiúil.

Ba í Cáit Uí Chionnaith an chéad Mhúinteoir i bhFeighil agus chuaigh sí i bhfeidhm go mór ar na tuismitheoirí uile le feabhas a cuid Ghaeilge maraon leis an gcúirtéis is an dínit a bhí go smior inti. Dhréachtaigh sí an mana scoile "Doras Feasa Fiafraí" a mhaireann go dtí an lá inniu. Is é an mana sin a bhí ag croílár gníomhaíochtaí uile Choláiste Pobail Osraí. Chuir Múinteoir Cáit rian na cáilíochta is na cuibhiúlachta ar an scoil nua is thuill sí gean is dílseacht na scoláirí nua is tuistí araon.

Arna chloisteáil gur bunaíodh an scoil, bhronn Aodhghán Brioscú, scoláire Gaeilge agus ailtire a lonnaigh i mBaile Átha Cliath, a leabharlann de leabhair as Gaeilge ar an gcoláiste nua. Diarmuid a d'inshealbhaigh iad sa scoil nua tar éis iad a chruinniú i mBaile Átha Cliath.

An Príomhoifigeach Feidhmiúcháin ag an am Brendán Ó Conbhuí, tionscnóir láidir na teanga Gaeilge é féin, a dhein réamhtheagmhála is moltaí thar ceann an choiste scoile is an Choiste Ghairmoideachais leis an Roinn Oideachais i mBealtaine 1990.

Lean turas crua achrannach le cuid mhór cur ar gcúl, díomá is dóchas leanúnach. Chuaigh grúpaí teagmhála is brú chun cainte le polaiteoirí áitiúla, lucht tionchair is spéis, ag dréim go mbeadh teacht i mbláth i mbrionglóid Mheánscoil Osraí. Sa deireadh thiar thall, dheonaigh an t-Aire Oideachais, Máire Uí Ruairc, cead dul ar aghaidh leis an dtionscadal. Shamhlaigh Coiste na scoile agus an Coiste Gairmoideachais gur chóir go mbeadh oideachas trí Ghaeilge ar fáil do na scoláirí go léir ar mhian leo tairbhe a bhaint as. D'osclófaí clárú do chách. Ba rud tábhachtach é don Choiste scoile go mbeadh an polasaí iontrála chomh cuimsitheach is ab fhéidir.

Sular bhog an chéad rang isteach theastaigh mórchuid oibre chun foirgneamh Sheosaimh Naofa a dhéanamh inchónaitheach. Fuarthas deontais ón gCoiste Gairmoideachais is ón Roinn Oideachais ionas go mbeadh an bhrionglóid ar áitreabh scoile indéanta. Múinteoir Cait Uí Chionnaith, i gcomhar le foireann dhíograiseach, mic léinn is tuistí spreagtha, a leag amach ardchaighdeáin agus meon na scoile. Caitheadh samhradh na bliana 1991, ag cur barr feabhais ar scileanna na foirne scoile mar ullmhúchán don dúshlán nua os a gcomhair amach.

I Meán Fómhair 1991, chonaic an dream beag seo tuistí is cairde chéad thorthaí a gcuid saothair nuair a osc:aíodh doirse na scoile. Ó shin i leith is ar dhúthracht tuistí, foireann theagaisc thiomnaithe agus scoláirí díograiseacha atá an scoil bunaithe, fíricí a d'iompair í ar bhóthar a leasa is a chuir lena hardú aitheantais.

I 1994, thóg Caoimhín Ó Conghaile an lóchrann ar aghaidh fad a chuaigh an scoil ó neart go neart.

Sa bhliain 1995, cinneadh ar Chúrsa na h-Ardteistiméireachta a chur ar fáil i gColáiste Pobail Osraí, ach dá thoradh san, níorbh fholáir dóibh bogadh ó láthair Sheosaimh Naofa le cur fúthu i seomraí réamhdhéanta ar láithreán an Choiste Gairmoideachais taobh thiar de Choláiste Urmhumhan.

Thar a bheith cúntach a bhí Coláiste Chiaráin agus an Príomhoide ag an am, Micheál Ó Diarmada, i soláthar agus fairsingiú mhúineadh ábhar áirithe ag leibhéal na hArdteistiméireachta ina scoil do mhic léinn Choláiste Pobail Osraí. Maireann an comhoibriú seo fós agus dá bharr san, tugtar níos mó rogha in ábhair scoile d'iarrthóirí Árdteiste.

Sa bhliain 1999, ghlac Póilín Uí Leannáin le ceannaireacht na scoile is threoraigh sí í chun neamhspleáchais laistigh den Choiste Gairmoideachais i 2003 - clochmhile mhór don Choláiste.

Tharla athrú mór i 2003 nuair a réitigh Ruairí Uas. Ó Corráin agus an Coiste Gairmoideachais tar éis mórchuid dul i gcomhairle agus plé le foireann uile na scoile go dtabharfaí neamhspleáchas iomlán do Choláiste Pobail Osraí le soláthar foirne agus buiséid dá chuid féin san áireamh. Ceapadh a chead Bhord Bainistíochta an bhliain sin faoi chathaoirleacht   Risteáird Uí Dhúbhlaing. Ba chéim ar aghaidh eile é san don scoil.

Trí Stádas Neamhspleách a chur i gcrích i 2007, leag Coláiste Pobail Osraí bonn don chéad mhodúl eile ina stair ghairid. Is an chloch is mó ar a paidrín sa ghearrthéarma ná "foirgneamh deisiúil nua-aimseartha" a sholáthar do na mic léinn is don scoil uile. Faoi láthair, cuirtear raon iomlán áiseanna ó fhoireann theagaisc shaineolach, saotharlanna eolaíochta, páirceanna spóirt agus seomraí don Ealaín, d'Eacnamaíocht Bhaile is d'Abhair Theicneolaíochta ar fáil don uile scoláire. Is mór an dul chun cinn atá déanta ag Coláiste Pobail Osraí ó na trí sheomra ranga tosaigh i bhfoirgneamh Sheosaimh Naofa go dtí an liosta cuimsitheach d'áiseanna ar láithreán Bhóthar Urmhumhan.

I dteannta le curaclam iomlán ilchineálach cuirtear gach ábhar ar fáil don uile mhac léinn. Ghlac an Coláiste rannpháirtíocht agus d'éirigh thar na bearta leis i raon ollmhór gníomhaíochtaí, mar atá, díospóireachtaí Ghael Linn, tionscadail staire áitiúla, Slógadh, Trátha na gCeist, Óráid Phoiblí Comórtais um Shábháilteacht ar na Bóithre, imeachtaí ceoil, Eolaí Óg, Fiontraí Óg, Foirmiú agus Comhtháthú, Co-operation Ireland, chomh maith le rathúlacht spóirt i gcluichí ar nós iománaíocht, caid, sacar, leadóg agus cispheil. I 2006 ghlac an scoil páirt lárnach san Leabhar Mór, togra a d'fhéach le ceangail a bhunú is a bhuanú idir Gaeil na hÉireann is na hAlban faoi choimirce Oifig Ealaíon an Choiste Ghairmoideachais. Faoi choimirce Oifig Ealaíon an Choiste Ghairmoideachais freisin bhí scríbhneoir cónaitheach, Jack Harte, ag an scoil.

I mbun na scoile go dtí seo bhí Múinteoirí i bhFeighil Cáit Uí Chionnaith (1991-1994), Caoimhín Ó Conghaile (1994-1998), agus Póilín Uí Leannáin (1999-2006). Ó baineadh stádas neamhspleách amach, maíonn an Coláiste as Príomhoide Cathnia Ó Muircheartaigh agus Príomhoide Tánaisteach Madailín Mhic Chana dá chuid féin.

Clochmhíle mhór don scoil stádas neamhspleách a bhaint amach. Táthar ag súil gur féidir le Coláiste Pobail Osraí borradh agus forbairt go buaiceanna nua éachtaí i bpáirtíocht oideachais tuistí, mac léinn agus múinteoirí a thosnaigh chomh rathúil sin i 1991.

"Never doubt that a small group of thoughtful committed citizens can change the World. Indeed, it is the only thing that ever has". Margaret Mead.

Coláiste Pobail Osraí, Kilkenny

Coláiste Pobail Osraí, the first Co-Educational all Irish School opened its doors to its first 13 students, on the 3rd of September 1991. That historic day in education in Kilkenny was reached, following long, exhaustive, protracted negotiations and lobbying of County Kilkenny VEC, the Department of Education and the then Minister for Education, Mary O'Rourke. Most of this work was done by a group of courageous dedicated and determined parents. Those parents were focussed on providing education through Irish at second level for all of those students who wished to avail of it in Kilkenny. It has to be noted that they were the parents of the very first group of students who had completed their primary education through the medium of Irish. The idea of an all-Irish second level school came about in 1989 when the issue was put on the agenda challenging Gaelscoil Osraí parents that a secondary school 'as Gaeilge' was the natural follow on from the Gaelscoil.

A number of meetings were held with the parents of those children who were due to leave the Gaelscoil that year and go on to attend one of the other secondary schools in Kilkenny at that time. Many questioned the wisdom of starting another secondary school when Kilkenny had already a rich choice of quality secondary schools. The key selling point was that the new school would continue the tradition of being committed to the speaking of Irish as the normal language of transaction among the students and teachers.

Other secondary schools were approached, namely the CBS and Presentation and their response was to offer an Irish stream as part of their existing services, it was the VEC under CEO Brendan Conway who offered the prospect of an independent school managed and staffed as a separate school within the VEC structure. This option was accepted by the parents as the preferred choice. The key issue was to now make this an immediate reality for the intake of September 1991.

A key group of parents, including Seán O Dulchaointigh, Eoin Ó Néill, Diarmuid Ó Druacháin, Micheál Ó Máirtín and Ray Hennessy, were now faced with the challenging task of getting the new school up and running.

A series of meetings with Brendan Conway followed regarding curriculum, staffing choice of subjects, teachers, and school location.

The VEC appointed Proinsias Ó Drisceoil as a link between the coiste bunaithe and the VEC. Members of the working group met the Minister Mary O Rourke when she visited Castlecomer and they also met her key civil servant at the Department of Education in Dublin. The Minister Mary O'Rourke and Brendan Conway have to be credited for the support which they gave at this time.

A grant from the Department of Education enabled the identification, selection and renovation of an unused building at St Joseph's on the Waterford Road . This was surveyed by Diarmuid Ó Druacháin. It was Ray Hennessy (RIP) who put in a huge voluntary effort to ensure that this building was made ready for the start of the school year. This involved plumbing, painting making classroom divisions etc.

Of special interest at this time was the design of the school emblem. This was the work of Diarmuid Ó Druacháin and was based on the old pre-1950s local authorities road sign for school, a torch symbol with a single flame. At around the same time that Diarmuid had drawn up his first sketch, a Tory party conference under Mrs Thatcher was getting under way in England. By a curious twist the conference was using a single flame torch. Diarmuid decided there and then that the emblem of the CPO would have three flames and this was accepted by all as the school emblem and with the help of Eoin Ó Néill who held the ladder, Diarmuid erected the emblem in time for the official opening.

Meanwhile Múinteoir Cáit Uí Chionnaith was the first Múinteoir-i-bhFeighil and greatly impressed all of the parents with her excellent command of Irish, and her innate courtesy and dignity. She was responsible for drafting the school motto, "Doras Feasa Fiafraí" which endures to this day. It is the motto which has been at the heart of all Coláiste Pobail Osraí activities. Múinteoir Cáit put a stamp of quality and decorum on the new school and won the affection and loyalty of new students and parents alike.

Aodhghán Brioscu a Dublin based Architect and Irish scholar who heard of the founding of the school donated his library of Irish books to the new Coláiste. These were collected in Dublin by Diarmuid and installed in the new school.

The Chief Executive Officer at that time Mr. Brendan Conway himself a staunch promoter of the Irish Language made the introductory contacts and proposals on behalf of the Coiste and the VEC to the Department of Education in May 1990.

There followed a tough and arduous journey with many setbacks, disappointments and continued hope. Contacts and lobby groups approached local politicians and people of influence and interest in the Meánscoil Osraí dream. Mrs Mary O'Rourke the Minister for Education finally gave the go ahead. The Coiste and the VEC envisaged that Education through Irish should be available to all students who wished to avail of it. The door was to be opened to all comers. It was important to the Coiste that the entry policy should be all inclusive.

Before the first class moved into the St. Josephs building, a lot of work had to be done to make the building habitable - grants were received from the VEC and the Department of Education to make the dream of a school premises possible. Múinteoir Cáit Uí Chionnaith set out the high standards and ethos of the school, in partnership with an enthusiastic staff and motivated students and parents. The summer of 1991 was spent honing the skills of the staff in preparation for the new challenge ahead.

In September 1991 that small and dedicated group of parents and friends saw the first fruits of their labours with the school opening its doors. Since then it has continued to be based on parental commitment, dedicated teaching staff and enthusiastic students, elements which have carried the school along the road to success and increased recognition.

In 1994 Caoimhín Ó Congaile continued and carried the torch forward while the school went from strength to strength.

In 1995 a decision was made to bring Coláiste Pobail Osraí through to Leaving

Certificate, but this meant that they would have to move from the site in St. Josephs to locate in prefabs in Ormonde College.

St. Kieran's College and the then Principal, Micheál Ó Diarmada were very helpful in facilitating and extending the teaching of some subjects to Leaving Certificate level in St. Kierans. This co-operation is still in place and provides a much greater choice of subjects to Leaving Certificate.

In the year 1999 Póilín Uí Leannáin took over and steered the school to getting VEC independence in 2003, a major mile stone for the Coláiste.

A big change around came when Mr. Rodger Curran and the VEC decided in 2003, after a lot of consultation and discussions with all staff, that Coláiste Pobail Osraí be given full independence with its own staff and budgets. That first Board of Management took up office that year under the Chair of Councillor Richard Dowling. The was another major step forward for the school.

The achievement of independent status by Coláiste Pobail Osraí in 2007 has set the foundation for the next module in the short history of Coláiste Pobail Osraí. The provision of a state of the art building for the students and the school is the next priority. Currently the full range of facilities from expert teaching staff, science laboratories, sports fields, art, home economics and materials technology rooms are available to all students. Coláiste Pobail Osraí has come a long way from the initial three classrooms at St. Josephs to the expansive list of facilities at the Ormond Road Campus.

Along with a full and varied curriculum, every subject is available to all students. The Coláiste has participated and been very successful in a huge range of activities from Gael Linn debates, local history projects, Slógadh, quizzes, public speaking, road safety competitions, music events, Young Scientist, Young Entrepreneur, Form and Fusion, Co-operation North as well as sporting success on the hurling, football, soccer, tennis and basketball fields.

The school has been led to date by M'inteoir i bhfeighil Cáit Uí Chionnaith (1991-1994), Caoimhín Ó Conghaile (1994-1998), Póilín Uí Leannáin (1999-2006) and since gaining independent status it now boasts its own Principal Cathnia Ó Muircheartaigh and Deputy Principal Madailín Mhic Cana.

Gaining Independent status has been a major milestone for the school. It is expected that Coláiste Pobail Osraí can only grow and develop to new heights of achievements in an educational partnership with of parents, students and teachers, which began so successfully in 1991.

'Never doubt that a small group of thoughtful, committed citizens can change the world. Indeed it is the only thing that ever has' Margaret Mead.

Diospóireachtaí Sóisearach Conradh Na Gaeilge 1995 An Chéad Duais
(L-R) Sinéad Ní Cashin,
Sorcha Ní Dhruachain,
Caoimhín Ó Chonghaile,
Ciara Ní Mhairtín."

Eolaí Óg
Eoin Ó hÓgáin,
Micheál Ó Muircheartaigh,
Dairine de Róisle,
Róisín Ní Chaoimh.

Young Entrepreneur 1999
(L-R) Cáit Ní Ógáin,
Póilín Uí Leannáin (Múinteoir i bhFeighil),
Síona Ní Fhearghail Fhionnlaoich,
Aoife Ní Dhúlaing.

Grúpa ón scoil ar thuras scoile

An Chéad Duais
Clár Raidió Slógadh 1992

Rang ceoil sa scoil,
Br. Phort Láirge i 1991

Bronadh a dhein na daltaí ar Cháit Ui Chionnaith nuair a d,éirigh sí as. A Presentation by the students to Cáit Uí Chionnaithe

217

Duiske College Staff 2007-08
Back Row L to R: Lillian Carr, Dolores Barron, Pat Kavanagh, Karen Spencer, Brigid Keoghan, Marie Hayles, Teresa Doyle, Mary Beck, Elaine Norton, Beibhinn O'Leary, William Watson, Tommy Quigley.
Front Row L to R: Kevin Cheesty, Eileen Moyles, Anne Foley(Deputy Principal), Seamus Knox (Principal), Brenda Foskin, Pauline Lalor, John Maddock.

Duiske College, Graignamanagh

On the 11th of May 1953 Kilkenny VEC held its monthly meeting in Graignamanagh to coincide with the turning of the first sod on the site of the new school. The tender price of the building was £10,557-5-6 and the site had been donated free of charge by Miss Keating.

The school was officially opened on the 9th of December 1954, and consisted of three classrooms, a woodwork store, office, and toilets.

Commerce teacher Gerry Daly was appointed as Headmaster with Sean Buckley as Science teacher, Connie Feeney as Home Economics teacher and Brian Hunt as Woodwork teacher. School caretaker appointed was Gerry Kavanagh.

The day Vocational Certificate Courses were taught, with the girls taking the Commerce and Home Economics group and the boys following the manual group. After completion of their Group or Secretarial Certificate, students left school to enter employment, take up apprenticeships, or work on their farm.

In the sixties the advent of free education and the extension of the intermediate certificate course to Vocational Schools led to increased numbers and the consequent need for more teachers and additional classroom accommodation.

Extra teachers were appointed and prefabricated classrooms were provided to cater for their immediate needs. Students could now do their Group and Intermediate Certificate in Graignamanagh, but had to transfer to Kilkenny City Vocational School or other schools to complete their Secondary education and sit for their Leaving Certificate Examination.

In order to address this situation and provide a more accessible Leaving

Certificate centre for the students, talks were held in the early seventies with the Department of Education, the VEC, and representatives from the three vocational schools in Ballyhale, Graignamanagh and Thomastown. After much discussion and negotiation it was eventually agreed that Thomastown would be the designated Leaving Certificate Centre for the three schools, and students would be provided with free transport to complete their secondary education there. Ballyhale was established as the Secretarial Centre for the three schools and similar transport arrangements were put in place. Over the succeeding years many students from Graignamanagh availed of these transport arrangements, and contributed greatly to the educational, sporting and social lives of both Ballyhale and Thomastown Vocational Schools.

During the next few years the Senior Cycle was introduced to other Vocational Schools in the county and by the start of the eighties the only Junior schools remaining were Castlecomer and Graignamanagh.

In April 1981 County Kilkenny VEC announced that it would introduce senior cycle courses in Castlecomer and Graignamanagh commencing in September 1981. Mr. Brendan Conway, CEO Kilkenny VEC, stated at the time that he felt the difficulties students encountered in travelling to other centres was discouraging some of them from continuing their studies beyond intermediate level. He also believed that the new courses would result in substantial increases in enrolments in both schools.

As forecast, student numbers in Graignamanagh increased substantially over the following years with a corresponding requirement for additional staff and accommodation. Extra staff were appointed and pre-fabricated classrooms were again provided. Department of Education sanction had still not been obtained for the senior cycle but following a comprehensive submission from the VEC detailing the lack of capacity in Thomastown, the transport cost involved, and the impact on the town of Graignamanagh of closing their Vocational school, Departmental approval for the course was finally approved at the September 1982 meeting of the Vocational Education Committee. Mr Jim Phelan on behalf of Graignamanagh Board of Management is recorded as expressing their gratitude to "God, VEC representatives, and the Department of Education in approximately that order of priority".

The continued growth in numbers and resultant need for extra classrooms was met over the years by the provision of pre-fabricated units, most of which had been transferred from other schools and had deteriorated badly. Following sustained pressure and lobbying by parents, teachers, and VEC members most of these were replaced by more permanent and better suited units, and while the ultimate goal of a new school remains, the present facilities and accommodation are vastly superior and much more suitable. New facilities were officially opened by Deputy Seamus Pattison on the 14th of February 1997 with the name of the school being changed to "Duiske College", an acknowledgement of the part that the Abbey of Duiske (Dubh Uisce) had played in medieval Graignamanagh.

Further developments came with the provision of hard-court facilities which were opened in September 1998. Credit for this is due to the enterprise of the parents who sought matching funding for basketball and tennis courts which they proposed to provide. Following from this came Departmental sanction for a woodwork room and the conversion of the existing woodwork room to a science laboratory. Approval was also obtained for replacing equipment in the home economics room.

Post Leaving Certificate courses continue to be an important part of the schools educational programme and this year there are forty students enrolled.

The school has always provided a relevant and innovative range of adult education courses. An example of this was the series of music recitals arranged in Duiske Abbey in the eighties with performances by such groups as the Cork Youth Orchestra, The Southwark Choral Singers from London, and the Army Band.

Sports and extra-curricular activities have always played an important part in school life in Graignamanagh, and students involve themselves in a wide range of team and individual events, successfully representing their school and their county at all levels.

With its natural assets of Brandon Hill and the River Barrow, Graignamanagh was seen as the ideal location for an outdoor pursuits centre. In 1977 the VEC appointed Kevin Higgins, a PE teacher with particular expertise in the area of outdoor pursuits, to establish and run an outdoor education centre based in Graignamanagh Vocational School. With funding from Cospóir, The National Sports Council showers and changing rooms were built and equipment was purchased. The centre operated successfully for many years attracting student groups from all over the country to spend a day, or a weekend, hill walking and orienteering on Brandon Hill and canoeing on the river Barrow.

In 1980 An Óige (The Irish Youth Hostel Association) leased the school from the VEC to be used as a Youth Hostel during the summer holiday months. This also operated very successfully for many years and the combination of hostelling facilities together with the outdoor pursuits made the school a very attractive location.

Around this time also, students from Graignamanagh were involved in an exciting and interesting educational cross border venture under the aegis of Co-Operation North, a body set up to promote contact and understanding between groups in the north and in the south of the island. Graignamanagh was invited to enter into a schools exchange with Dundonald Boys School in Belfast. After exploratory contacts had been made the students travelled in the school minibus across the border to stay for a few days with their host schools students in Belfast. The event attracted huge media attention and television cameras recorded the journey from the symbolic crossing of the border to the students meeting and greeting their host families in Belfast. During their stay the students visited and stayed in an Outdoor Pursuits Centre taking part in a wide range of water based sports activities, and were given a civic reception by the Mayor of Belfast in City Hall. The reciprocal visit by the Belfast students took place later in the year. They stayed with their host families in Graignamanagh, took part in a wide range of activities, and were given a great welcome by the people of the town and of the county.

While those kinds of visits became more commonplace in the following years the Graignamanagh one was fairly unique at the time and was a great experience for the students, parents, and teachers involved.

Duiske College, with its modern refurbished buildings and its up-to-date facilities and courses, provides an excellent educational opportunity and experience for all its students. Student achievements have been consistently high, many have gone on to further education, and past pupils of the school can be found pursuing rewarding career in all walks of life.

From a teaching staff of four and accommodation of three classrooms in 1954, Duiske College now has a staff of 16 and has 14 classrooms.

Mr. Gerry Daly, Principal and
Ms. Anne Foley with students on a
day trip to Tramore.

Marie Foley in the Laundry Class in
the 1970s.

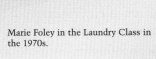

**Debs Night for Graignamanagh
Students**
Included in the staff picture are:
Ms. Anne Foley, Mr. Joe Mackey,
Ms. Teresa Buggy, Mr. Chris Greene,
Ms. Anne Maloney,
Mr. William Norton and
Ms. Caroline Graham

Presentation to Post Leaving Certificate Students
Back Row
L to R: Sadie Doherty, Joan Earls, Essie Phelan, Liam King, Nellie Grace, Kitty Blanchfield, Ray Talbot, Marget Talbot, Cllr. Matt Doran, Seamus Hogan
Front Row L to R:
Cllr Anne Phelan,
Karen Somers, Carl Irwin, Kathleen Lauran, Marie Widger, Anne Doyle, Brigid Murphy

Scene from Grease performed by Duiske College Students

Students on a Walk up Brandon Hill 2005

Duiske College Soccer Team 2007

Girls Basketball Team 2007
Marian Ryan, Kelly Ann Bolger, Aine Ryan, Shauna McGrath, Rebecca Connolly

224

Kilkenny City Vocational School

Kilkenny City Vocational Staff 2007-08
Back row L to R: Bernadette O'Brien, Emer White, Elizabeth Thornton, Niamh Hoyne,
Virginia Kennedy, Fr. Mark Condon, Micheál Seoighe, Michelle Mulhall, Sharon Bryan,
Anne-Marie Ryan, Kathleen Hogan, Brendan Brennan.
Front row L to R: Kay Muldowney, Deirdre Cullen, Helen Duggan, Catherine Connery,
Deirdre Dowling, John Collins, Cathy McSorley, Principal.

Ormonde College Staff 2007-08
Front Row L to R: Anne Kiely, Anne Campion, Billy Burke, Deputy Principal,
Bronwyn Keane, Deirdre Dowling, Canice Ryan, Sheena McKeon,
Back Row L to R: Olive Keyes, Margie Wall, Kathleen Hogan, Mary Ann Gelly,
Pat Gleeson, Mary McTiernan, Vincent Andrews, Tony Brennan, Marian Fitzpatrick.
Inset: Mary Dermody

Our records show that the early days of the present City Vocational School were spent in the ACC Bank in Parliament Street.

Mr. George Phillips, later the first CEO of the VEC, was appointed Principal in 1903. He was to continue in that position until the early 1930s. By 1907 the school had 3 centres:

(a) The trades preparatory school in the 'library' (ACC Bank)

(b) Rooms in the model school on the Ormonde Road for domestic economy subjects, commercial subjects and for practical tailoring.

(c) Rooms in the courthouse for use as a place for evening classes.

The Model School was built to accommodate Church of Ireland children and was not used to its full capacity at this time. Rooms became available to the City Technical Instruction Committee and as numbers began to grow the pressure on space mounted. The Committee sought to purchase the building in the early years of the 20th century. However the model school project was a protracted one.

In fact the saga of the 'Model School' was to occupy the attention of the City Technical Instruction Committee later the Joint Technical Instruction Committee and finally the Vocational Education Committee for many years.

The committee procured a site on the Castlecomer road to house a new 'Model School' for the Protestant children as part of purchase agreement. This new 'model school' was in use on this site until the opening of the newest model school adjacent to Kilkenny College in the late 1990s. This phase of the saga ended on the 9th January 1940 when the Bishop of Ossory, Dr. Patrick Collier, officially opened the newly extended partially reconstructed and refurbished school on the Ormonde Road.

The three centres, occupied for a number of years, were now amalgamated into the New Model School as the Kilkenny City Technical School.

The school had a staff of 13 teachers and was under the leadership of the then headmaster Mr. James Henry. At the time of the amalgamation as there were two people already equally positioned for the position of headmaster it was decided by 'Gentleman's Agreement' that the position would be filled by the more senior of the two Mr. James Henry therefore became headmaster to be succeeded on his retirement in 1955 by Mr. James J. Byrne. Mr. Byrne led the school until 1966. The school was called the Technical School because it was involved so much in trades and the training of apprentices.

Student enrolments were at this time in the region of 140 and remained below 200 until around 1966. The school was coeducational and multi-denominational. It was divided into three sectors:

The Trades Side, which provided skills for all male students interested in this; The Commerce Side, which provided skills in the field of commerce for both boys and girls; and the Domestic Science Side, which provided Homemaking skills solely for girls and had the smallest intake. In 1958 (Ms. Moyra McCarthy reports) there were but nine students attending Domestic Science classes. These numbers had grown to 32 by 1961. Michael O'Neil was 'assistant to the headmaster' until 1965.

Growth in numbers led to the purchase of lands belonging to the County Club from the Marquis of Ormonde in 1966 to house prefabricated classrooms and an extension. A garage workshop and fitter's workshop to accommodate apprentices on block release and a Bord na Móna Apprentice Training Course was approved by the Department. Kilkenny City was designated at a centre for Senior Stage courses for Motor Trade Apprentices; the apprentice block was located on the newly purchased site behind the 'Model School'' building. This complex provided training for 'Day-Release' Motor Mechanics for five days per week. There were two 'Block-Release' groups from Board na Mona and ANCO who attended for eleven weeks each. There were three groups each of eleven weeks accommodated each year.

Following the retirement for Mr. James J. Byrne in 1966, Mr. Sean Dignan was appointed Headmaster. He was assisted by Mr. Paddy Taffe as assistant to the headmaster until 1970.The appointment of Mr. Dignan ushered in an era of great change at the City Technical School. In that year the first year intake which had increased to 125 students was allowed prepare for the Group Certificate Examination and sit it in Year Two followed by the Intermediate Certificate in Year Three.

The beginnings of a new link with neighbours, St. Kieran's College also was initiated around this time. Students from St. Kieran's College took woodwork, metalwork, mechanical drawing, agricultural science and biology at the City Technical School.

The school had its first cohort of students sit for the Leaving Certificate in 1969. These students came from the City Technical School as well as the VEC scheme schools around the county. The arrival of the Leaving Certificate to the school forged an even greater link with neighbours St. Kieran's College. Ms. Moyra McCarthy was appointed Vice-Principal in 1970.

By 1971 Kilkenny City Technical School had an enrolment of 432 students and provided facilities for some 224 pupils from Saint Kieran's College. During the early 1970s numbers continued to grow to a high of 475 students.

During all this period the school on Ormonde Road was acclaimed both academically and in the sporting arena. It was regarded as the premier school in the region for gymnastics and also excelled in hurling and other sporting activities. In the 1970s the City Technical School was a vibrant educational establishment which was highly respected in the community. It contributed enormously to local, business professions and sport. The first 'Book Lending Scheme' was conceived and developed by the school which had one of the earliest Parent/Teacher associations up and running in 1972.

There are as many views as there are people involved about the 'co-operation' arrangements with neighbours St. Kieran's College. Planning for a new school to replace the model school and the multitude of prefabs that dotted the City Technical grounds began in mid 1970. Discussions conceived of the ideal of a 'community of schools' - two new school buildings on one site with shared facilities and enrolments. Reports show some serious unease on the VEC staff side and efforts were made to seek to have agreement on common or shared enrolments.

Agreement was finally reached, however, regarding a 'capping' of numbers, teaching and facility co-operation.

The outcome of 'co-operation' discussions resulted in the completion of the New Street School in 1979 which was officially opened as the City Vocational School by Minister Gemma Hussey TD in 1984. The City Vocational School experienced some falling numbers, in the mainstream area, which were offset by the development and promotion in 1980 of VPT 2 courses. These became known as PLC courses sometime later. Mr. Sean Dignan retired in 1994 to be replaced by Ms. Fiona O'Sullivan who served as Principal until 1999. Ms. Moyra McCarthy retired 1998 and was replaced by Mr. Seosamh O'Floinn as Deputy Principal until 2005. Today, Ms. Cathy McSorley is Principal at the City Vocational School and Mr. W. Burke is Deputy Principal with responsibility for Ormonde College.

The old 'Model School' is today the home of a growing PLC college with the title Ormonde College of Further Education. Opened in 1991 under the auspices of County Kilkenny VEC, the garden at the rear of Ormonde College has since then housed Kilkenny's only Coláiste Lán Ghaeilge, Coláiste Pobail Osraí.

View of Ormonde College in the 1970s

*For Sam Dunlop, the highlight of his school
career was a momentous sporting occasion,
here recollected thirty-five years on.*

**Kilkenny Vocational Schools team which won the All-Ireland senior
hurling final in 1972; beating Cork by 3-9 to 3-7.**
Back Row(from left): Tony Murphy, Eamon Lalor, Michael Hogan, Sam Dunlop,
John Knox, Pat Kiely, Pat Treacy, Martin Orr, Dick O'Hara, Murty Kennedy.
Front row(from left): Paudie Lannon, Tom O'Shea, Kevin Robinson, Joe Tierney,
Joe Connolly, Willie Doheny, Noel Drennan, Tom Phelan, Ian Doyle, Martin Joyce.

All Ireland Final - 1972

Our manager, Billy Burke had us gathered together at James Stephens, Larchfield
grounds in May 1972. We had one final hurdle to jump on a journey which started
the previous October. This journey had taken a momentum beyond our wildest
dreams, since our initial encounter with Kildare. We were a group consisting of
hurlers selected from the various Vocational schools - Kilkenny, Thomastown,
Slieverue, Ballyhale and Johnstown. Our task against our Cork counterparts was to
win an All-Ireland Vocationals Schools title, a first since 1963. A group of lads who
had never met prior to our first training session the previous October, 'soft townies'
and 'tough culchies' had matured and bonded.

We were to be the curtain raiser to the National Hurling League Final on the
famous Thurles sod. The scene was set for us and for our four bus loads of
supporters from around the county. On the scale of things in a county such as
Kilkenny it was a low key affair, especially since our Seniors were not contesting
the League Final. For most of us it would be our only chance to represent our
county at any level. Of course a significant number of the players on this panel
went on to enjoy success at Minor, U 21 and Senior level, winning All Ireland titles
in all grades.

With Kildare beaten, and victories under our belts over Antrim and Offaly, both after replays, we waited to see what the heavyweights from Cork had to throw at us. We were ready, thanks to the meticulous tactical preparation of Billy Burke and jumping out of our skin following Nicky McGrath's thorough physical preparation

Our convoy of buses left Ormonde Road at 11.00am decked with black and amber.

Unlike previous matches there were ladies on the team bus today! We are on the brink of stardom and could not be distracted. The team bus stopped in a small café in Urlingford for tea and sandwiches. No dieticians on board so the townies were telling the country lads to go easy on the beef sandwiches. 'Sure all ye're used to is bread and tea', was the reply from the country lads. That country town banter was typical of the banter and friendship that bonded this group together.

No distractions with injuries, all fit and well was Billy's opening address, so every reason to go out there and do it. No banging of hurleys. Not required! The determination was tangible, the focus visible in each and every pair of eyes. The run on to the pitch has to be the highlight of any sporting occasion and this was no different. You could feel the hair standing on the back of your neck. If you can play on the rough sod of O'Toole Park, Dublin you can certainly play on this green carpet. Like all big sporting occasions once the match started time flew. After a slow start we managed to lead by 2-5 to 1-3 at half time.

Billy suggested in the half time team talk that these boys will come at us. Keep focused. Sure enough the third quarter heralded a magnificent rally by the rebels. With ten minutes to go we were 3-8 to 1-5 ahead. Cork raised two green and two white flags to our one white flag in the last ten minutes, A final last gasp effort by Cork with three minutes left resulted in a Cork substitute scoring a goal which would have left us beaten by one point, but all our prayers were answered, when the goal was disallowed for a square infringement. Kilkenny 3-9 Cork 3-7. We were All-Ireland Vocational Schools Champions for 1972.

A group of unknowns became a statistic in Tom Ryall's book of Kilkenny GAA victories. It cemented lifelong friendships between the whole panel. We got a chance to renew this friendship when we met as a team for the first time since 1972 at a reunion of past pupils from Kilkenny Vocational Schools at the Club House Hotel, Kilkenny earlier this year-2007.

A noted absentee from that night was Noel Drennan (Ballyhale) who unfortunately passed away earlier this year. Ar dheis Dé go raibh sé.

Post Leaving Certificate Awards Evening 2006

Presentation to Mr. Paddy Fahy, Caretaker on the occasion of his retirement from Kilkenny City Vocational School.

Official Launch of the Beauty Therapy College on the 9th November 2007
Back Row (from left): Natasna Scott, Sandra Holloway, Cathy McSorley Principal,
Ms. Pat Gleeson, Director of Ormonde College, Helen Barry, Marie Cahill, Jacqui Hynes, Sandra Kelly,
Margaret McKenna, Kathleen Carroll, Mr. John McGuinness, Minister of State with Special Responsibility for
Trade and Commerce, Ms.Margie Wall, Career Guidance Counsellor.
Front Row (from left): Ann Marie Stone, Ms. Bronwyn Keane, Beauty Therapy Co-Ordinator,
Mr. William Burke, Deputy Principal with responsibility for Ormonde College, Pamela Broaders,
Ann Marie Sweeney.

231

Retirement Presentation for Ms. Moyra McCarthy 1998
L to R: Ms. Catherine Connery, Ms. Fiona O'Sullivan, Principal, Ms. Moira McCarthy,
Mr. John Sheehy, Fr. Richard Scriven, Mr. Michael Brett, and Ms. Rita Neary.

Kilkenny City Vocational School first Parent/Teachers Association met in 1972
Back Row(LtoR): Eddie Holohan, Tom Kerwick, David Gunner,
Sean Dignan(Principal), Billy Tyrell, Paddy Mc Grath, Peadar Flanagan.
Front Row (LtoR): Mrs. Maher, Mrs.Walsh, Michael Muldowney, Maura Tyrell, Moyra McCarthy (Vice Principal).

Tina Connolly, County Winner of B.I.M. Fish Cookery Competition
Tina later won 1st Place in the National Final in Waterford.
L to R: Sean Dignan, Principal, John Holohan, Chairman of County Kilkenny VEC, Moira McCarthy, Vice Principal and Home Economics Teacher, Tina Connolly, Barbara Byrne, B.I.M., Eamonn Gibson, C.E.O.

14 year old Patty O'Farrell winner of the National Cookery Competition in Killarney in 1960
The prize was a one year training course as Hotel Cook in Rosslare. Patty was later to become the first cook in Rose Hill Hotel in Kilkenny.

Sineád Delahunty, All-Ireland College Cross County Champion showing her medal to team-mates Margaret Matthews and Hazel Mullen.

KCVS Senior Camogie Team 1998

Presentation by Bill Hennessy to the Under 16 Hurling Champions: 1993-94

Grennan College, Thomastown

Grennan College Staff 2007-08
Back Row Left - Right
Edmond Murphy, Elisabeth Byrne, Donal Dunne, Mary Shasby Furlong, John O'Brien, Derek Dooley,
Fiona Page, Eleanor Reddy, Jennifer Finn, Denis Kelly, Mairead Frisby, Ann-Marie Donnelly, Maura Cottrell
Front Row Left - Right
Denise Phelan, Mary Brennan, Elizabeth Kett, Edel Cleary, Nicola Murphy, Aviva Walsh,
William Norton, Principal, Denis Doyle, Angela Browne, Anne Teague, Barbara Comber, Christine Kehoe
Inset: Miriam O'Donnell, Deputy Principal.

Grennan College Craft School Staff 2007-08
(L to R) Peter Donovan, Niall Harper,
Catherine Ryan, Alexandra Meldrum, Course Director,
George Vaughan, Christine Shanahan,
William Norton, Principal.

Equestrian Staff 2007-08
William Norton, Principal, Bridgette McCarthy,
Jenny Reid, Fiona Loughnanae

Vocational Education commenced in Thomastown in 1958 with the opening of the Technical School. It was built on a site purchased from Mr O'Carroll. It had a historic start because when the first roof was completed on the building it was set on fire. Luckily it was seen by a householder on Newtown Terrace who called the fire brigade, but the roof had to be replaced. A night watchman was then employed but once again the roof was set on fire. This time less damage had been done when the fire brigade arrived on the scene, so only a percentage of the roof had to be replaced. Finally the school was finished and opened with Mr. Walter Cleary as its first Principal.

This was an important development for the area because it was the only second level school except for the Secondary Top established by the Mercy Sisters in 1950 which provided education for girls only.

The original school was small by today's standards. It consisted of three classrooms - kitchen, general classroom and woodwork room with store attached. Beside the school a very ornate bicycle shed was built. The original buildings still stand and are currently in use as classrooms but the bicycle shed has found another use. At first the students (boys and girls) were prepared for the Day Vocational Certificate (Group Cert) and achieved excellent results. The range of subjects was limited to General Subjects, Woodwork, and Domestic Science and Typing. Following Group Certificate, students left to take up employment, go into trades and farming.

Adult education classes at night were a very important element of education for people whose full time education finished at primary school. Many practical skills were taught at these night courses.

In 1967 with the advent of free education the Technical School and the Secondary Top amalgamated. The Mercy Sisters were given two reserved teaching positions in the school. Two Sisters of Mercy (Sr. Carmel and Sr. de Sales) joined the staff bringing with them first, second and third year students. This, together with the introduction of free education, caused an explosion in the number of students. While it was welcomed, it posed accommodation problems. The promised new "state of the art" school was delayed until 1985. Meanwhile it was common practice to have two classes in each room even in the relatively small prefabs. Other classes were held in the entrance hall, the woodwork store, the bicycle shed, while others had to walk to the CYMS hall and to the Concert Hall where they would remain for two or four class periods at a time.

At that time teachers had to be very versatile as many new teachers moved to "Greener Pastures" as soon as they got jobs elsewhere. These were difficult days but staff and students accepted the conditions and the school flourished. Sr. Carmel remained on the staff until 1986. The link with the Mercy Order ceased at this stage as she was not replaced by a Mercy Sister.

Despite these difficulties, new subjects were added to the curriculum and students sat two exams, Group Certificate in second year and Intermediate Certificate in third year. This continued until the two exams were amalgamated into the Junior Certificate in 1993.

Under Mr. Luke Murtagh, who replaced Mr. Walter Cleary as Principal, the school was given permission to do the Leaving Certificate programme. The first group of students sat the Leaving Cert in 1975. This included many who had to transfer from Ballyhale because Ballyhale did not have Leaving Certificate at that stage. This was a huge step forward for the students, the school and the population of the surrounding area because now the students could compete for places in third level education and for occupations demanding Leaving Certificate. Bishop Laurence Forristal, a native of Thomastown, has said that prior to this only those students in Thomastown who could afford to go to boarding school were able to do the Leaving Certificate. Since then many of the students have gone on to Third Level education where they have been very successful studying to the highest level and can now be found in all walks of life.

The school has always been to the forefront in developing new courses and meeting new challenges. Under the Principal Mr Luke Murtagh it was one of the first schools to develop a Transition Year programme in 1976/77 in conjunction with the Department of Education. It was then called a Work Experience class because of the introduction of work experience into the curriculum which was unheard of at that time. This was a pilot programme for later transition year programmes.

The school was a pioneer also in the area of Equestrian Studies and was one of the first schools to provide equestrian education when the course commenced in 1978. Since then other schools have modelled their courses on the Thomastown course. Another development under Mr. Pat Cronin was the establishment of Grennan Mill Craft School to provide education in the arts in 1981. The establishment of these courses is a tribute to County Kilkenny VEC and the school principals and staff who saw the need for courses in Equestrian Studies and Craft which are indigenous to County Kilkenny. The Equestrian course and the Craft course brought students from all over Ireland and even from abroad to Thomastown which was a boost to the local economy. The Secretarial/ Reception course, which is one of the original areas of education in technical schools continued in the school but it has developed and changed over the years to meet the needs of the world of work and changes brought about by new technology.

Under Mr. Tim O'Mahony the school developed a gardening course - a joint venture between the school and Kilkenny County Council. The practical work of the course is undertaken in Woodstock Gardens, Inistioge which are being restored. These Post Leaving Certificate courses are to this day very important areas of education.

After many years the Deptartment of Education sanctioned the building of the "state of the art" new school. This was built on the site of the original school and incorporates it. It consists of two science laboratories, a home economics room, an engineering room, a woodwork room, an art room, eight general purposes rooms, a computer room, offices and a canteen. The provision of a canteen meant that students could avail of hot meals at lunch time. This school was officially opened by Ms. Gemma Hussey, Minister for Education in 1986.

The school underwent a major refurbishment programme in 2005 which means that the facilities now are the most updated and modern in the area. These refurbished rooms were officially opened by Ms. Mary Hanafin Minister for Education and Science in May 2005.

The building of the new school on the school's playing fields necessitates students having to go to the Community Hall, Grennan GAA grounds and the Soccer Club grounds to train and play matches and the school is indebted to these for their use. Despite these difficulties the pupils have always taken part in a wide range of sports and extra curricular activities. In the sporting field there have been many successes, some at national level, in Camogie, Basketball, Ladies Football, Hurling, Gaelic Football, Soccer, Athletics and Badminton. Famous sportspeople who are past pupils are Dick O'Hara and Michael Reddy. Music, drama and debating are just some of the extra-curricular activities of the school. While the school continues to meet new challenges, develop new curricula and new programmes, these extra- curricular activities are fostered and contribute to the life of the school.

The school changed its name to "Grennan College" in 1996 and is a school which hasn't stood still. It has always adapted and changed to meet the needs of the students, the changing world of work and with its Principal Mr. Willie Norton and staff it faces the 21st century with the optimism and the enthusiasm needed to meet any new challenges.

Grennan visit
The refurbished rooms at Grennan College were officially opened by
Ms. Mary Hanafin, Minister for Education and Science in May 2005.

Students at work

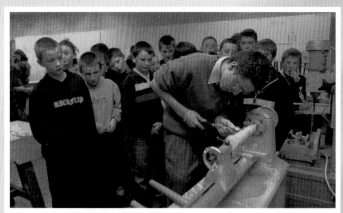

Thomastown Vocational School Senior Camogie Team Leinster Colleges Champions 1990-91
Back (L to R): Dolores Lanigan, Susan Laherty, Vanessa Butler, Patricia O'Keeffe, Deirdre Lannon, Susan Malone, Siobhan Whelan, Georgina Foley, Gillian Dillon
Front(L to R): Brenda Murphy, Mary Comerford, Anita White, Siobhan Delaney, Jennifer Walsh, Theresa White, Una Murphy.

1992 Vocational Schools Camogie All Ireland Finalists and Leinster Champions
Back Row (L to R) Olivia Burke, Pauline Grace, Sandra Kenny, Deirdre Lanigan, Liz Dempsey, Florence Lanigan, Elaine Dunne, Brenda Murphy.
Front Row(L to R): Michelle Power, Olivia Hayden, Theresa White, Yvonne Malone, Dolores Lanigan, Mary Norris, Jennifer Walsh, Georgina Foley.

All Ireland Vocational School 1987 Champions
Back Row (L to R): Billy O'Keeffe, Matt Bookle, John Conlon, Kevin Maher, Johnny Cullen, Declan Ryan, John Skehan, Robbie Maher, Eoin O'Neill, Colm Mullins, Shem O'Neill, Joe Bookle.
Front Row(L to R): Declan Lannon, Barry Doyle, Richard Keirns, Alan Aylward, Paul Tracey, Paul Cullen, Robert Finan, Willie Holden, Larry Fenlon.
Thomastown Managers were Joe Mackey and Ned Byrne.

All Ireland Soccer Winners against Dungarvan Community School in Buckley Park, Kilkenny 1995
Front (L to R): Eugene O'Neill, Ray Dack, JJ Roche, Martin Hughes, Paul Dempsey, Alan Meegan, Sean Cassin, David Dempsey, Stephen Croke O Neill.
Back(L to R): Ned Dack, Tim O'Mahony, Principal, Rob Stapleton, Michael Reddy, Derek Brennan, Paul Dunne, Niall Nevin, Tony O'Mahony, Paul Doyle, Denis Walsh, Eleanor Reddy, William Grace.

240

Sr. Carmel, Ned Byrne (R.I.P.) and Gerry Daly (R.I.P.) walking back from Mass for the opening of the new school in Thomastown.

Young Entrepeneur Winners 1996
L-R Mr. Denis Kelly, Michael Reddy, Michelle Treacy, Sarah Quinn, Maria Walsh, Pat Hackett with Ms. Mairead O'Dwyer, T.S.B.

Group of officials and recipients pictured in November 1986 at awards dinner in the Newpark Hotel when Certificates in Equestrian Science were presented to students attending the course organised by County Kilkenny Vocational Education Committee and Bord na gCapall at Thomastown Vocational School. Seated (from left): Bridgette McCarthy, Assistant Instructor, Pat Cronin, Principal, Patricia Kinahan, John Kinahan, Manager, equestrian training, Bord na gCapall, Eileen Conway, Brendan Conway, CEO, County Kilkenny VEC and Faith Ponsonby, Instructor.

Scoil Aireagail Staff 2007-2008
Back Row L to R. Mick McGrath, Bobby Hearne, Aidan Walsh, Ronan Murphy, Tom Hunt, Colin Madden,
Catherine Phelan, Shirley Mills, Svetlana Tchaikovskaya, Joe Foster.
Middle Row L to R. Canice Corr, Majella O'Neill, Mary T. Dalton, Anne Marie Fogarty, Andrew McDonald,
Maureen Roche, Brid Kennedy, Mary Dunne, Valerie Dempsey, Marie Butler, Valerie O'Callaghan.
Front Row L to R. Carmel Raggett, Kathleen Farrell, Mai Murphy, Ashling McCarthy Suzanne Maher,
Rita Dooley,Angie O'Meara, Theresa Ryan, Susan Brophy, Alice Kiernan, Annette Muldowney.

Scoil Aireagail, Ballyhale

Ballyhale Vocational School opened in 1959. Forty students were enrolled. There
were just two classrooms. Students were accepted to study for their Group
Certificate Examination. The Intermediate and Leaving Certificate courses were
not allowed to be taught in the initial stages. Quite a lot of work also went on at
night, particularly in Home Economics and Woodwork for adults. Teachers gave
night classes in Home and Food Management, Animal Husbandry, Crop Rotation
and items relevant to the location of the school. Teachers could be timetabled to
work during the day and also four nights a week. This could be seen as the
forerunner of what later became known as adult education. Another feature of
Vocational Schools at that time was their support for rural development,
particularly in the area of farm buildings. Jim Devereaux was appointed first
Principal. Michael Cahill worked on the construction of the school and then
became its caretaker.

In the 1970s Ballyhale Vocational School won a Leinster Minor Camogie Final
and two years later lost a Senior Camogie final. Bridget O'Neill became the first
student to secure a place in St. Patrick's Training College in Drumcondra. She had
been a student in Ballyhale up to Intermediate Certificate, but had to transfer to
Kilkenny City Vocational School to do her Leaving Certificate, as there was no

Leaving certificate allowed in Ballyhale at that time. Later in the 1970s Leaving Certificate status was conferred on Ballyhale. The Senior Camogie team won the All-Ireland Vocational Schools title, beating Mallow comprehensively in the final.

In 1979 the VEC set up a sub-committee to examine the physical conditions in all of the schools in the county. This group was to recommend to the VEC a schedule of building programmes for all the schools. Ballyhale was given absolute priority over all the other schools. In the event Ballyhale was the last school to be re-built being officially opened twenty years later in 1999.

The physical conditions of the school, throughout the seventies, was dreadful. In the eighties there was an on-going campaign by teachers and parents to have a new school provided, but problems with the site and educational cutbacks ensured that nothing happened. The Junior Minister for Education, Donal Creed paid a visit to the school. He inspected the pre-fabs from the outside. He was invited in to see the insides of one pre-fab classroom where water was coming in onto electric wiring. He refused the invitation saying 'it's too dangerous'. He promised to do something.

Five students built a boat and came third in the national boat building competition. Ronnie Delany of Cospoir and Olympic fame presented the prizes. John Wilson, Minister for Education sanctioned a new school, It was election time. After the election nothing happened. The conditions in the school became a national issue when Pat Holmes, Education Correspondent with the Irish Press, accompanied by a photographer, did an extensive article on the school. The headline on the article said it all 'Even the bicycle shed was taken over for classes'.

However though the physical conditions in the school were far from ideal, there was a tremendous energy within the school. During the eighties students from the school won National titles in Drama in Slógadh and Scoil Dramaíocht. Ballyhale also became a force to be reckoned with in debating and public speaking, competing at national level in a number of competitions. During this time also we had the first student from the school to win the Europe at School Competition, setting in train a line of winners for the next twenty-five years. This period also gave a first of a different kind to Ballyhale. A student gained direct entry to Oxford University. Definitely the only student from County Kilkenny VEC to do so and probably the first from any Vocational School in the country to do so. Another 1980s student from the school was later to become a lecturer at Oxford in the late 1990s. The school had its first success in The Young Scientist Exhibition. Students from Ballyhale were beginning to take up places in Universities and Institutes of Technology in greater numbers. One student won the United World College Scholarship to Pearson College in Vancouver, Canada. This scholarship allowed our student to complete the last two years of his secondary education in the company of two hundred and fifty students from seventy-five different countries. This scholarship was later won by two other Ballyhale students, one in the 1990s and the other in 2004.

By the beginning of the 1990s pressure for a new school had really come to a head. The growing numbers in the school made this imperative. It was a time when promises were made in respect of a new building which were then quickly broken or ignored. The 1990s also was the end of an era. Mr. Devereaux retired as Principal of the school and was replaced by Mr. Tom Hunt. Ms. Marie Butler became Vice-Principal. Mr. Devereaux was the first Principal of the school, having been appointed when the school first opened. At a celebration dinner to mark his retirement the community, former students and their parents came to say thanks. Also, all the teachers who had taught in the school during Mr. Devereaux's time came to the function, to join the celebration. It was a wonderful thank you to the man who had seen the school grow from 40 students to its present enrolment of 250 students.

Promises, promises about a new building and then President Robinson came to visit us. She came to thank the students for the money they had raised for famine relief in Somalia. She praised the parents for their commitment to have a new school established in their community. It was a wonderful boost to everybody that the President of Ireland should grace us with her presence.

The first phase of the new school was built but immediately was inadequate to meet the needs for classrooms. Pre-fabs sprouted up everywhere. The second phase was built and officially opened in 1999 by the then Minister for Education, Micheál Martin. This building contained a unique feature, in that it had a purpose built Hairdressing Salon. A Hairdressing PLC course had been operating in the school since the early 1980s. Now it had a proper facility. In sport a Senior Hurling Leinster title was won in 1996. The students became involved in the Chernobyl Children's Project and over the next ten years more than a quarter of a million euro has been donated to this cause in terms of ambulances, food and medical supplies and cash. This project is carried out each year by the Transition Year students.

The students' work for Chernobyl was recognised nationally when they were awarded the Gulbenkian Gold Medal in Áras an Uachtaráin for their 'commitment to world issues'. The public speaking team won the All Ireland Mental Health Public Speaking Competition. Two other teams reached the national finals during this time. The Business and Professional Women's National Public Speaking Competition for girls was won twice during the 1990s. In the Young Scientist Competition we had three category winners and a number of highly commended projects during the 1990s. During this decade also, a group of students wrote a series of poems in response to an atrocity in the North of Ireland when a gunman walking into Sean Grahame's bookmaker shop on the Ormeau Road and killed 5 people. These poems received national recognition in the press and illustrated copies of them were presented to President Mary Robinson when she visited the school in May 1994.

A feature of the school in the 1990s was the development of a support system for students with learning difficulties. This structure has become a central feature of our holistic approach to learning and child development. The system has also provided some remarkable results with quite a number of students with specific learning difficulties going on to achieve university entry.

An aspect of the 1990s can best be summed up in the epilogue of the Student's

Magazine 'Ballyhale Times' October 1999, 'WE HAD OUR DAY AT LAST'. *The new school was officially opened by Micheál Martin, Minister for Education. This a full eighteen years after it was first sanctioned in 1981. We left the mud, the prefabs, the wet, the wind, the cold, the hurt, the neglect, the anger, the strikes, the let-downs, the promises, the threats, the lies, the hopes, the failures, all behind us and basked in the glow of survival. We knew when the minister cut the ribbon that an era was over and as Gar says in Philadelphia here I come 'It's all over and its all about to begin'. Goodbye to Ballyhale Vocational School, welcome to Scoil Aireagail.*

In the new millennium, student numbers increased. Students competed in the Young Scientist with a number of category winners being achieved. The senior boys competed in the All Ireland Colleges B soccer cup finals three years in a row and won two of them. Handballers won national titles in 60 x 30 and 40 x 20 colleges and vocational school competitions. The under 16 boys hurling team won a Leinster title. A senior boys football team won a Leinster title. The girl's camogie team won a Leinster title. The girls Gaelic Football team won a Leinster title also. Winners in track and field and cross-country kept up a long tradition of participation in these events. The senior girls reached the All-Ireland Colleges Badminton final. A student won a major award in the Texaco Art Competition. A senior student gained second place in the All-Ireland Inter Schools Hunter Trials. A junior student won a poetry competition organised by the Department of Foreign Affairs in Ireland and in Newfoundland.

In the space of two weeks, thousands of euro was raised for a boat to be given to victims of the tsunami disaster. The boat is called 'The Scoil Aireagail'. It is now a fishing boat in south east Asia. It is perhaps a fitting symbol of our school, that our boat is giving a life to people we have never met on the other side of the world.

All Irealnd Finalists Public Speaking 1991-1992
L to R:
Mairead O'Sullivan, Ita O'Brien, Suzie Cunningham

Retirement function in Kiltorcan House
1981 for Seán Delaney, Science Teacher and
Elizabeth Phelan, Maths Teacher.

Jim Devereaux, first Principal in Scoil
Aireagail been presented with Waterford
Glass on the occasion of his retirement
by Tom Hunt.

**Young Scientist Senior Winners Group
Category 2006**
Project was 'Haemochromatosis! Do we
know enough?' Picture of Annette O'Shea
and Paula Butler been presented with their
trophy.

Green Schools Committee
carrying out a rubbish audit.

Cleve Cuddihy, Sharon Hughes and
Kenneth O'Shea winners of the National Finals
of the Mental Health Public Speaking Project
held in Trinity College, Dublin. The prize for
winning was a cycling trip in Belgium.

Pictured receiving their prizes from the adjudicators are Louise Healy, Carol Cottrel and Katriona Holden for
the All Ireland Cup for the best team in the Business and Professional Women's Public Speaking Project in
Trinity College, 1998.

The Chernobyl Children's Project, Food, Medical Supplies and Toys for the Orphanage in Belarus.

Louise Healy, Brendan Moore and Emmeline O'Brien all won national prizes in the 1997 'Europe at School Competition' run by the Department of Education.

U14 Boys Hurling Team 2003

Winners of the South East League are the U15 Girls Soccer Team 2002

Tsunami Disaster-Boat Appeal. Donated by Scoil Aireagail Students' January 2005

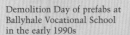

Demolition Day of prefabs at Ballyhale Vocational School in the early 1990s

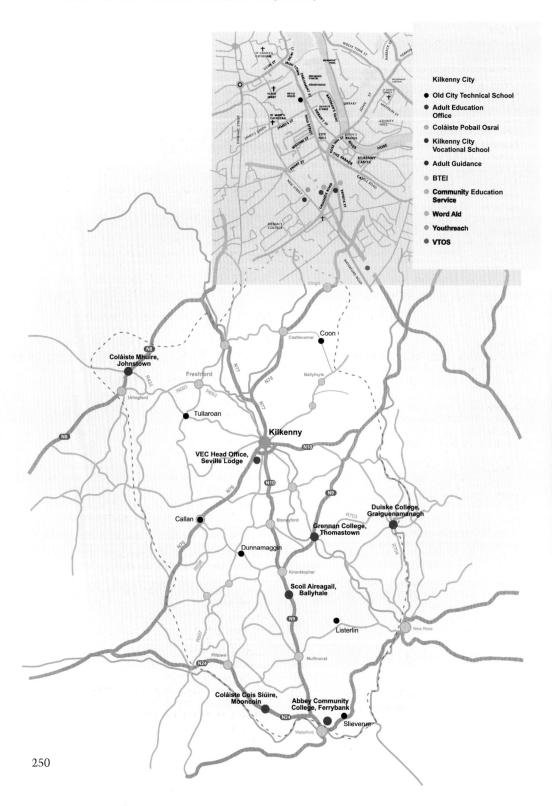

Kilkenny City

● Old City Technical School

● Adult Education Office

● Coláiste Pobail Osraí

● Kilkenny City Vocational School

● Adult Guidance

● BTEI

● Community Education Service

● Word Aid

● Youthreach

● VTOS

Coon

Castlecomer

Ballyfoyle

Coláiste Mhuire, Johnstown

Freshford

Urlingford

Tullaroan

Kilkenny

VEC Head Office, Seville Lodge

Callan

Stoneyford

Duiske College, Graiguenamanagh

Grennan College, Thomastown

Dunnamaggin

Knocktopher

Scoil Aireagail, Ballyhale

Listerlin

New Ross

Piltown

Mullinavat

Coláiste Cois Siúire, Mooncoin

Abbey Community College, Ferrybank

Slieverue

Waterford

Index